THE MARKETING PLAN HANDBOOK

THIRD EDITION

Marian Burk Wood, M.B.A.

PEARSON
Prentice Hall

Upper Saddle River, New Jersey 07458

Library of Congress Cataloging-in-Publication Data

Wood, Marian Burk.
    The marketing plan handbook / Marian Burk Wood.—3rd ed.
        p. cm.
    Includes bibliographical references and index.
    ISBN 0-13-223755-5
    1. Marketing—Management—Handbooks, manuals, etc. I. Title.
    HF5415.13.W66 2007
    658.8'02—dc22

                                                            2007002233

Editor in Chief: David Parker
VP/Editorial Director: Jeff Shelstad
Product Development Manager: Ashley Santora
Assistant Editor: Keri Molinari
Editorial Assistant: Christine Ietto
Marketing Manager: Anne Howard
Marketing Assistant: Laura Cirigliano
Associate Director, Production Editorial: Judy Leale
Managing Editor: Renata Butera
Production Editor: Renata Butera
Permissions Coordinator: Charles Morris
Associate Director, Manufacturing: Vinnie Scelta
Manufacturing Buyer: Michelle Klein
Design/Composition Manager: Christy Mahon
Cover Art Director: Jayne Conte
Cover Designer: Bruce Kenselaar
Cover Illustration: Chris Spollen / Stock Illustration RF / Getty Images, Inc.
Composition: ICC Macmillan Inc.
Full-Service Project Management: Mohinder Singh; ICC Macmillan Inc.
Printer/Binder: Hamilton Printing Company
Typeface: 10/12 Times

Credits and acknowledgments borrowed from other sources and reproduced, with permission, in this textbook appear on page 181.

Pearson Education, Ltd
Pearson Education Singapore, Pte. Ltd
Pearson Education, Canada, Ltd
Pearson Education—Japan

Pearson Education Australia PTY, Ltd
Pearson Education North Asia Ltd
Pearson Educación de Mexico, S.A. de C.V.
Pearson Education Malaysia, Pte. Ltd

10 9 8 7 6 5 4 3 2
ISBN-13: 978-0-13-223755-0
ISBN-10: 0-13-223755-5

BRIEF CONTENTS

CONTENTS

Preface

Never has a carefully crafted, properly implemented marketing plan been more important to business success. Because thousands of new goods and services are introduced every year, a good marketing plan makes all the difference between profit and loss. Although marketing textbooks often discuss the general use of a marketing plan or contain a brief outline of one, they don't explain exactly how to develop an effective plan—yet that's what student marketers really need.

The Marketing Plan Handbook fills this gap with concise step-by-step coverage of the structured process for formulating a creative and actionable marketing plan, including preparations for measuring marketing performance and controlling implementation. The award-winning *Marketing Plan Pro* software bundled with this book makes documenting decisions fast and easy so readers can concentrate on putting marketing principles into practice.

REAL-WORLD VIEW OF MARKETING PLANNING

How does Yum! Brands use marketing planning (see Chapter 1)? What changes in business demographics are helping Caterpillar grow globally (Chapter 2)? How has Marriott used ethnographic research to better understand the needs of business travelers (Chapter 3)? Why does HomeBanc Mortgage's segmentation and targeting strategy include the use of personas (Chapter 4)? What role do objectives play in the not-for-profit Heifer International's plans for marketing communications (Chapter 9)? How does Endeca Technologies use a marketing dashboard to monitor marketing effectiveness (Chapter 10)?

These and dozens of other examples featured in *The Marketing Plan Handbook* illustrate how marketing planning is actually applied in consumer and business markets, in large and small companies, in traditional and online businesses, and in not-for-profit organizations. To reinforce this real-world view, key examples also demonstrate how today's global economy and dynamic business environment can cause marketers to change their plans as new competitors emerge, budgets are cut or shifted, and new technologies overtake existing strategies. Thus, long after the marketing plan is written, savvy marketers continue charting paths to profitability and watching for threats and challenges every working day.

SPECIAL FEATURES SUPPORT EFFECTIVE PLANNING

The Marketing Plan Handbook supports the hands-on development of imaginative yet realistic marketing plans through a series of special features.

Sample Marketing Plan

What does a marketing plan look like? The Appendix presents a sample plan for the SonicSuperphone, an enhanced, multifunction cell phone. This hypothetical sample, based on current market conditions, serves as a model for the content and organization of a typical marketing plan.

In particular, the sample plan demonstrates how a company might analyze market needs and trends, examine environmental factors, look at the competitive situation, and set objectives to be achieved. It also touches on segmentation, targeting, positioning, and the variety of marketing strategies and programs needed to launch a new product.

Checklists

What questions should marketers be asking? Checklists in Chapters 2 to 10 summarize nine key areas to be examined during the planning process. Topics include:

- environmental scanning and analysis
- analyzing markets and customers
- setting marketing plan objectives
- identifying and evaluating market segments
- analyzing and planning product strategy
- planning pricing strategy
- channel and logistics issues
- planning marketing communications strategy
- elements of a marketing audit

Practical Planning Tips

What important points and pitfalls should marketers be aware of? Each chapter includes a number of special tips, shown in the margin, to help readers make the transition from theory to application. These tips emphasize various practical aspects of planning and mention specific issues or questions to consider when developing a marketing plan.

Current Examples of Marketing in Action

How are companies and not-for-profit organizations actually putting marketing plans to work? Every chapter features 10 or more recent examples of consumer and business marketing in action. In all, this book includes more than 100 examples that illustrate specific planning and implementation activities, looking at marketing in organizations such as: Apple, Bluefly, Bluenile.com, Citigroup, Ent Federal Credit Union, Escada, GE, Google, Harley-Davidson, ING Direct, Kellogg, McDonald's, Monro Mufflers, Nestlé, Netflix, Nike, Onslow Memorial Hospital, PepsiCo, Procter & Gamble, Rock Bottom Restaurants, Sony, Sprint-Nextel, Toyota, Wal-Mart, and Wyndham Worldwide.

Powerful New PowerPoint Presentation

Created by John Newbold of Sam Houston University, the new PowerPoint presentation is a powerful supplement to *The Marketing Plan Handbook*. Expanded content and eye-catching graphics make this a high-impact presentation package for instructors to download.

Online Features

Visit this book's Web site, www.prenhall.com/wood, for access to a variety of additional materials, including:

- hotlinks to selected online marketing resources
- discussion questions for each chapter
- an outline showing the main sections of a marketing plan
- faculty materials, including the new PowerPoint presentation

MARKETING PLAN PRO SIMPLIFIES PLANNING

Palo Alto Software's highly rated *Marketing Plan Pro* software, which comes with this book, is a professional, user-friendly program for documenting marketing plans. The software includes an introductory video, help wizards, and other valuable features to guide users through marketing analyses and plan for each element in the marketing mix. It also helps users prepare for implementation, compare actual to planned results, and assess the financial value of marketing programs through profitability, ROI, and customer lifetime value calculations.

   Marketing Plan Pro offers a structured plan format and dozens of spreadsheets, tables, and charts to help users organize and present data about marketing decisions. It also includes sample marketing plans from a variety of organizations, including manufacturers, retailers, consulting firms, service businesses, and not-for-profit groups. Once the marketing plan is complete, the software allows it to be printed, translated into a read-only document, exported to other programs, or exported for posting on the Web.

SUPPLEMENTING PEARSON PRENTICE HALL MARKETING TEXTS

A value package of *The Marketing Plan Handbook* with *Marketing Plan Pro* software is available at a deeply discounted price to supplement the following Pearson Prentice Hall textbooks:

- *Marketing Management* by Philip Kotler and Kevin Lane Keller
- *A Framework for Marketing Management* by Philip Kotler and Kevin Lane Keller
- *Principles of Marketing* by Philip Kotler and Gary Armstrong
- *Marketing: An Introduction* by Gary Armstrong and Philip Kotler
- *Marketing: Real People, Real Choices* by Michael Solomon, Greg Marshall, and Elnora Stuart
- *Marketing Management* by Russell S. Winer
- *Market-Based Management* by Roger Best

ACKNOWLEDGMENTS

Throughout the process of planning, writing, and revising three editions of *The Marketing Plan Handbook,* I was extremely fortunate to have the support of many good people. I deeply appreciate the dedication and hard work of the many talented Pearson Prentice Hall professionals who have contributed so much to this book's success: David Parker, Editor in Chief; Melissa Pellerano, Project Manager; Ashley Santora, Project Development Manager; Christine Ietto, Editorial Assistant; Anne Howard, Marketing Manager; Renata Butera, Managing Editor and Production Editor; and Charles Morris,

Permissions Coordinator. An extra special thank you, from my heart, goes to Assistant Editor Keri Molinari, who went above and beyond again and again. Her enthusiasm and know-how kept this edition on track from beginning to end. And my sincere thanks to Mohinder Singh of ICC Macmillan Inc., my genial, meticulous, and efficient Project Manager. What a pleasure it has been to work with everyone on this great team! Last but not least, a tip of the hat to Tim Berry, Sabrina Parsons, and all the folks at Palo Alto Software who are responsible for *Marketing Plan Pro*—many thanks for your ingenuity, ideas, and expertise.

I'm very grateful to the many faculty reviewers who graciously shared their insights and provided helpful suggestions to shape this third edition: Mel Albin, University of Maryland University College; Ismet Anitsal, Tennessee Tech University; Tim Becker, University of San Diego, University of Phoenix, Webster University; Cathleen Behan, Northern Virginia Community College; Normand Bergeron, Bristol Community College; Robert Blanchard, Salem State College; Brian Bourdeau, Auburn University; Michaelle Cameron, St. Edwards University; Ravi Chinta, American University of Sharjah; Yun Chu, Frostburg State University; Patricia Clarke, Boston College; Earl Clay, Bristol Community College; Greg Combs, Methodist College; Mary Conran, Temple University; Larry Crowson, University of Central Florida; Don Eckrich, Ithaca College; William Fillner, Hiram College; Douglas Friedman, Penn State Harrisburg; B. Christine Green, University of Texas at Austin; Tom Gruen, University of Colorado at Colorado Springs; James Hansen, University of Akron, John Carroll University; Harry Harmon, Central Missouri State University; Betty Jean Hebel, Madonna University; Jeffrey Heilbrunn, Columbia College of Missouri; David Hennessey, Babson College; James Hess, Ivy Tech Community College; Stacey Hills, Utah State University; Mahmood Hussain, San Francisco State University; Lynn Jahn, University of Iowa; Michelle Jones, NC State University College of Textiles; Michelle Kunz, Morehead State University; Ada Leung, University of Nebraska at Kearney; Nancy Lowd, Boston University; Terry Lowe, Heartland Community College; William Machanic, University of New Hampshire; Gordon McClung, Jacksonville University; Margaret Mi, University of Mary Washington; Chip Miller, Drake University; Peter Mooney, Embry-Riddle Aeronautical University; Charlene Moser, Keller Graduate School of Management; Michael K. Mulford, Des Moines Area Community College; Keith Nickoloff, Rochester Institute of Technology; Ralitza Nikolaeva, University of Wisconsin– Milwaukee; Bernadette Njoku, College of Saint Rose; Margaret O'Connor, Penn State Berks Campus; Carol Osborne, University of South Florida; Peggy Osborne, Morehead State University; Joseph Ouellette, Bryant University; Elizabeth Purinton, Marist College; Ruby Remley, Cabrini College; Mark Rosenbaum, University of Hawaii, Northern Illinois University; Bennett Rudolph, Grand Valley State University; David Saliba, Duquesne University; John Schibrowsky, University of Nevada, Las Vegas; Camille Schuster, California State University San Marcos; Chris Shao, Midwestern State University; Annette Singleton, Florida A&M University; Allen Smith, Florida Atlantic University; Jim Stephens, Emporia State University; Bala Subramanian, Morgan State University; Ronald Thomas, Oakton Community College; Scott Thorne, Southeast Missouri State University; Beverly Venable, Columbus State University; Ven Venkatesan, University of Rhode Island; Edward Volchok, Stevens Institute of Technology; Kathleen Williamson, University of Houston-Clear Lake; Katherine Wilson, Johns Hopkins University; Wendy Wysocki, Monroe County Community College; Mark Young, Winona State University.

Let me also express my appreciation to the following reviewers who kindly shared their thoughts and valuable suggestions during the development of earlier editions: Brent Cunningham, Jackson State University; Ralph M. Gaedeke, California State University, Sacramento; Dennis E. Garrett, Marquette University; Kathleen Krentler,

San Diego State University; Ron Lennon, Barry University; Byron Menides, Worcester Polytechnic Institute; Henry O. Pruden, Golden Gate University; Scott D. Roberts, Northern Arizona University; Gary R. Schornack, University of Colorado, Denver; and Michael J. Swenson, Brigham Young University.

This book is dedicated to my beloved husband, Wally Wood; my beloved sister, Isabel Burk; and my wonderful extended family. A great big hug to the Biancolo, Burk, Goodwin, Hall, Mazzenga, Weiner, and Wood families—you're the best!

—Marian Burk Wood
MarianBWW@netscape.net

About the Author

Marian Burk Wood has held vice presidential-level positions in corporate and not-for-profit marketing with Citibank, Chase Manhattan Bank, and the National Retail Federation, as well as management positions with national retail chains. In addition to *The Marketing Plan Handbook,* she is the author of *Marketing Planning: Principles into Practice,* geared to the European market. Over the years, she has collaborated with well-known academic experts to coauthor college textbooks on principles of marketing, principles of advertising, and principles of management.

Wood has extensive practical experience in marketing planning, having formulated and implemented dozens of marketing plans for a wide range of goods and services. She also has developed numerous chapters, cases, sample plans, special features, exercises, and print and electronic supplements for college textbooks in marketing and related disciplines. A long-time member of the American Marketing Association, Wood holds an MBA in marketing from Long Island University in New York and a BA from the City University of New York. Her special interests in marketing include ethics, segmentation, channels, and B2B marketing.

1

Introduction to Marketing Planning

In this chapter:

PREVIEW

In a world where customers are surrounded by marketing—at work, at home, in the streets, in stores, at play, in virtually every medium or daily activity—businesses must fight simply to capture attention before they can start to demonstrate the value they provide. Because customers have more choices and more power than ever before, a good product, brand, commercial, price, Web site, or store is no longer good enough. Not when consumers and business buyers can quickly and easily research products and companies, compare prices, check specifications and delivery options, and buy with the click of a mouse. Not when reputation counts: Customers (and suppliers) prefer to deal with organizations and brands that have credibility and a positive public image. And

not in today's global economy, in which local and international competitors alike are vying to start and strengthen relationships with their customers.

This emphasis on relationship building is reflected in the American Marketing Association's current definition of **marketing** as "an organizational function and a set of processes for creating, communicating, and delivering value to customers and for managing customer relationships in ways that benefit the organization and its stakeholders." This definition emphasizes the importance of **value,** the difference between the perceived benefits received (to satisfy a want or need) and the perceived total price. Of course, the way a company gains value (in the form of higher sales and profits, more market share, and so on) is by providing value to its customers. If value is present for both parties, the resulting relationship may take the form of a one-time purchase or repeat purchasing and referrals to other potential customers.

Thus, effective marketing covers everything the company is and does, and it all must consistently provide value to win customers and earn their ongoing loyalty. However, marketing that is effective today may not be as effective tomorrow because of ever-accelerating change—the only constant that marketers can depend on when formulating a marketing plan.

OVERVIEW OF MARKETING PLANNING

The best way for any business, nonprofit organization, or government agency to move toward its goals is one marketing plan at a time, over and over. Start-ups, multinational corporations, and charitable foundations all need marketing plans to chart paths to their goals (whether defined by profits, donations, or people helped). Consider the plan that China's Nanjing Automobile Group is using to enter the U.S. and European markets.

Nanjing Automobile Group. This Chinese automaker recently bought the equipment and name of Britain's MG Rover to form MG Motors. Now it is preparing to leverage the MG brand's reputation in the global marketplace. "We don't want to be a company that simply exports out of China," states Duke T. Hale, head of MG Motors. Instead, he says, the company will design and build cars in local markets, profiting from the competitive advantage of "a brand name that still resonates" with European and American drivers. Following its plan, MG Motors is recruiting dealers in Europe and the United States, readying U.K. and U.S. factories, updating the MG car designs, and determining the package of pricing and features that will attract buyers and build profits.[1]

Rapidly expanding companies, including those going global for the first time, face special challenges in defining their short-term and long-term objectives, researching and analyzing the marketing environment, and developing effective strategies to build (and retain) a solid customer base in new areas. Oasis Hong Kong Airlines, a recent start-up, sees opportunities in flying from Hong Kong to London and other long-range destinations. To compete with Cathay Pacific Airways and Air China, Oasis will have to keep fares and costs low; this is not an easy task, given the high fuel prices in recent years.[2] Well-established companies have much more experience with their customers, markets, and competitors, but they are subject to the same environmental dynamics. Nestlé, for example, has been in business for more than a century but is still learning new things about customers and competitors.

Nestlé. Based in Switzerland, Nestlé has a diverse product portfolio of foods, beverages, and pet foods for global markets. Alert to an increase in health problems such as diabetes and obesity, the company has begun dishing up diet-friendly foods such as cereal bars that do not cause blood sugar levels to spike. The company is also more active in China, which an executive calls "the fastest and most competitive market in the world" because of burgeoning demand and intense rivalry from both international and local firms. Nestlé has profited by creating food items specifically for China—such as sesame-chocolate cubes—and developing an adaptable distribution system to get products to outlying communities. In Argentina, the company has prospered, despite a difficult economic situation, through brand-building campaigns, product introductions, and periodic price promotions.[3]

The marketing plans of Nestlé, Oasis Hong Kong Airlines, and MG Motors center on how to provide value to their customers in ways that will result in value (profit, in particular) for the companies. Every day brings new decisions about using marketing to profitably acquire, retain, and satisfy customers in a competitively superior way. Online businesses such as Amazon.com have the added complications of developing, updating, and operating a Web site, handling customer service, and managing order fulfillment as they work on all the other elements of marketing strategy. Still, marketers for younger firms, like their counterparts in older companies, are most effective when they follow a structured series of steps for marketing planning.

The purpose of this handbook is to provide an overview of the process that contributes to the development of a viable marketing plan. This process enables marketers in every organization, regardless of industry or product, to make informed decisions about the most appropriate marketing paths to profits, market share, and other objectives. Marketing principles and techniques are explored in the context of each step in the process, along with numerous examples illustrating their use. Despite company-by-company variations in the formality and timing of the process, the aim is to emerge with a plan documenting appropriate strategies and programs for the chosen markets.

Planning Tip

A structured process helps you identify, assess, and select appropriate marketing opportunities and strategies.

Marketing Planning Defined

Marketing planning is the structured process of determining how to provide value to customers, the organization, and key stakeholders by researching and analyzing the current situation, including markets and customers; developing and documenting marketing's objectives, strategies, and programs; and implementing, evaluating, and controlling marketing activities to achieve the objectives. This systematic process enables marketers to identify and evaluate opportunities for satisfying needs that might lead to achieving overall goals, as well as emerging threats that could interfere with goal achievement (see Exhibit 1.1). As noted in the preview, any aspect of the marketing environment can change at any time; thus, marketing planning must be viewed as an adaptable, ongoing process rather than a rigid, annual event.

The outcome of this structured process is the **marketing plan,** a document covering a particular period that summarizes what the marketer has learned about the marketplace, what will be accomplished through marketing, and how. All marketing plans should explain intended strategies for building relationships by creating, communicating, and delivering value to customers; outline the activities that employees will undertake to reach objectives, including gaining value for the organization; show the mechanisms for measuring progress toward objectives; and allow for adjustments if actual results are off course or the environment shifts.

EXHIBIT 1.1 Marketing Planning

A marketing plan is one of several official planning documents created by a company. These include the business plan, which outlines the organization's overall financial and operational objectives and strategies; and the strategic plan, which discusses the organization's general long-term strategic direction. Sir George Bull, former chairman of the U.K. supermarket chain J. Sainsbury, stresses that the marketing plan is distinguished from the business plan by its focus. "The business plan takes as both its starting point and its objective the business itself," he explains. In contrast, "the marketing plan starts with the customer and works its way round to the business."[4]

The company's strategic plan falls in between, laying out the broad strategies that will guide the strategic management of all divisions and functions over a three- to five-year planning horizon. The marketing plan is created at a lower level than either the business or the strategic plan, and it is intended to provide shorter-term, specific operational direction for how the organization will implement strategies and move toward achieving the targeted results.

In the past, marketing planning often was sequestered in the marketing department until the plan was reviewed by management, revised, and then distributed to sales and other departments. These days, however, marketing planning encompasses more bottom-up, organizationwide input and collaboration. At Nokia, for example, managers and employees from different units contribute ideas to be incorporated into the plan. With tweaking to allow for endless environmental shifts such as new technology and competition, this is the plan used to guide the company's marketing. Such collaboration is a necessity when, like Nokia, a company introduces dozens of new products yearly.[5] In addition to building internal consensus and cooperation, this two-way flow of information provides valuable input for strategies and implementation at all levels.

Larger organizations such as Yum Brands frequently require a marketing plan for each unit (e.g., individual stores or divisions) as well as for each product or brand.

Yum Brands. KFC, Pizza Hut, Taco Bell, Long John Silver's, and A&W are among the well-known fast-food brands in Yum's global empire. Within the United States, the company is pursuing growth by developing new products based on studies of customer needs. After research found that a large percentage of office workers eat lunch at their desks, KFC created a marketing plan to introduce the Mashed Potato Bowl, a convenient, one-bowl take-out lunch featuring bite-size pieces of chicken, cheese, corn, and potatoes or rice. Testing at several KFC locations helped marketers gauge consumer appeal and refine the ingredients to make preparation easier. Interestingly, the company has learned that customers prefer Yum restaurants that feature more than one brand, such as KFC and Pizza Hut. Putting several brands under one roof gives family members with different tastes a wider variety of choices (and boosts sales and profit margins for Yum). The company also has a separate marketing plan for expanding in Asian markets.[6]

Contents of a Marketing Plan

Although the exact contents, length, and format may vary, most marketing plans contain the sections shown in Exhibit 1.2. (The sample plans accompanying the *Marketing Plan Pro* software and the sample in Appendix 1 show how plan contents and length differ depending on the organization and its purpose.) The executive summary at the beginning of the plan is actually the final section to be written, because it serves as a brief overview of the main points. The other sections are generally drafted in the order in which they appear in the plan, with each successive section building on the previous one. Managers are unable to prepare marketing budgets and schedules, for example, until their objectives, strategies, and action programs have been set. Note that when a company changes one part of the plan, it may have to change other parts as well (such as programs and budgets), because of the interrelated nature of the sections.

Planning Tip
Get a fresh perspective by creating a new plan every year rather than adapting last year's plan.

Even after receiving management approval and being implemented, marketing plans should be reexamined in accordance with changes in competition, customers' needs and attitudes, product or company performance, and other factors. Sometimes changes are warranted, sometimes not, as PepsiCo's experience shows.

PepsiCo. The U.S. soft-drink market is barely growing and intensely competitive, yet New York-based PepsiCo is growing through higher sales of diet sodas, bottled water, energy drinks, and snacks. The company is always testing different activities; for instance, it recently gave Wal-Mart an exclusive on the introduction of Slice One fruit-flavored diet soda. Another marketing move involved a slight recipe change to make Mountain Dew and Diet Mountain Dew taste more alike—a move that drew both complaints and compliments. After the chief marketing officer listened to customers on both sides, she ultimately decided against switching back to the old formula. Now, she says, "the calls have died down and the [sales] volume is up. We definitely made the right call." Although Pepsi's North American beverage volume continues to rise, its international volume is rising even faster, suggesting higher profit potential overseas.[7]

EXHIBIT 1.2 Main Sections of a Marketing Plan

Section	*Description*
Executive summary	Briefly reviews the plan's highlights and objectives, linking the marketing effort to higher-level strategies and goals.
Current marketing situation	Summarizes environmental trends: • Internal and external situational analysis (mission, offerings, markets, previous results, competitors, other environmental forces) • SWOT (internal strengths and weaknesses, external opportunities and threats) analysis
Objectives and issues	Outlines the specific marketing plan objectives to be achieved and identifies issues that may affect attainment of some objectives.
Target market, customer analysis, positioning	Explains the segmentation, targeting, and positioning decisions. Also discusses the segments to be targeted, with an overview of customers' and prospects' needs, wants, behavior, attitudes, loyalty, and purchasing patterns.
Marketing strategy	Shows the overall strategy to be used in achieving the marketing plan objectives by creating, communicating, and delivering value to the target market.
Marketing programs	Lays out the programs supporting the marketing strategy, including specific activities, schedules, and responsibilities for: • Product • Price • Place (channel) • Promotion (marketing communications) • Service • Internal marketing
Financial plans	Details expected revenues, budgets, and profits based on the marketing programs in the plan.
Implementation controls	Indicates how the plan will be implemented, including metrics for measuring performance; shows how adjustments will be made to keep programs on track toward objectives; and includes contingency plans as needed.

The success of a marketing plan depends on a complex web of internal and external relationships as well as on uncontrollable environmental factors. In many cases, unexpected or fast-developing circumstances can alter the environment so profoundly that even the most carefully crafted marketing strategy becomes obsolete in short order. Here is how Sony's competitive situation has been changing.

Sony. Known for its sleek, innovative electronics, Sony is under competitive attack from more nimble companies introducing value-added products that are commanding customers' attention and building a loyal following. Among its competitors are: Apple, which is always updating its stylish iPod digital media player with new capabilities or increased storage; Dell, which is promoting feature-packed home theater equipment; and Microsoft, which markets the popular Xbox videogame console. Rivals have made inroads because Sony didn't anticipate how quickly digital technology would sweep the consumer electronics industry; it was therefore unprepared for the demands of this new environment. "The bridge between content [such as music] and hardware [such as a player] is software, and that was something we didn't master," says Sony's CEO. In response to technological advances and increased competitive pressure, Sony has changed its marketing plan by eliminating a number of product lines and unrelated businesses, cutting costs and prices, streamlining product development, and researching new ways to satisfy customers' needs.[8]

As these examples indicate, no marketing plan is ever really final. Rather, the marketing plan must be updated and adapted as the market and customers' needs evolve and the organization's situation, priorities, and performance change.

DEVELOPING A MARKETING PLAN

Marketing plans generally cover a full year, although some (especially those covering new-product introductions) may project activities and anticipate results farther into the future. The marketing planning process starts several months before the marketing plan is scheduled to go into operation; this allows sufficient time for thorough research and analysis, management review and revision, and coordination of resources among departments and business units.

The Phoenix Suns basketball team, for instance, starts planning for the following season even before the current year's playoffs are over. During the early stages of working on the marketing plan, team management reviews the current season's ticket and merchandise sales performance, analyzes game-by-game attendance, weighs fan feedback and market research, and swaps best-practices ideas with other National Basketball Association teams. With months of lead time, management can examine the team's current situation, identify market segments for special attention, set objectives, and prepare forecasts of future results. Then the team is ready to plan team marketing initiatives and special events such as community appearances by players and the gorilla mascot.[9]

The following sections introduce each of the six marketing planning steps shown in Exhibit 1.1, providing an overview for the remainder of this handbook.

Research and Analyze the Current Situation

The first step is to study the current situation before charting the organization's marketing course. Externally, marketers study environmental trends to detect demographic, economic, technological, political-legal, ecological, or social-cultural changes that can affect marketing decisions, performance opportunities and threats, and potential profits. Marketing managers also assess the company's capabilities and the strategies of competitors so they can build on internal strengths while exploiting rivals' weaknesses and making the most of emerging opportunities. In addition, they analyze how customers, competitors, suppliers, distributors, partners, and other stakeholders might influence marketing results.

Look at Netflix's situation.

Planning Tip
This analysis helps you identify influences on your objectives, strategies, and performance.

Netflix. This online DVD rental firm, founded in 1999, today serves more than 5 million subscribers. Its first marketing plan called for customers to rent and pay for DVDs one at a time, plus a late fee if the DVD was not returned within a week. However, this approach attracted few customers, so the company changed its marketing plan. Now customers pay a flat monthly fee to have one or more DVDs out at one time, with no return deadlines. Customers like the convenience of renting DVDs by mail, selecting from 60,000 movies, and browsing personalized recommendations from Netflix's automated system. Using technology to best advantage, Netflix will soon offer movie downloads. Despite competition from Blockbuster and from cable companies like Comcast, CEO Reed Hastings believes that Netflix's convenience and value will gain it a solid customer base of 20 million by 2012.[10]

Chapter 2 contains more detail on gathering and analyzing data to examine the organization's current situation and the issues and opportunities it may face.

Understand Markets and Customers

The second step in marketing planning is to analyze markets and customers (whether consumers or businesses) by researching market-share trends, product demand, and customer characteristics such as buying habits, needs, wants, attitudes and behavior, and satisfaction. Among the many questions to be studied are: Who is doing the buying, when, why, and how? Are buying patterns changing—and why? What products and categories are or will be in demand? Consider how McDonald's marketers have become expert at analyzing customers' preferences in different countries and then adapting menu items for local tastes: aloo tikka in Mumbai, gourmet burgers in Tokyo, and kosher meats in Tel Aviv. It also knows when to pull a new product from the regular menu, as it did when customers did not warm to Hot 'n' Spicy McChicken.[11]

Planning Tip
Market and customer analyses help you decide which customers to target and how to provide value by meeting their needs.

With cutting-edge technology, marketing managers can examine detailed customer buying behavior based on sales by product, by time and place, and other factors. Wal-Mart uses sophisticated software to track each item in each store, determine how quickly it is selling (or not selling), what other items it is usually purchased with, and the likely revenue and profit consequences of cutting an item's price. Carphone Warehouse Group, a 1,400-unit chain of cell phone stores in 10 European countries, checks sales every 15 minutes so it can react quickly to problems or shift resources to better-performing areas.[12]

However, marketers must not overdo customer research. To illustrate, different groups within IBM used to conduct 48 or more surveys measuring customer satisfaction with products, sales, and service; one survey involved 40,000 interviews spread over 58 countries. Some IBM customers complained about being surveyed up to five times a year. "When you're the CEO of one of our major customers, and you hear from IBM three times in a month on a survey that sounds identical to the last one you answered, you get a little annoyed," notes IBM's director of worldwide customer satisfaction management, who consolidated the surveys and responses to make research data available across the corporation.[13] (More information about analyzing markets and customers can be found in Chapter 3.)

Plan Segmentation, Targeting, and Positioning

Planning Tip
Use segmentation and targeting to focus on opportunities, then use positioning for competitive advantage.

Because organizations can never be all things to all people, marketers have to apply their knowledge of the market and customers to select groups within the market, known as **segments,** for marketing attention. In the past, this meant dividing the overall market into separate groupings of customers, based on characteristics such as age, gender, geography, needs, behavior, or other variables. With today's technology, however, some companies can now identify and serve segments as small as a single customer, based on what they know (or can find out) about that consumer or business.

The purpose of segmentation is to group customers with similar needs, wants, behavior, attitudes, or other characteristics that affect their demand for or usage of the good or service being marketed. For instance, Bank of the West identified a small but growing customer segment in Kansas not being served by traditional banks: time-pressured factory workers, mainly immigrants, who need access to basic services like check-cashing. Therefore, Bank of the West built a special waterproof ATM inside a local meatpacking plant so employees could cash checks and handle banking transactions during lunch or break periods. As a side benefit, when the factory is washed, the ATM can withstand the washing as well. Another customer segment being targeted is Asian Americans in California, for which Bank of the West has created a "Pacific Rim Banking" program offering services in English, Chinese, Japanese, and Korean.[14]

Once the market has been segmented, the next set of decisions centers on **targeting,** including whether to market to one segment, several segments, or the entire market, and how to cover these segments. Segmentation and targeting are vital in **business-to-business (B2B) marketing,** as well as consumer markets.

Intuition Publishing. Based in Dublin, Ireland, Intuition Publishing creates online and classroom training courses targeted to financial services firms. Recently the company recognized an even more profitable opportunity in a subsegment of the overall market: banks that require training customized to their specific locations, policies, procedures, and employee competence levels. By customizing its off-the-shelf educational programs for individual banks, Intuition Publishing has achieved revenue growth of 20 percent per year.[15]

Next, the organization formulates suitable **positioning,** using marketing to create a competitively distinctive place (position) for the brand or product in the mind of targeted customers. This positioning sets the product apart from competing products in a way that is meaningful to customers. For example, Apple Computer uses design to differentiate its Macintosh computers and iPod digital media players; the European discount airline EasyJet promotes cheap fares to communicate its differentiation. To effectively create a particular image among targeted customers, companies must convey the positioning through every aspect of marketing. This is why most Apple iPod ads focus on the product's sleek styling and EasyJet's Web site emphasizes ticket price rather than in-flight service. Chapter 4 discusses segmentation, targeting, and positioning in further detail.

Plan Direction, Objectives, and Marketing Support

Planning Tip
Be sure marketing plan objectives fit with the organization's overall mission and goals.

Marketing managers are responsible for setting the direction of the organization's marketing activities, based on goals and objectives. **Goals** are long-term performance targets, whereas **objectives** are short-term targets that support the achievement of the goals. Setting and achieving shorter-term marketing, financial, and societal objectives will, over time, move the organization forward toward its overall goals, whatever they may be and however they may be expressed.

To illustrate, executives at Target Stores established a detailed mission during the 1970s to guide future growth. Although the mission has been revised periodically, one basic tenet unchanged for 30 years is the idea that Target sells "the best products at the best value," specifically, "affordability and great design." Another tenet is that the

EXHIBIT 1.3 Six Approaches to Growth

	·········· **Product Offers** ··········		
Markets	Penetrate existing markets with current product offers	Modify current product offers for existing markets	Innovate product offers for existing markets
	Market current product offers in expanded geographic areas	Modify current product offers for dispersed markets	Innovate product offers geographically
	Expand current product offers to entirely new markets	Modify current product offers for entirely new markets	Diversify by innovating product offers for entirely new markets

company will "give generously to the communities" in which it does business. This mission provides direction for the top managers, who set long-term growth goals and for marketing managers who set and are held accountable for shorter-term marketing, financial, and societal objectives documented in the marketing plan.[16]

Like Target, most businesses use their marketing plans to support growth strategies. As shown in Exhibit 1.3, growth can be achieved in six ways; in practice, some companies pursue growth through two or more of these methods.[17] For example, Boeing has developed new products (like the 787 Dreamliner jet) for its existing market of air carriers; in addition, it develops new configurations of current products (like the 737 jet) for new and existing markets.[18] Note, however, that marketing an existing product (or variations on that product) is not as risky as marketing a new product or diversifying into other offerings.[19] Also, the chosen direction and objectives require marketing support, as discussed below.

More organizations are adopting **sustainable marketing,** "the establishment, maintenance, and enhancement of customer relationships so that the objectives of the parties involved are met without compromising the ability of future generations to achieve their own objectives."[20] This requires balancing long-term goals with the short-term realities of current objectives and budgets. For instance, FedEx has set a goal of cutting air pollution by buying 30,000 low-emission diesel-electric vans over the next decade. It is also arranging to power more of its FedEx Kinko's stores with electricity from environmentally friendly renewable sources. Although the initial outlay is high, savings in fuel and maintenance will eventually offset the entire cost; the program also positions FedEx as a "green" company.[21] (See Chapter 5 for more about planning direction and objectives.)

Develop Marketing Strategies and Programs

At this point, the company has examined its current situation, looked at markets and customers, targeted segments and determined its positioning, and set both direction and objectives. Now management formulates strategies for providing value using the basic marketing-mix tools of product, place, price, and promotion, enhanced by service, to build stronger customer relationships and internal marketing to bolster support within the organization. Note that some companies can profit by developing a marketing mix for segments of one. Both Boeing and Airbus do this by adjusting the configuration of their jets, their product pricing, their delivery schedules, and their sales approach to the needs and buying cycle of each airline customer.

Marketing strategies and programs must be consistent with the organization's overall direction, goals, and strategies, as Rock Bottom's experience demonstrates.

Planning Tip
Check that your strategies fit with segmentation, targeting, and positioning decisions.

Rock Bottom Restaurants. Headquartered in Louisville, Colorado, the growing Rock Bottom Restaurants chain develops marketing programs with a strong local connection, because "our brand is built on community involvement," says the director of marketing. Its biggest promotion focuses on Fire Chief Ale, with nearby fire companies receiving a cash donation for every pint sold in the local Rock Bottom Restaurant. Since the program started more than a decade ago, the company has donated $1 million to local firehouses, while the chain increased in size from 12 to 30 restaurants. When a new Rock Bottom Restaurant opens, the marketing plan calls for selecting a local charity to receive the proceeds of the grand-opening fund-raiser. This generates positive publicity while helping the restaurant build relationships with customers and community members.[22]

External marketing strategies are used to build relationships with suppliers, partners, and channel partners such as wholesalers and retailers. In addition, an internal marketing strategy is used to build support among employees and managers, demonstrate marketing's value and importance to the organization, ensure proper staffing to carry out marketing programs, and motivate the proper level of customer service. (Chapter 5 contains a section on internal marketing and customer service; Chapter 6 covers product and brand strategy; Chapter 7 covers pricing; Chapter 8 explores channels and logistics; and Chapter 9 examines integrated marketing communication).

Track Progress and Control Implementation

Before the marketing plan is implemented, the final step is to identify mechanisms and methods of measuring progress toward objectives. Most companies use sales forecasts, budgets, schedules, and other tools to establish and record standards for market share, sales, profitability, productivity, and other measures against which to evaluate results. By comparing actual outcomes against yearly, quarterly, monthly, weekly, daily, and even hourly projections, management can see where the firm is ahead or behind and where adjustments are needed to return to the right path. Tracking progress is essential because marketing is accountable for producing the results specified in the marketing plan and providing value to the organization. Many companies use specific financial measures to evaluate marketing outcomes; these may include return on marketing investment and return on sales.[23]

Planning Tip
Make your forecasts, budgets, and schedules realistic to better support your objectives.

Writing a good marketing plan is not enough; proper implementation is just as critical, as numerous businesses have learned the hard way. The online furniture retailer Living.com, for example, wanted to revolutionize the way consumers buy furniture. Its marketing plan centered on the sale of upscale sofas and other home furnishings; too late, the company found out that few top-end manufacturers would agree to sell through Web retailers. The company also assumed that consumers would visit local furniture stores to browse, then buy online. In reality, consumers looked at Living.com's site, then went to local stores to buy. Living.com burned through millions of dollars before closing down.[24]

To control implementation, marketers measure interim performance of the planned programs against preset standards, diagnose the results, and then take corrective action if results fail to measure up. This **marketing control** process is iterative; managers should expect to retrace their steps as they implement strategies, assess the results, and take action to bring performance into line with expectations (see Exhibit 1.4). Chapter 10 covers in more detail the topics of measuring progress and controlling implementation.

EXHIBIT 1.4 Marketing Control

Set marketing ⟶ set standards ⟶ measure ⟶ diagnose results ⟶ take corrective action
plan objectives   performance   if needed

PREPARING FOR MARKETING PLANNING

The complex and volatile business environment as well as intense competition in many industries and current trends in consolidation and globalization make marketing planning more challenging than ever before. Therefore, marketers must develop a number of professional and organizational strengths, including:

- *Knowledge of markets and customers.* Marketers need current, in-depth knowledge of what their customers want, how and why they buy, how they perceive the value of competing products, and so on. Often, technology can be used to collect and analyze data about specific customers instead of relying on a composite picture of the average customer. This allows fine-tuning of marketing actions to build one-to-one customer relationships, rather than relying on general knowledge, such as knowing that the median age of the U.S. population is 35.3 years old and the average U.S. household consists of 2.59 people.[25]

- *Core competencies.* **Core competencies** are skills, technologies, and processes—not easily imitated—that give the company competitive superiority in providing value by effectively and efficiently satisfying customers. Marketers identify these by looking at employees' talents and expertise and the organization's technologies and operational processes. How can marketing build on these core competencies to provide customer-satisfying value and achieve marketing plan objectives? Just as important, how can management handle activities outside the organization's core competencies through outsourcing, forging alliances, and other methods?

- *Relationships.* Strong, mutually beneficial links with suppliers, distributors, ad agencies, and others form the chain through which the organization creates, delivers, and communicates value. For example, Cardinal Health Care coordinates its suppliers' activities to get the right mix of medical products to hospitals at just the right time. Cardinal's hospital customers value the benefit of having prepackaged trays of sterilized surgical tools delivered immediately before operations are to begin.[26] And because the marketing function must work with every other company function in satisfying customers, good internal relationships are also critical.

Primary Marketing Tools

Planning Tip
Use your marketing plan to provide value in a competitively superior way.

In addition to relying on these three main strengths, marketers need to be creative in their use of the primary marketing tools: product, channel, pricing, and promotion. Some of the key elements in the marketing mix are shown in Exhibit 1.5 (and discussed further in Chapters 6, 7, 8, and 9).

Product Offering

Although the product can be either a tangible good or an intangible service, many offerings are actually a combination of tangibles and intangibles.[27] Lexus is selling luxury cars, but it's also selling intangible aspects of a car purchase: "A free espresso, an

EXHIBIT 1.5   The Marketing Mix

Product Offering
Product variety
Quality
Features
Brand
Packaging
Labeling
Warranty
Other product issues

Pricing
List price
Discounts
Credit terms
Payment period
Other pricing issues
New product pricing
Price competition

Marketing Mix

Channel
Coverage
Assortments
Locations
Inventory
Transport
Order fulfillment
Other channel issues
Levels

Promotion
Advertising
Sales promotion
Public relations
Personal selling
Direct marketing
Internet activities
Other promotion issues

explanatory meeting in the service drive, and a detailed car afterward was 'wow' back in 1994," comments the general manager of Lexus. Now, he says, "when you purchase a Lexus, the ownership experience will be better than anywhere in luxury retail." The offering must therefore include both a great car and competitively superior dealer sales and service.[28]

In planning product strategy, it is important to think about all the components and about customers' perceptions of the offering as a whole. Piaggio, for example, has learned that customers buying its Vespa motor scooters particularly value styling and technology, not just ease of operation and fuel efficiency.[29] Branding is another key aspect that is so vital in certain categories that large retailers are cashing in by introducing their own brands: The drug-store chain CVS has its Gold Emblem brand; Home Depot markets the Hampton Bay brand.[30]

Pricing

What should the organization charge for its product offering? Pricing decisions are based on a number of factors, including how customers perceive the value of the offering; how the organization positions the product; what the product's development, production, and distribution costs are; the competitive structure of the market; and the value that the organization expects to gain. Pricing can be so complex that companies such as General Electric and Home Depot use special software to set and change prices.[31] Technology is bringing new practices and new flexibility to pricing, as eBay, Orbitz, and other Web-based businesses have demonstrated.

Higher pricing can support an upscale image or better quality, but it also carries the risk that customers may perceive the price as too high relative to the product's perceived benefits. A low-price strategy can attract new customers, boost market share,

NEED HELP CHECKING VEGETABLES OFF YOUR DAILY "TO DO" LIST?

Three Full Servings of Vegetables

V8®

100% VEGETABLE JUICE

12 FL. OZ.

DON'T JUST LIVE, THRIVE.™

1 serving of vegetables = 1/2 cup. 3 servings in 12 oz. V8. Daily recommendation of 2-1/2 cups of vegetables for a 2,000 calorie diet (USDA MyPyramid).

Both demographic and social trends affect the marketing of V8 vegetable juice.

and fend off rivals; however, it requires a careful balance between building relationships and building profits. Nintendo is a case in point.

Nintendo. Competing with Microsoft's Xbox and Sony's PlayStation models, Nintendo was able to stimulate U.S. sales and reduce its inventory of GameCube videogame consoles by reducing prices up to 45%. This also helped Nintendo sell more of its profitable game programs. Later, the successful launch of the much-anticipated Nintendo DS portable game device led to shortages in some areas because the device and its games had widespread appeal for adults, teens, and younger children. Thanks to the Nintendo DS, company profits soared. Now Nintendo has priced its new easy-to-operate Wii game console lower than Xbox or PlayStation to attract consumers who think videogame devices are too complicated. Will Nintendo again profit by selling more games to this newer segment?[32]

Channel

Channel (place) strategy involves decisions about how, when, and where to make goods and services available to customers. Many consumer products pass through one or more layers of wholesalers and retailers in the course of reaching buyers. Thus, manufacturers must check frequently with their channel partners to learn about customers' buying patterns, needs, and requests. "What happens in Ohio at Best Buy is going to be quite different [from what happens] at Dixons in Manchester [U.K.]," says the head of worldwide manufacturing for Cisco Systems, which makes networking equipment under the Linksys brand, among others.[33] Cisco also makes components and products for direct sale to business customers through a channel without wholesale or retail participation. In addition, transportation, inventory management, and other logistics issues are an integral part of channel strategy. As an example, Boeing buys 6 million parts for use in assembling its jets. The company's global suppliers must have sufficient stock and arrange transportation to get parts to Boeing's Seattle-area factory on time and within budget.

Promotion

Promotion covers all the tools used to communicate value to the target market, including advertising; public relations; sales promotion; personal selling; and direct marketing techniques such as catalogs, e-mail, and wireless messages. Because of media proliferation and audience fragmentation, some companies are adding nontraditional communications programs and reducing their use of mass media like network television. Small businesses are finding keyword search ads particularly cost-effective. When Internet users use a search engine like Google or Yahoo! to find information or merchandise, they usually see sponsored links (paid for by business advertisers) alongside the results. Ralph Loeff, who owns a copier sales and repair shop in Los Angeles, is so delighted with the keyword search ads that he now budgets $300 a month for this activity. "I've got a lot of customers I never would have had if I didn't have the Internet," he says.[34] Of course, when using a variety of messages and media, marketers must carefully manage the overall content and impact through the use of integrated marketing communication.

Supporting the Marketing Mix

No marketing plan is complete without strategies for supporting the marketing mix with customer service and internal marketing. Why is customer service so important? First, it reinforces positive perceptions of a brand, product, and company—and customers expect it (or even demand it). Second, good service can clearly differentiate a

Planning Tip
Remember that good internal relationships are a prerequisite to good customer service.

company from competitors. Third, poor or inconsistent customer service simply will not satisfy customers; even worse, customers are likely to tell others about their dissatisfaction, generating negative word of mouth communication.[35] Fourth, great service can help the organization retain current customers and bring in new ones through reputation and referral.

At the very least, marketing plans should allow for handling customer inquiries and complaints; some may also cover installation (e.g., for appliances, floor coverings, or giant turbines), technical support (e.g., for computer products), and training (e.g., for software). Web-based FAQs and help indexes, e-mail, live text chat, live online telephony, and/or toll-free telephone contact are common customer service tactics. Even the U.S. government is focusing on customer service, speeding up answers to inquiries submitted by mail or e-mail to the Federal Citizen Information Center (www.firstgov.gov) or by phone to the National Contact Center.[36]

The internal marketing strategy focuses all employees on serving customers and builds support for the marketing plan. For example, Green Hills Farms Store, a family-owned supermarket in Syracuse, New York, pretests store promotions on its 200 employees. Once marketers receive employee feedback, they adjust a program if needed before opening it to customers. Employees also serve as goodwill ambassadors, telling their friends and family about new promotions. In addition, to add value and strengthen customer relationships, Green Hills' employees use technology to prepare and deliver product promotions tailored to individual customers' purchasing patterns.[37]

Guiding Principles

Supplementing the marketing strengths and tools discussed above, today's marketers should follow five guiding principles to contribute to customer value and stay competitive as they proceed through the marketing planning process: (1) expect change; (2) emphasize relationships; (3) involve everyone; (4) seek alliances; and (5) be innovative in providing value. These guiding principles, summarized in Exhibit 1.6, are explored below.

Expect Change

Planning Tip
Expect change and stay alert for new partners, rivals, customers, opportunities, and threats.

The global networked economy is a fact of business life, with buyers and sellers able to connect anywhere in the world. In practical terms, this means marketers can more easily link with the best suppliers, partners, resellers, and deals, because geographical distance is not the obstacle it used to be. Still, competitors can more easily explore the territory of their rivals, so marketers must expect change and be ready to fend off rivals from anywhere at any time.

EXHIBIT 1.6 Guiding Principles of Marketing Planning

Compete effectively
- Expect change
- Emphasize relationships
- Involve everyone
- Seek alliances
- Be innovative

Create, communicate, deliver customer value

Build internal/external relationships

In the dynamic business environment, trends can come and go without warning. Here is how the retailer Escada plans for change.

Escada. Fashion never stands still, which is why Escada, a women's apparel chain based in Germany, introduces as many as 15 full product lines every year. The company also watches for suddenly hot looks or colors and makes these the basis of periodic "minicollections" produced between regularly scheduled line introductions, bringing shoppers back again and again in search of the latest styles. "It is a reaction to the ever-faster fashion cycle and to retailers like H&M and Zara, who react to new trends very quickly," says an Escada official. The company continues to revamp its offerings, adding "more modern and youthful" clothing to "attract the daughters but keep the mothers," according to the design director.[38]

Emphasize Relationships

All customers—consumers, businesses, not-for-profit organizations, and government agencies—have more information and more choices in today's marketplace, which means they have more power. Therefore, for long-term success, marketers need to strengthen relationships with their customers as well as suppliers, channel members, partners, and other key **stakeholders** (people and organizations that are influenced by or can influence company performance).

Traditionally, companies kept up a monologue by sending information to customers through advertisements and other promotion techniques. With a dialogue, however, information flows both ways—from the firm to customers and from customers to the firm. This dialogue provides clues to what customers think, feel, need, want, expect, and value, helping marketers adjust current programs and plan new programs to reinforce loyalty.

Some marketers are taking dialogue a step further, connecting customers with each other and taking the pulse of the community. The auction site eBay, for example, also serves as a forum for buyers and sellers to exchange ideas and research areas of interest. Having buyers rate sellers is "a really important part of eBay's chemistry," says the CEO. With 200 million people worldwide using eBay, she adds, "A cardinal sin is not knowing what the community's concerns are." And, to help sellers build relationships with each other and build their businesses online, the company also holds an annual eBay Live convention, complete with success stories and practical tips.[39]

Involve Everyone

At one time, marketing and sales personnel were the only people responsible for an organization's marketing functions. Now all employees must be involved in marketing, and all contact points must be seen as opportunities to add value and strengthen customer relationships. Everything about the company sends a signal, so companies must project the right impression and meet customers' expectations through more than marketing.

To keep employees involved, they must be informed about products, promotions, and whatever else they need to satisfy customers. Many firms circulate printed newsletters, post news on internal Web sites, or send updates via e-mail to keep employees informed. Japanese beauty products manufacturer Shiseido connects employees in 16,000 stores worldwide with cell phones that can download corporate information and upload comments on fast-selling products. This keeps manufacturing, sales, and home-office personnel updated about inventory, requests, sales, and more.[40]

EXHIBIT 1.7   Building a Network of Alliances to Provide Value

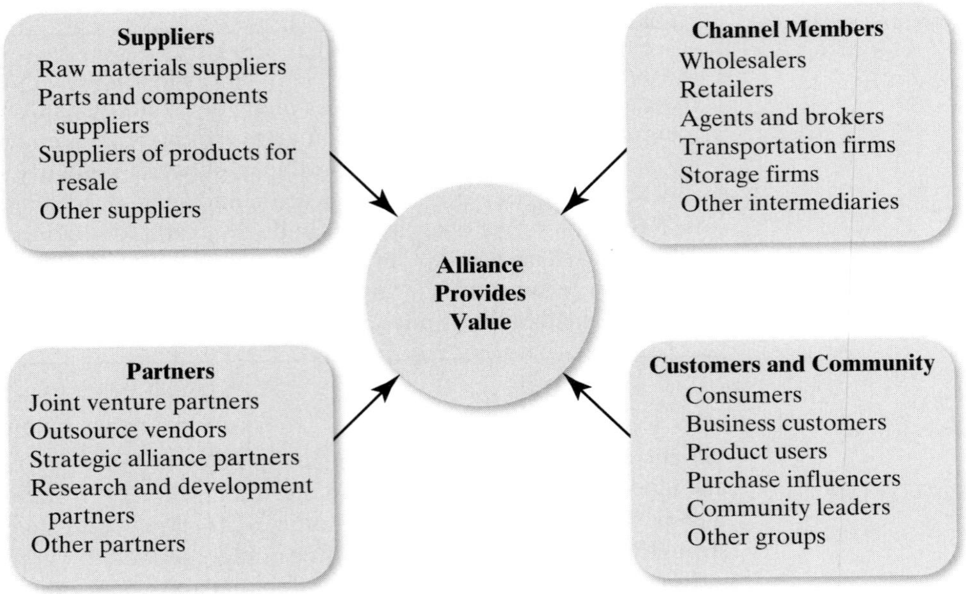

Suppliers
Raw materials suppliers
Parts and components
  suppliers
Suppliers of products for
  resale
Other suppliers

Channel Members
Wholesalers
Retailers
Agents and brokers
Transportation firms
Storage firms
Other intermediaries

Alliance Provides Value

Partners
Joint venture partners
Outsource vendors
Strategic alliance partners
Research and development
  partners
Other partners

Customers and Community
Consumers
Business customers
Product users
Purchase influencers
Community leaders
Other groups

Seek Alliances

Planning Tip
Seek out creative ideas
and insights from
suppliers and other
value-chain members.

Successful marketers work through a network of alliances with carefully chosen suppliers, channel members, partners, customers, and community leaders (see Exhibit 1.7). The purpose is to provide the mutual support, capabilities, and innovations that participants need to satisfy their customers, meet their objectives, and be competitive. In essence, the company's network of alliances is in competition with the networks that rival companies have assembled.[41]

- *Suppliers* not only provide raw materials, parts, and other inputs; they can offer insights regarding the external environment. Increasingly, companies are connecting with suppliers to lower costs and exchange data for mutual profitability. These alliances are critical because the quality of a product depends, in large part, on the quality of suppliers' materials.
- *Channel members* such as wholesalers and retailers have daily contact with customers and can provide vital feedback about buying patterns and preferences. Channel choices are critical because customers associate the firm's brand and value with the quality and convenience of their shopping experience.
- *Partners* in joint ventures, outsourcing, or other arrangements contribute their core competencies and market knowledge. Linking up with a partner that has complementary capabilities and strengths gives both more marketing power. This is why consumer products manufacturer Procter & Gamble develops new products by coordinating the efforts of 600 partners around the world.[42]
- *Customers* can be excellent partners because they are eager for products that solve their problems or, in the case of businesses, want to better serve their own customers. 3M, for example, brings in business customers to discuss their needs, and its scientists visit customer sites to see products in use. Groups within 3M that forge customer partnerships generate four times as many new product ideas compared with other groups, helping to boost revenues by $1.2 billion annually.[43]

- *Community* leaders from civic groups, charities, school groups, and other parts of the community can contribute feedback about the organization's image and activities and inform management thinking about social issues, local concerns, and sustainable marketing ideas. One example is Home Depot, which donates materials for community projects like playground construction and encourages employees to volunteer locally. Why is community involvement so important? "Things have become a lot more interdependent," says Home Depot's CEO. "There are a broader range of constituents." He also believes that community involvement is "just the right thing to do."[44]

Innovate to Provide Value

To succeed, companies must seize every opportunity to be innovative in providing value. A return to old-fashioned personal service is a welcome "innovation" in industries in which automation has reduced human contact. To illustrate, Patriot National Bank in Connecticut competes with regional and national banks by hiring employees who are known in the community and by emphasizing personal service at its 11 branches. The bank's marketing plan calls for high-tech as well as high-touch operations: "We serve muffins and cookies in our offices, but we still have Internet banking," says the bank's president.[45]

Many innovations involve technology. John Deere, which has been making agricultural equipment since 1837, sees technologically advanced new products as the key to growth; its technology now helps farmers better manage crops while improving productivity.[46] Online, companies are applying technology to deliver good service and provide value that satisfies customers. Here's how Blue Nile sells expensive jewelry on the Internet.

Blue Nile. Business is clicking along for Blue Nile (www.bluenile.com), which invites customers to review pages of information about diamonds and design the jewelry of their dreams before they buy online. Customers can zoom in on 32,000 gems and try the stones in settings of different sizes and shapes. Because Blue Nile's jewelry sells for up to $300,000, it is not surprising that customers typically view 200 Web pages before ordering. More than half the company's revenue comes from the sale of engagement rings, although the site also features other jewelry to attract new customers who, once satisfied, are likely to return for bigger purchases. Such enthusiastic customer response has helped Blue Nile expand quickly, adding a U.K. division as it surpasses $200 million in annual sales.[47]

Companies can pursue innovation in a variety of ways. Ben & Jerry's, for instance, sends tasters around the world in search of ideas for novel ice cream flavors. After its travels, the team concocts 150 recipes and narrows the decision to about 12 new flavors each year. Given that Ben & Jerry's marketing plan calls for selling fewer than three dozen flavors at any one time, 12 newcomers represent considerable innovation. The company, a Unilever division, is also known for its commitment to social responsibility causes. Its American Pie flavor, for example, was launched with a nationwide campaign promoting greater U.S. federal funding of children's education and health care programs.[48] Innovations perceived as providing superior value attract like-minded customers, suppliers, and investors, thus building stronger relationships for long-term success.

SUMMARY

Marketing planning is the structured process of determining how to provide value to customers, the organization, and key stakeholders by researching and analyzing the current situation, including markets and customers; developing and documenting marketing's objectives, strategies, and programs; and then implementing, evaluating, and controlling marketing activities to achieve the objectives. The marketing plan documents the results of the marketing planning process and explains strategies and programs for building relationships by creating, communicating, and delivering value to customers. It also serves an important coordination function and allows for accountability by showing how results will be measured and adjustments made if needed. With internal consensus, the plan provides direction for employees and managers; encourages collaboration; outlines resource allocation; and delineates the tasks, schedules, and responsibilities planned to accomplish objectives.

The six broad steps in marketing planning are (1) research and analyze the current situation; (2) understand markets and customers; (3) plan segmentation, targeting, and positioning; (4) plan direction, objectives, and marketing support; (5) develop marketing strategies and programs; and (6) track progress and control plan implementation. For marketing purposes, marketers need a number of professional and organizational strengths and the know-how to create an effective marketing mix supplemented by customer service and internal marketing. Five broad guiding principles for marketing planning are to expect change, emphasize relationships, involve everyone, seek alliances, and innovate to provide value.

CHAPTER

Analyzing the Current Situation

In this chapter:

PREVIEW

A change in one element of the marketplace or organization—even a small change—can make a big difference in decisions about marketing strategies, customer service, choice of channels, pricing, and other aspects of the marketing plan. This chapter explores the use of environmental scanning and analysis to understand the dynamic forces and trends affecting the current marketing situation. First is a discussion of the internal environment, including the organization's mission, resources, product offerings, previous results, business relationships, keys to success, and warning signs. The second half of the chapter examines the external environment, including demographic, economic, ecological, technological, political-legal, and social-cultural trends, as well as competitor analysis. Coverage of SWOT (strength, weakness, opportunity, threat) analysis ends the chapter; this lays the foundation for market and customer analysis, which is discussed in Chapter 3.

demand; meanwhile, Fording and other firms must consider substitutes like retreaded tires.[8] Sometimes companies can arrange external sources or supplement existing resources through new strategic alliances and new supply-chain relationships. But only by analyzing internal resources will marketers learn about gaps and strengths that can affect marketing planning, implementation, and control.

Offerings

This part of the analysis looks at what the organization is currently offering in the way of goods and services. At a minimum, it is necessary to look at the product mix and the lines within that mix, asking questions such as: What products are being offered, at what price points, and for what customer segments? What value does each product provide by solving a customer's problem or fulfilling a need? What is the age of each product and its sales and profit trend over the years? How are newer products faring in relation to older products? What is the market share of each product or line? How does each product support sales of the line—are some sold only as supplements or add-ons to others? How does each product contribute to the company's overall performance? Does one product account for a large portion of sales and profits? Where is each product in its life cycle, and how can marketing extend or enhance the life cycle?

Just as important, marketers must determine how the organization's offerings relate to its mission and to its resources. Do the products use the firm's resources most effectively and efficiently while following the mission? Are other offerings needed to restore the focus or fulfill the long-term purpose described in the mission? Answering these questions will give management a better sense of internal strengths and weaknesses in preparation for future marketing activities.

Previous Results

Planning Tip
Put results into context by examining the influence of environmental factors on the organization's performance.

The company's previous results also offer important clues to internal strengths and weaknesses that can affect results. By analyzing last year's unit and dollar sales, profits, and other financial results—and comparing these results with trends over several years—marketers can get a big picture of overall performance. Marketers also need to analyze the results of the previous years' marketing programs to see what worked and what did not.

In addition, marketers should look carefully at customer acquisition and retention costs to be sure they are appropriate for the value of the relationship. As an example, traditional catalog retailers spend about $38 to acquire a new customer. Some consumer products marketers may spend less; B2B companies and new online businesses may spend more. Netflix, for instance, spends about $35 to acquire each DVD rental customer as part of its aggressive growth strategy. "Because we're a subscription service, with an ongoing revenue stream from each customer, we expect total marketing costs will fall as a percent of revenue," notes the CEO, explaining the financial rationale.[9]

The point of analyzing previous results is to separate effective from ineffective activities and to understand related costs as a prelude to planning marketing programs. Consider the situation at Procter & Gamble, where marketers examine results over time when formulating marketing plans:

Procter & Gamble. With $57 billion in yearly sales, P&G owns some of the best-known brands on the planet, including Crest, Tide, and Gillette. In fact, 22 of its brands each generate more than $1 billion in annual sales. P&G is always studying results, product by product and category by category, to build on its successes and identify areas for satisfying the needs of even more customers. Thus, Crest debuted in 1955 as a toothpaste brand and, more than 50 years later, the brand remains so strong that it powers a broad range of products in the oral-care category. P&G spends heavily to develop and promote new products; when the company introduced Crest Pro-Health Toothpaste, it backed the launch with a $100 million multimedia ad campaign. Each campaign is then carefully evaluated in the context of expected results, overall performance, and historic sales trends.[10]

Business Relationships

A closer look at relationships with suppliers, distributors, and partners can help determine whether changes should be made in the coming year. Although cost is always a critical factor, companies also must ask whether their suppliers and distributors (1) have the capacity to increase volume if needed; (2) maintain a suitable quality level; and (3) can be true partners in providing value to satisfy customers. How has the roster of suppliers and dealers changed over time? Is the company overly dependent on one supplier or channel partner? Does the company expect its partners to provide special expertise or services? All these questions are geared toward getting a well-rounded picture of strengths and identifying weaknesses that can affect the organization's offerings and marketing plans.

Keys to Success and Warning Signs

Not everything in a marketing plan is equally important. Marketers should identify, in just a few sentences, the special factors that most influence the firm's movement toward fulfilling its mission and achieving superior performance. Pinpointing these keys to success can put the focus on the right priorities in planning the year's marketing strategies and programs. For example, Wal-Mart has built its retail empire on two major keys to success: (1) controlling costs and logistics to keep prices low and (2) entering markets underserved by competitors.

Every organization should scan for the major warning signs that indicate potential problems with leveraging the keys to success and performing as planned. For Wal-Mart, one such issue might be rising fuel and transportation costs: unless the chain can contain or lower such costs, it may be forced to hike prices—a problem when low prices are a key to success. Other possible warning signs for Wal-Mart: shifts in U.S. trade policy that affect imports, and community resistance to new-store construction.[11] Paying close attention to these issues will help Wal-Mart's marketers plan to reach their objectives.

ANALYZING THE EXTERNAL ENVIRONMENT

Planning Tip
Use this analysis to identify opportunities and threats that must be factored into your marketing decisions.

Within the external environment, marketers need to examine broad demographic, economic, ecological, technological, political-legal, and social-cultural trends. They also must pay special attention to strategies and movements of competitors. Whereas scans of the internal environment are designed to uncover strengths and weaknesses, scans of the external environment are designed to uncover opportunities and threats that can be effectively addressed in the marketing plan. Exhibit 2.3 shows an example using Southwest Airlines.

EXHIBIT 2.3   The External Environment of Southwest Airlines

Element and Potential Impact	*Possible Changes in Marketing*
Demographic trends: Population shifts and changes in business concentration can affect demand; household income can affect affordability.	Consider entry into new markets; examine pricing for targeted segments; plan promotions in line with trends.
Economic trends: Growing inflation can push costs higher; economic recovery can boost demand.	To maintain profitability, trim costs or raise prices in response to inflation; gain pricing flexibility if demand is higher.
Ecological trends: Community concerns about airports being expanded and flight-related noise can affect the number of available gates and flight slots.	Research airport plans and local reaction in new markets; research local rules about early-morning flights; train flight crews for noise-abatement.
Technological trends: Higher Internet usage can shift more customers to online reservations; advanced plane design can increase fuel efficiency.	Reduce off-line customer service support, increase marketing use of Web site; consider applying fuel savings to lower ticket prices.
Political-legal trends: More stringent security rules are forcing changes in check-in procedures and baggage handling.	Consider communications to alert customers about security requirements and offer reassurances about air travel safety.
Social-cultural trends: Money-saving choices are gaining widespread acceptance; public interest in social responsibility can affect company reputation.	Communicate the financial benefits of flying Southwest and the money-saving advantages; expand Adopt-A-Pilot community educational program for fifth-grade students.
Competitive trends: Start-up airlines can increase competitive pressure; price wars can affect revenue and profits.	Continue to enhance brand image and awareness; communicate competitive superiority; maintain competitive pricing in each market.

Demographic Trends

Consumer and business markets are moving targets—never static, always changing. For marketers of consumer products, population trends and characteristics suggest the size of the market and strength of demand. For marketers of business products, indicators of market size and strength include trends in business formation and certain organizational characteristics. However, these point-in-time examinations of demographic trends must be routinely updated to reflect any changes.

Consumer Demographics

Population growth is creating and expanding markets around the world, whether through higher birth rates, longer life spans, or immigration. Yet the population is actually shrinking in some areas as people move elsewhere, such as from urban to suburban or rural markets or from one state or country to another. For this reason, marketers need to follow the population trends in the markets where they currently do business or are considering doing business, using U.S. Census data and other research. They must also explore the composition of the consumer population: age, gender, ethnic and religious makeup, education, occupation, and household size and income, as well as trends over time.

When P&G, for example, examined U.S. demographics through Census reports and other data, it noticed sizable increases in certain segments, such as Hispanic consumers. Then it looked closer, says P&G's vice president-general manager of multicultural development: "While Hispanic household income is about $33,000 a year versus $43,000 a year for the general market, Hispanics consume more in our product categories than the general population—diapers, detergents, etc." Based on this opportunity, the company now spends more than $150 million annually to reach Hispanic consumers and is active in Avanzando con tu Familia and other causes.[12]

Business Demographics

Companies that operate in business markets need to scan the environment for information about the size and growth of the industries that they sell to, as measured by number of companies, number of locations or branches, number of employees, and sales revenues. They also should pay attention to trends in new business formation, which can signal emerging opportunities to market products such as office furniture, computers, accounting services, telecommunications services, and cleaning supplies. Palo Alto Software, which makes the *Marketing Plan Pro* software packaged with this text, is particularly interested in new-business formation as an indicator of demand for its marketing-planning software as well as its *Business Plan Pro* business-planning software.

Just as consumer marketers examine population trends in different geographic markets where they are selling or want to sell, business marketers must look at business population trends. For instance, B2B marketers might determine which cities and states host the most new start-ups as a factor in identifying promising markets for B2B products such as business loans, computers, and insurance. Often urbanization and business demographics suggest opportunities for marketing to government and business customers, as in the case of Caterpillar.

Caterpillar. This Illinois-based manufacturer of bulldozers, backhoes, and other earth-moving equipment targets areas being transformed by infrastructure projects, urbanization, or business development. It is planning to grow through higher global sales, particularly in Asia. Caterpillar recently sold the Chinese government equipment for modernizing the country's dams, railways, and roads and for generating electricity. Private construction in India represents another opportunity for equipment sales to support the expansion of business centers and new housing. However, the company also faces rivals such as Sweden's Volvo, South Korea's Hyundai and Daewoo, and Japan's Komatsu and Hitachi, all of which are active in Asia. And if economic growth slows significantly, Caterpillar may have difficulty reaching its ambitious objectives.[13]

Economic Trends

Planning Tip

Notice how regional, national, and international economic trends affect customer buying power, supplier strength, and competitive pressures.

In today's interconnected global economy, deepening recession in one part of the world can affect consumer and business buying patterns thousands of miles away. For Caterpillar, unfavorable economic conditions in Asia would likely slow the pace of development, thereby affecting sales of construction-related products. Thus, marketers have to keep a close eye on local, regional, national, and even global economic trends, watching for signs of change.

To better understand the buying power of consumers (or business customers), marketers should analyze buyer income, debt, and credit usage. When personal income is rising, consumers have more buying power; lower debt and more available credit also

FEDERAL TRADE COMMISSION - FACTS FOR BUSINESSES

FACTS FOR BUSINESSES

D⚫T C⚫M DISCLOSURES

Overview

Although the number of companies advertising online—and the number of consumers shopping online—are soaring, fraud and deception may dampen consumer confidence in the e-marketplace. But cyberspace is not without boundaries, and fraud and deception are unlawful no matter what the medium. The FTC has enforced and will continue enforcing its consumer protection laws online to ensure that products and services are described truthfully in online ads and that consumers get what they pay for. These activities benefit consumers as well as sellers, who expect and deserve a fair marketplace.

Many of the general principles of advertising law apply to Internet ads, but new issues arise almost as fast as technology develops. This booklet describes the information businesses should consider as they develop online ads to ensure that they comply with the law. Briefly,

1. The same consumer protection laws that apply to commercial activities in other media apply online. The FTC Act's prohibition on "unfair or deceptive acts or practices" encompasses Internet advertising, marketing and sales. In addition, many Commission rules and guides are not limited to any particular medium used to disseminate claims or advertising, and therefore, apply to online activities.

2. Disclosures that are required to prevent an ad from being misleading, to ensure that consumers receive material information about the terms of a transaction or to further public policy goals, must be clear and conspicuous. In evaluating whether disclosures are likely to be clear and conspicuous in online ads, advertisers should consider the *placement* of the disclosure in an ad and its *proximity* to the relevant claim. Additional considerations include: the *prominence* of the disclosure; whether items in other parts of the ad *distract attention* from the disclosure; whether the ad is so lengthy that the disclosure needs to be *repeated*; whether disclosures in audio messages are presented in an adequate *volume and cadence* and visual disclosures appear for a sufficient *duration*; and, whether the language of the disclosure is *understandable* to the intended audience.

Federal Trade Commission guidelines are part of the political-legal environment.

fuel consumer buying. Similarly, businesses with higher debt may not buy as much or as often as businesses with lower debt and more available credit. For planning purposes, consider how specific trends may affect the company's industry, its products, its competitors, and targeted geographic markets.

Ecological Trends

The natural environment can influence companies in a variety of ways. Shortages of raw materials such as water, timber, oil, minerals, and other essentials for production can cause major headaches for companies. To illustrate, after drought hurt cotton crops in China and Australia (and hiked cotton prices), Nike, Adidas, and Reebok introduced polyester sports apparel.[14]

In addition, marketers have to examine the various environmental issues that affect their organizations because of government regulation or social attitudes. What pollution or environmental problems directly and indirectly affect the business? Operating in northern Canada, Diavik Diamond Mines Inc. must factor in the consequences of global warming. Simply bringing products to market is problematic and costly because ice roads are melting earlier, forcing Diavik to use helicopters and planes to ferry supplies and mined materials in many cases.[15]

Some companies are building on growing interest in environmentally safe goods and services. WorldWise, for example, responded to this trend by creating "green" products such as rainforest snack foods sold through Costco, Target, and other retailers. As another example, New Leaf Paper sells a line of top-quality recycled paper products.[16] Even businesses that don't position their products as ecologically sound must watch ecological trends and anticipate movements or regulations that can influence performance.

Technological Trends

Technology reaches into every aspect of the marketing mix, from digitally enhanced advertisements to new packaging materials and methods and beyond. Key trends include the ongoing global penetration of cell phones, computers, digital media, speedy Internet access, and the incorporation of electronic capabilities into a wider range of products. The Internet alone has spawned countless opportunities, from online retailing and wholesaling to security solutions for viruses, stolen data, and other problems. Here is how Citigroup is addressing value opportunities using technology.

Citigroup. Based in New York, this financial services giant has long been known for its innovative use of technology to make banking and purchase transactions faster and more convenient for customers. New Yorkers can wave the Citi PayPass, for example, to pay for subway rides (among other goods and services); cell phones with Citibank debit-card capabilities are in the testing phase. The company was also the first credit-card issuer to sign up for Google Checkout, an online payment system that competes with PayPal. "We think that being the first to market here will give us an advantage," says a Citigroup executive.[17]

Broad questions about technological trends include: What cutting-edge innovations are being introduced, and how do they affect the organization's customers, suppliers, distributors, marketing, and processes? How are these technologies affected by, or generating, industrywide standards and government regulations? What substitutes or innovations are becoming available because of new technology, and how are these changes likely to affect suppliers, customers, and competitors?

For instance, AU Optronics originally predicted high demand for its LCD panels because flat-screen televisions have been growing more popular. It wasn't alone: other suppliers also foresaw high demand and opened huge factories to manufacture LCD panels in quantity. However, because of lower-than-projected demand and increased competition, AU's marketers wound up lowering prices more quickly than they had planned.[18] Understanding such trends can reveal threats (such as inventions likely to supplant older technology) and opportunities (such as quickly adopting a new technological standard).

Political-Legal Trends

As part of the external scanning process, marketers need to examine the legal and regulatory guidelines that govern diverse business and marketing practices. Numerous state and federal laws cover competitive behavior, pricing, taxation, promotion, distribution, product liability, labeling, and product purity, among other elements, in the United States. Moreover, government agencies such as the Federal Trade Commission and the Department of Justice watch for questionable business practices.

Political developments also can signal changes in legal and regulatory priorities—posing new threats or opening new opportunities. The Sarbanes–Oxley Act, which requires companies to collect and retain internal documents about their financial performance as a way of improving corporate accountability, has opened opportunities to sell software for storing e-mail, voice mail, and other messages; it has also opened opportunities for info-tech systems providers.[19]

Political pressure to deregulate U.S. industries has resulted in both threats and opportunities. Deregulation freed airlines to compete through schedules, destinations, fares, amenities, and loyalty programs. Eventually price wars, global economic woes, and high costs took a toll, sending several major airlines (such as United and Delta) into severe financial turbulence. Low-fare carriers such as Southwest have survived because of low-cost structures and controlled expansion. Another low-fare carrier, AirTran, is drawing customers and building loyalty with in-flight extras like satellite radio access.[20]

Companies that operate globally need to monitor the political and regulatory climate in all the countries and regions where they operate while recognizing that surprises can derail any marketing plan. Consider Motorola's situation in Russia.

Motorola. Russia is a fast-growing market for mobile phones: 33 million are sold each year, and Motorola (which makes the stylish RAZR) is among the top five handset marketers. But the company recently clashed with Russia's Interior Ministry, which seized 167,500 Motorola handsets after first saying they were fakes, then saying they didn't meet safety standards, and then implicating the products in a smuggling case and a patent dispute. Motorola filed legal protests but could not stop the government from destroying 50,000 handsets (117,500 were later returned to the company). Meanwhile, RussGPS, a Russian company, said some Motorola models violated its patents and demanded licensing fees. Motorola's senior legal counsel says this is "an abusive attempt to use the criminal law to extort license fees from Motorola and its customers." Motorola's manager in Russia comments: "It is very much evident that the transition of Russia to a market economy, ruled by well-defined laws, is still going on."[21]

Social-Cultural Trends

Increased diversity in markets—and in the workforce—is a key social-cultural trend affecting today's marketing. Using U.S. Census data and other sources, marketers can learn more about the cultural diversity of specific geographic markets. These include nation of origin, primary language, and other details that can help in tailoring the offer and the message to specific groups. Wider exposure to other societies also creates new opportunities. Sawanee Engblom started Tuk Tuk Foods in Stockholm after she noticed that Swedish travelers returning from Thailand wanted to buy authentic Thai dishes locally. Now Tuk Tuk markets Thai meals in Swedish supermarkets and also exports to Denmark, Norway, and Finland, where there is increasing interest in trying Thai foods.[22]

Remain alert to the unexpected opportunities and threats created by popular culture; makers of fad products are quite familiar with the pattern of meteoric sales increases followed by sharp sales declines as another craze takes the spotlight. Yet the core beliefs and values that pervade a society or subculture, which change only slowly over time, also create opportunities and threats. Attitudes toward ethical and social responsibility issues, influenced by core beliefs and values, can affect marketing plans and corporate image, as cigarette marketers have learned.

A few years ago, the U.K.-based Co-operative Insurance Society (CIS) surveyed its 5 million customers about whether CIS should invest its $37 billion portfolio in certain countries or types of companies. "We think that the social, ethical, and environmental issues on which we engage should reflect the values of our customers," the CEO said. Based on customer input, the company developed ethical engagement policies and began lobbying other businesses to "improve their ethical and environmental performance on a range of ethical issues: from human rights to the transfer of arms to oppressive regimes; and from the environment to animal welfare."[23]

Competitor Analysis

Planning Tip

Look for new ideas by probing customers' reactions to competitors' strengths.

Analyzing competitors can help marketers better understand market dynamics, anticipate what rivals will do, and create more practical marketing plans. Start by identifying current competitors and possible sources of competition in the near future, to avoid being blindsided by a new entrant. Also look at trends in market share to get a sense of which competitors are becoming more powerful. Look at the fast-changing competitive situation confronting Giant Food.

> **Giant Food.** In just five years, Giant Food's share of the grocery retailing market in and around Washington, D.C., fell from 45 percent to 38 percent. It is still the area's leading supermarket chain, but the intense competition has prompted Giant to change its marketing plans. In the past, Giant's main competition was Safeway. Today it also faces competition from Wegmans Food Markets, Harris Teeter, Whole Foods Market, Shoppers, Ukrops Super Markets, and Food Lion, among others. This is why Giant's current marketing plan focuses on making the shopping experience more appealing and convenient by remodeling existing stores, adding multiple services, and locating new stores in growing neighborhoods. In addition, the plan calls for changing each store's product selection to reflect changes in local customers' tastes and behavior—including adding hundreds of organic food products.[24]

Exhibit 2.4 depicts Michael Porter's model of the competitive forces affecting industry profitability and attractiveness. As this model suggests, it is important to examine competitive barriers to entry and exit, which can affect the number of new entrants

EXHIBIT 2.4   Competitive Forces Affecting Industry Profitability and Attractiveness

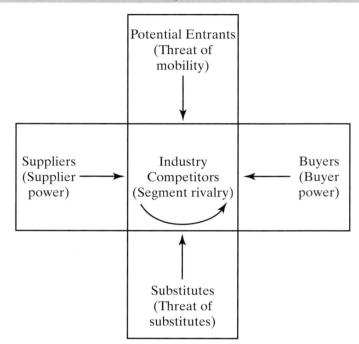

and the number of firms that leave the industry, as well as the power of both suppliers and buyers and the potential threat presented by substitute products. For example, one barrier to entry may be political-legal (such as regulation); another might be financial (such as high costs).

During this competitive analysis, marketers should learn about the unique competitive advantages of each rival (such as Wal-Mart's global buying power and ability to sell at unusually low prices). Yet customers ultimately determine the value of a firm's competitive advantage, which means that any organization can build advantage by discovering what customers need or desire and delivering it more effectively and efficiently (and perhaps more distinctively) than competitors. That's how Starbucks turned a run-of-the-mill product, coffee, into an everyday luxury and an experience for which millions of customers pay handsomely. Now any new entrants to the upscale coffee market must contend with Starbucks's established brand and leadership position.

Competitive analysis helps marketers determine which of Porter's generic competitive strategies is most appropriate for the company's unique situation.[25] With a **cost leadership strategy,** the company seeks to become the lowest-cost producer in its industry. With a **differentiation strategy,** the company creates a unique differentiation for itself or its product based on some factor valued by the target market. With a **focus strategy,** the company narrows its competitive scope to achieve a competitive advantage in its chosen segments. Which strategy a company chooses depends, in part, on its analysis of internal strengths and weaknesses and external opportunities and threats.

SWOT Analysis

All the information gathered through scanning and analysis is now distilled into a **SWOT analysis,** showing the strengths, weaknesses, opportunities, and threats of the

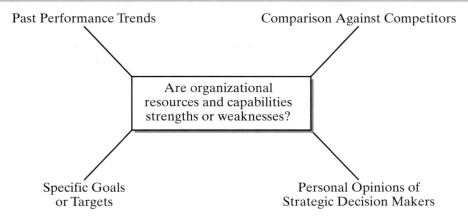

EXHIBIT 2.5   Judging Organizational Strengths and Weaknesses

Past Performance Trends

Comparison Against Competitors

Are organizational resources and capabilities strengths or weaknesses?

Specific Goals or Targets

Personal Opinions of Strategic Decision Makers

Planning Tip
See how your strengths fit with opportunities and strategies for providing value and building relationships.

organization. Marketers should also conduct a SWOT analysis of each current and emerging competitor to examine the possible influence on the marketing situation, the overall industry, and the overall market.

The purpose is to understand key strengths that can be exploited through marketing and defend against vulnerabilities that competitors might detect and use against the organization. What is a strength and what is a weakness? Exhibit 2.5 shows four criteria to be used in assessing organizational resources and capabilities.

Coach uses SWOT analysis in planning the marketing of its luxury products.

Coach. One of Coach's main strengths is its well-known brand, which is associated with quality. Ten years ago, seeing Gucci and other upscale marketers give new fashion life to their brands, the CEO hired new designers to enhance the styling of Coach's handbags and accessories. By testing products through ongoing consumer research, Coach's marketers learned that consumers were willing to pay more than $300 for the Hamptons Flap Satchel, which became a company best-seller. Every proposed product is evaluated in terms of whether it detracts from the brand image (a possible weakness) or enhances the strength of the brand. Coach has also opened stores in the United States and Japan (two market opportunities with major profit potential) to build on its strengths by offering luxury service along with luxury goods. Careful SWOT analysis has enabled Coach to sharply increase both sales and profit margins as it moves toward the goal of overtaking Vuitton, the world's largest luxury-goods company.[26]

SUMMARY

Environmental scanning and analysis is the process of gathering data about the environment and analyzing the findings to understand the company's strengths, weaknesses, opportunities, and threats in preparation for marketing planning. The macroenvironment consists of key environmental factors that affect organizational performance, including broad demographic, economic, ecological, technological, political-legal, and social-cultural forces. The microenvironment consists of groups that more directly influence performance, such as customers, competitors, channel members, partners, suppliers, and employees.

In scanning the internal environment, marketers examine the organization's mission, resources, offerings, previous results, business relationships, keys to success, and warning signs. In scanning the external environment, they examine demographic, economic, ecological, technological, political-legal, and social-cultural trends, as well as the competitive situation. Using the data gathered during these environmental scanning steps, marketers conduct a SWOT analysis so they can plan to take advantage of strengths and opportunities while defending against weaknesses and threats.

3

Understanding Markets and Customers

In this chapter:

PREVIEW

All the world's a market—but clearly, no company can afford to sell to or satisfy everyone. Even well-heeled giants like PepsiCo, Honda, and Nordstrom must make informed decisions about which local, regional, national, and international markets to serve and, within each, which potential buyers they can satisfy most profitably. Likewise, smaller businesses must carefully define their markets so they can use their resources most efficiently and effectively.

This chapter discusses how to research and analyze markets and customers. The chapter starts with a discussion of how to define the broad market, research overall characteristics, and calculate market share, a prelude to selecting markets and segments to target. The next section shows how to examine the needs and behavior of consumers and business customers in light of the constant change that affects marketing activities. The chapter closes with an overview of planning for primary and secondary marketing research, including key issues such as privacy concerns.

As you read this chapter and move ahead with marketing planning, continue to record your conclusions and decisions using *Marketing Plan Pro* software or in a

written marketing plan. This chapter's checklist features questions to help you understand both markets and customers.

ANALYZING MARKETS

A **market** is defined as all the potential buyers for a particular product. As Exhibit 3.1 indicates, market analysis is a backdrop for understanding customer needs and buying behavior—because people, not statistics or projections, constitute markets. Whether buying for themselves (or their families) as part of the **consumer market,** or buying for their companies (or nonprofit or institution) as part of the **business market,** customers are ultimately the primary focus of every marketing plan. Knowing this, marketers must perform a comprehensive market analysis so they have a context within which to understand the requirements, behavior, and attitudes of customers in the marketplace.

CHAPTER 3 CHECKLIST Analyzing Markets and Customers

Broad Market Definition
- ✔ How can the market be described in terms of product, customer need, and geography?
- ✔ What general demographics, characteristics, needs, behavior, and preferences pertain to this product and category in this market?

Changes in the Market and Market Share
- ✔ What needs and behavior do people exhibit relative to the product, and how are these changing?
- ✔ What are the current and projected sales of or demand for the product in this market?
- ✔ What do projected demographic and demand trends suggest for market growth and profitability?
- ✔ In units or dollars, what is the market share of the company, brand, or product?
- ✔ What is the market share of each competitor, and how is each share changing over time?

Customers in Consumer Markets
- ✔ What consumer needs, wants, behaviors, and attitudes pertain to the product and category?
- ✔ What value do consumers perceive in competing offerings that could satisfy their needs?
- ✔ Who are the customers in each market, and what are their buying patterns?
- ✔ How do users, culture, subculture, class, social connections, and personal factors influence needs and buying behavior?
- ✔ How can the marketing plan build on these influences to provide value and strengthen relationships?

Customers in Business Markets
- ✔ Who is involved in the buying decision, what is each participant's role, and what does each need to know during the buying process?
- ✔ How do the company's demographics, share and growth, competitive situation, buying policies, finances, needs, and buying cycle affect marketing planning?
- ✔ Does the company buy from competing suppliers, and how does it evaluate suppliers?
- ✔ How can the marketing plan build on these influences to provide value and strengthen relationships?

EXHIBIT 3.1 Market and Customer Analysis

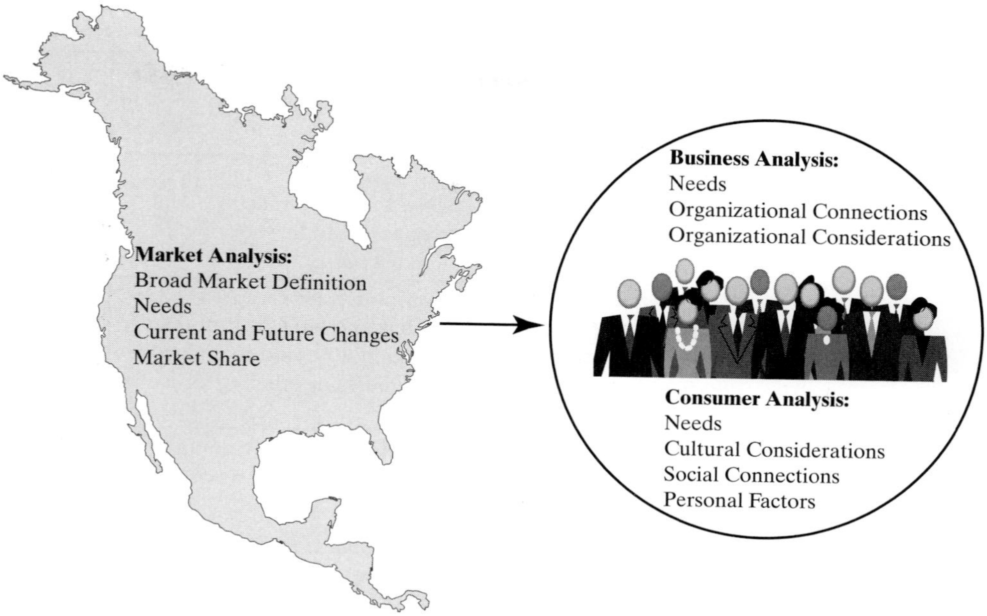

Market Analysis:
Broad Market Definition
Needs
Current and Future Changes
Market Share

Business Analysis:
Needs
Organizational Connections
Organizational Considerations

Consumer Analysis:
Needs
Cultural Considerations
Social Connections
Personal Factors

McDonald's has successfully dealt with different market situations by studying each market and understanding the needs and concerns of local customers.

> **McDonald's.** McDonald's France has expanded to 1,035 restaurants by offering convenient, fast, and affordable meals in a family-friendly environment. After McDonald's became the target of anti-American and anti-globalization protests in France, local executives reexamined consumers' attitudes and changed the marketing plan. Finding that the public didn't know how French McDonald's France really is, they started advertising to communicate that nearly all the ingredients and the employees are, in fact, French. The plan worked: Now one million French customers crowd McDonald's restaurants every year. The same aptitude for analyzing markets has helped McDonald's expand in China with drive-through restaurants attached to gas stations. "We see the future of China with cars, communities, and houses spreading out," says the CEO of McDonald's China. "We think the potential for drive-throughs is huge."[1]

McDonald's recognizes that every market is different, and it plans its offerings and communications with that in mind. The first step for McDonald's, as for other marketers, is to broadly define the market and its needs.

Broad Definition of Market and Needs

It is helpful to think about five basic levels of market definition, explained in Exhibit 3.2: (1) potential market, (2) available market, (3) qualified available market, (4) served or target market, and (5) penetrated market.[2] The potential market contains the maximum number of customers that exist for a company's product; in reality, however, no single product can appeal to every possible customer. Note that if the product already exists, the penetrated market consists of people who are already buying it. The remainder of the market consists of nonbuyers (potential customers)

EXHIBIT 3.2 Defining the Market

Type of Market	Definition	Rental Car Example
Potential market (broadest definition)	All customers who may be interested in a particular offering	Any driver who needs temporary transportation
Available market (subset of the potential market)	Customers who are interested, possess sufficient income, and have access to the offering	Any driver who can afford the rental fees and is in the area served by rental-car services
Qualified available market (subset of the available market)	Customers who are qualified to buy based on age (for products that cannot be sold to underage consumers) or other criteria	Drivers in the available market who have valid licenses and meet minimum or maximum age restrictions
Target market (subset of the qualified available market to be served)	Customers that the company intends to target for a particular offer	Drivers in the qualified available market who need to travel from airports to final destinations in the area
Penetrated market (subset of the target market)	Customers who are already buying the type of product sold by the company	Drivers in the target market who have previously rented cars

Planning Tip

When formulating your marketing plan, research and analyze the broad market for your product.

who are aware of the offering or value its benefits, have access to it, are of the proper age or have the skill to buy or use it, and can afford it.[3] Marketers, therefore, want to narrow their focus by gaining a thorough understanding of the potential, available, and qualified available markets.

For planning purposes, markets may be described in terms of geography as well as by product or customer definition. "The U.S. cell phone market" is a broad description of one target market that Nokia seeks to serve. Because it markets internationally, Nokia must define each target market geographically: "The British cell phone market" and "the London cell phone market" are two examples. Another way to define the market is in terms of customer need: "the Philadelphia market for pain relief" is an overall description of the group of customers and prospects who feel pain (from an injury or illness) and would benefit from a product that would relieve that pain (such as aspirin and other medications, specialized pads or patches, and so on).

The geographic description must be more precise to distinguish different markets being served. The online auction firm eBay, for instance, offers global auction listings as well as local auction listings in certain areas. Thus, eBay can define a series of markets for its services, including "the Orange County, California, market for online auction services," "the San Francisco market for online auction services," and "the Vancouver, Canada, market for online auction services." This helps eBay's marketers focus on the needs and preferences of a particular set of buyers in each location.

Next, the company conducts research into the broad needs of the available market. Here, the emphasis is on identifying general needs prior to a more in-depth investigation of each segment's particular needs. This research also helps the company identify what customers value and how its image, products, services, and other attributes can be positioned for competitive differentiation. Consider the situation of Thor.

> **Thor.** Thor is the U.S. market leader in towable recreational vehicles (RVs), with a variety of offerings for different markets and customer segments. Each brand (including Airstream and Dutchmen) and vehicle is differentiated by styling, size, features, capacity, price, and other elements. Thor has been driving for more growth with new products targeting the motorized RV market (designed to be driven, not towed). Studying the U.S. market, it uncovered higher consumer interest in driving vacations, learned that the median income of RV households is $56,000, and noted increased availability of longer-term loans for more expensive RVs. In response, Thor has introduced luxurious RV models like the Damon Tuscany, outfitted with most of the comforts of home at a home-like price of $194,000.[4]

Along with a broad understanding of needs, marketers need to look at general demographics, such as the number and characteristics of the consumer or business population, to get a sense of what each market is like (in the aggregate). As an example, U.S. Census information shows the number of people and households in specific areas of the country. Then marketers look beyond sheer numbers, researching gender, age, education, marital status, income, and other characteristics that relate to their products. Thor considers income a key characteristic; Marriott's retirement complexes would look at the population and incomes of consumers aged 55 and older.

In the business market, marketers can use the **North American Industry Classification System (NAICS)** to classify industries and investigate industry size; the main source for such data is the U.S. Census Bureau. Additional research about industries, products, and geographic markets is available from a wide variety of sources, including international trade organizations, global banks, foreign consulates, universities, and business publications. As with consumer markets, the next step is to obtain meaningful characteristics that relate to the product, such as the annual sales, number of employees, or industries served by the businesses in the market.

Texas Instruments, for example, sells computer chips to manufacturers of high-tech products. Because only some businesses are potential buyers, the company must identify and research industries and products that incorporate chips in their products, such as digital cameras and mobile phone handsets. Then TI's marketers can examine each market in more detail.

Markets as Moving Targets

Planning Tip
Consider tomorrow's markets as well as today's markets when developing objectives and strategies.

Markets are always changing: Consumers move in or out, are born or die, start or stop buying a good or service; businesses change location, go into or out of business, expand or divest units, start or stop buying a product. Thus, at this stage of the market analysis, marketers need to locate projections of demographic changes in the markets and forecast future demand for (or sales of) their type of product, as a way of sizing the overall market over time. (Common forecasting methods are discussed in Chapter 10.)

Is the population expected to grow or shrink, and by how much? How many new businesses are projected to enter or leave the market? What are the projections for total industry sales of the product over the coming years? Do these projections suggest a sizable market, a stagnant market, or a shrinking market? The answers to these questions influence decisions about targeting markets and segments, and setting objectives. Consider the situation at Texas Instruments.

Texas Instruments. Projections by this chipmaker indicate huge growth potential in handheld and mobile devices. In particular, its forecasts focus on how many and what kind of electronic devices a consumer is likely to own and carry in the coming years. This helps TI's marketers think about the types of computer chips that will power tomorrow's most popular devices. Although established manufacturers like Motorola and Nokia are good customers, TI also considers high-tech start-ups an important segment. Successful technologies can emerge from companies of any size and, notes a TI executive, "We aren't smart enough to know which of these small guys is going to be big."[5]

Much research is publicly available for major markets and for products, but marketers of ground-breaking products often must conduct their own research to project demand and sales. This part of the marketing planning process also feeds into the SWOT analysis discussed in Chapter 2, because it can reveal new opportunities or threats that must be addressed.

Market Share as a Vital Sign

Planning Tip
Keep market share in mind to set realistic objectives and establish suitable metrics for assessing results.

The market share held by a company and the shares held by competitors usually change over time as companies court customers, the market grows or shrinks, and competitors enter or exit. Market share information serves as a baseline for understanding historical market dynamics and a standard for setting and measuring objectives to be achieved through the marketing plan.

Market share is the percentage of sales in a given market held by a particular company, brand, or product, calculated in dollars or units (ideally, both). In simple terms, a company's share can be determined by dividing its product unit or dollar sales by the entire unit or dollar sales of that type of product in that market. Thus, if a firm sells 2 million units in the 50 states and overall market sales for all competitors selling that kind of product are 10 million units, the firm holds a 20% share of the U.S. market. Calculated in dollars, the same firm's share would be 15% if its product sales totaled $15 million and overall market sales totaled $100 million.

Market share calculation is only a point-in-time snapshot showing the relative positions of competitors during a particular period—positions that can and do constantly change. At one point, Thor had a market-leading 26% share of the towable RV market but a much smaller share of the motorized RV market (in which Winnebago, Fleetwood, and Monaco are leaders). However, Thor's new RV models could very well attract customers who might otherwise have bought towable RVs, affecting Thor's share in that market as well. If Thor acquires other RV companies, its market share will increase. In an industry with more than six dozen competitors marketing hundreds of brands, higher share can fuel economies of scale, strengthen relations with dealers, and enhance profitability.[6]

Clearly, market share is one of the vital signs of a business, to be monitored over time as a way of spotting potential problems as well as potential opportunities in the marketplace. Companies should develop share information for each product in each market, regularly update share numbers to track shifts, and examine shifts as possible triggers for control measures (discussed in detail in Chapter 10).

In addition, market share directly affects segmentation and targeting, because a company with marketing strategies to capture a larger and larger share of a shrinking market segment could end up with nearly 100% of a market too small to be profitable. On the other hand, most companies take special notice of markets in which demand is projected to skyrocket, using share over time to identify opportunities, understand competitive dynamics, and set and measure progress toward objectives. Consider Kirin Brewery's situation in Japan.

Kirin Brewery. Kirin closely monitors its market share in the Japanese market for beer and beer-like beverages, interpreting share trends in the context of overall industry sales, customer tastes, and seasonal purchasing patterns. In one recent six-month period, Kirin narrowly edged out rival Asahi Breweries to become the market leader—the first time in five years that Kirin had held the top spot from January to June. Better-than-expected sales of low-malt beers and flavored beer-like drinks helped Kirin gain market share, along with strong sales of a new low-priced beer introduced during the previous year. Kirin's objective was then to retain its market leadership for the entire year, despite Asahi's aggressive marketing activities during the summer gift-giving season.[7]

ANALYZING CUSTOMER NEEDS AND BEHAVIOR

Planning Tip
Analyze market needs in the context of competing offers.

With the market analysis as backdrop, marketers use research to analyze the needs, buying behavior, and attitudes of the customers in their markets. This research forms the foundation for decisions about which segments to target, the most effective way to position the product in each market, and what marketing strategies and tactics are most appropriate for profitably satisfying customers. The chapter-ending section on marketing research briefly discusses how marketers can study and understand customers' behavior and buying decisions.

Forces in the external environment can play a key role in affecting the who, what, when, where, why, and how of consumer and business buying behavior (see Exhibit 3.3). This is one of the reasons for studying the current situation, as discussed in Chapter 2. For example, when the economy is not doing well, many consumers and business customers change their buying patterns—sometimes purchasing less or less

EXHIBIT 3.3   Analyzing Customer Needs, Behavior, and Influences

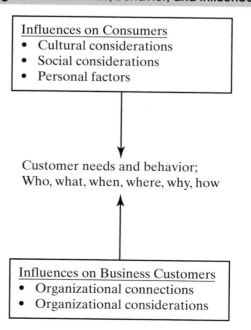

often, sometimes seeking out lower-priced alternatives. Social-cultural issues such as corporate ethics and social responsibility also affect buying habits. To illustrate, more than half of all U.K. consumers have purchased a Fairtrade food product, a designation showing that the growers in developing countries receive a fair price for their coffee and other crops.[8]

The attitudes and habits of consumers and business customers are clearly affected by the marketing-mix programs implemented by different companies competing for their attention, loyalty, and buying power. From the customer's perspective, no marketing tactic stands in isolation: it is only one tactic used by the company and one of many stimuli in the market (some of which are noticed and acted upon, most of which are not). As a result, marketers must not only understand their markets and the environmental forces shaping customer actions, but also learn to see the totality of their marketing activities and the actions of competing firms through their customers' eyes.

Marketers can harness sophisticated technology to identify, research, and analyze the behavior of individual customers in particular markets, instead of relying solely on averages or aggregate data. As they establish relationships with individuals in their consumer or business markets, the firms can gather even more customer behavior data and track changes over time, leading to more effective marketing plans. Here's how Wells Fargo does it.

Wells Fargo. Wells Fargo examines every interaction with its 10 million banking customers and correlates the data with customer-specific personal information. The bank has solidified its customer relationships by understanding both current and future needs; its customers buy, on average, four financial products from Wells Fargo—considerably more than the industry average of 2.2 products per customer. It also uses the data to determine which channels customers prefer. As a result, the bank has found that online banking is even more popular with customers than its extensive network of ATMs, prompting marketers to communicate the convenience of electronic services such as online bill payment.[9]

Delve below the surface when researching what customers need and want. Stated needs are generally the tip of the iceberg; customers also have unstated needs (e.g., good service) and sometimes secret needs (e.g., relating to their self-concept or other internal needs). Thus, it is vital to understand the problem each customer seeks to solve and what that customer really wants from the solution.[10] Remember that the needs, wants, attitudes, behavior, and decision-making processes of consumers differ, in general, from those of business customers. The next sections highlight important attributes that marketers need to understand when preparing plans for consumer and business markets.

Consumer Markets

As shown in Exhibit 3.3, marketers need to analyze the needs and behaviors of consumers from every angle. Who in the household or family is buying or using the product? What, exactly, are these consumers buying or using, and when, where, how, and why? What is their decision-making process for buying that product? What are consumers buying now, what did they buy before, how often are they buying, and how are their buying patterns changing? Look at both internal and external sources of data for this analysis of consumer needs, decision making, and behavior.

When making decisions about more complex purchases, such as an RV, consumers generally take more time, gather more information about alternatives, weigh

Planning Tip

Customize your research to fit the characteristics of your products and markets.

the decision more carefully, and have strong feelings in the aftermath of the purchase. Inexpensive items bought on impulse, such as candy, are not usually subjected to as much analysis and scrutiny before or after the purchase. By investigating the entire process consumers follow to buy, use, and evaluate their products, marketers can determine how, when, and where to initiate suitable marketing activities.

Planning Tip
Simply asking about needs is not enough, because many consumers are unaware of what influences their behavior.

Early in the buying process, for example, marketers may need to emphasize benefits that solve consumer problems. Later in the process, marketers may need to communicate where the product can be purchased; still later, marketers may want to stress the security of a product's warranty. The exact nature and timing of the marketing activities will depend on what the marketer learns about consumer decision making (as well as on the marketer's strategy and resources, of course).

Although the exact level of influence varies from individual to individual, consumer needs, wants, and behaviors are affected by cultural considerations, social connections, and personal factors.

Cultural Considerations

As buyers, consumers feel the influence of the culture of the nation or region in which they were raised as well as the culture in which they currently live. This means that consumers in different countries often approach buying situations from different perspectives because of differing values, beliefs, and preferences. Without research, marketers can't know exactly what those differences are or how to address them. Consider Hering's experience selling harmonicas in different countries.

Hering. Alberto Bertolazzi, head of Brazilian harmonica maker Hering, competes with Hohner, Suzuki, and Tomba for a share of the $130 million global harmonica market. He targets two main markets: Japan, where consumers annually buy $10 million worth of harmonicas, and the United States, where consumers annually buy $7.5 billion worth of all musical instruments. Bertolazzi has found different expectations in each culture. "In the [United] States, people said Hering harmonicas were great but looked cheap, so we upgraded the plates from brass to bronze," he says. For Japan, he added markers to indicate the three octaves on each harmonica, because "the Japanese prefer them that way." Now the company offers harmonicas tuned to international standards as well as custom-tuned to country preferences; it also sells recorders and harp-tuning accessories.[11]

Subcultures are distinct groups within a larger culture that exhibit and preserve distinct cultural identities through a common religion, nationality, ethnic background, or lifestyle. A variety of subcultures drive U.S. consumers' decisions and behavior. Cuban Americans frequently have different food preferences than, say, Chinese Americans. Teenagers—an age subculture—have different food preferences than seniors.

To create an effective plan for reaching each subculture, marketers must research that group's behavior and buying patterns. To illustrate, Kroger, a leading U.S. grocery chain, is targeting Hispanic customers in certain states with its Buena Comida private-label foods and specially designed Fry's Mercado stores, featuring Spanish-language signage and distinctive décor. Other supermarkets are also targeting this subculture: United Supermarkets is opening Super Mercado stores with a wide array of fresh and packaged foods geared to Hispanic shoppers.[12]

Class distinctions, even when subtle, also influence consumer behavior. The members of each class generally buy and use products in a similar way; in addition, people who aspire to a different class may emulate the buying or usage patterns of that class.

Savvy marketers learn how such distinctions operate and then apply this knowledge to decisions about products, marketing communications, distribution arrangements, price levels, and service strategies.

Social Connections

Consumers have a web of social connections that influence how they buy—connections such as family ties, friendships, work groups, and civic organizations. Family members, for example, directly or indirectly control household spending for many goods and services. Children ask parents to buy products advertised on television; parents buy things to keep children healthy or safe; families make group decisions about vacations. Understanding how these connections affect the buying decision is critical for marketers creating plans for products intended for specific family members, usage, or occasions, as Heinz well knows.

Heinz. Heinz, which dominates the U.S. ketchup market, designed its EZ Squirt ketchup packages and developed colored ketchups to appeal to children yet be acceptable to parents, knowing that children can influence food-buying patterns. Company research revealed that "3-year-olds use almost twice as much ketchup as adults," according to a Heinz executive. That was another reason to redesign the package for smaller hands. The result: 25 million bottles of colored EZ Squirt ketchup were sold in the first 30 months. Now Heinz has new kid-friendly packaging: Silly Squirts, a bottle that comes with three different tops for squeezing out ketchup designs. "Our objective was to deliver on what we call the top three 'Kid Insights,' which are fun, independence, and control," says a Heinz manager.[13]

As with class distinctions, aspirations to different social connections can be a powerful influence on buying behavior. In apparel, for example, preteens want to look as grown up as possible, so they emulate teen fashions; teenagers dress like the movie stars they admire; and managers seeking to move up follow the clothing cues of higher-level managers. Within each social group, consumers look to certain opinion leaders for advice or guidance about buying decisions. Judith Leiber, which makes upscale handbags, taps into social connections for marketing purposes by featuring socialites such as Vanessa Getty in its print ads. "The Getty name is an American icon," says Judith Leiber's CEO. "Lately we have been really targeting and speaking to younger, more contemporary customers, and the social celebrities of today speak to a younger audience a lot better."[14]

Personal Factors

Personal factors are another major category of influences on consumer buying, covering life cycle, lifestyle, and psychological makeup, among other factors. *Life cycle* refers to the individual's changing family situation over time—single, cohabiting, engaged, married, married with children, divorced, remarried, and so on. Each of these life-cycle phases entails different buying needs, attitudes, and preferences that, in turn, can be identified through research and addressed through marketing. Engaged couples, for instance, are targeted by marketers selling formal wear, wedding invitations, catering services, and other wedding products; new parents are targeted by marketers selling entirely different products (such as Huggies disposable diapers).

Lifestyle is the pattern of living that a person exhibits through activities and interests—how the individual spends his or her time. To understand the complexities of lifestyle and its influence on consumer buying, marketers use sophisticated techniques to examine variables known as **psychographic characteristics,** which together form a

Reader surveys help *The Economist* understand the audience's needs.

picture of the consumer's lifestyle. Some markets are better approached through psychographics. For example, Carnival Corporation markets to consumers who enjoy cruises, although age, income, and other demographic elements are helpful descriptors of this market. At the top end of its offerings, the *Queen Mary 2* and the new *Queen Victoria* are geared to the luxury lifestyle. Marketing according to lifestyle does not work for all products and segments: when marketing the *Carnival Paradise* as a "no smoking" ship did not stimulate the expected sales, the company changed the ship's port and strategy.[15]

Internal elements such as motivation, perception, and attitudes—all part of the consumer's psychological makeup—can strongly influence consumer behavior. **Motivation** stems from the consumer's drive to satisfy needs and wants. For example, the popular search engine Google is constantly adding new features—such as Google Trends and Google Earth—to motivate users to return to the site again and again when searching for virtually anything. The more people who click on Google, the bigger its audience for advertising, which fuels profitability.

Perception is how the individual organizes environmental inputs (such as ads, conversation, and media) and derives meaning from them. When marketers talk about "cutting through clutter," they are discussing how to make the marketing message stand out among many messages bombarding consumers throughout the day—not just to capture attention but to motivate consumers to respond. **Attitudes** are the individual's lasting evaluations of and feelings toward something, such as a product or a person.

Only through careful research can marketers become knowledgeable about the personal factors that influence their customers, as De Beers well knows.

> **De Beers.** When the Diamond Information Center researched women's attitudes toward jewelry on behalf of the De Beers Diamond Trading Company, it found many women who believe that diamond rings should be gifts of love, rather than being self-purchased. To modify this attitude and encourage women in the target audience (30 to 54 years old with household incomes of $100,000 and above) to buy diamond rings for themselves, it launched a campaign emphasizing that "Your left hand says 'we,' your right hand says 'me.'" This marketing boosted sales of nonwedding diamond rings. Because 40% of global sales are made in the last six weeks of the year, Diamond Trading Company's next two campaigns for multiple-diamond jewelry have appeared throughout the year, to influence attitudes toward purchasing for occasions other than year-end gift-giving.[16]

Business Markets

Like consumer markets, business markets are made up of people—individuals who buy on behalf of their company, government agency, or not-for-profit organization. In the context of business buying, however, these people are generally influenced by a different set of factors. Marketers therefore need to examine organizational considerations and connections when analyzing business buying decisions and behavior.

Organizational Connections

Although exactly who does the buying differs from company to company, officially designated purchasing agents are not the only people involved with the buying decision. Buyers are usually connected with other internal players. For instance, another employee or manager may initiate the buying process by suggesting a purchase; those who actually use the product may play a role, by providing specifications, testing alternatives, or evaluating purchases; and buyers may need connections to the managers who are authorized to approve a purchase. In a business that buys express delivery services, as an example, a manager in one department may make the actual decision but managers in other departments may have a say or request assistance. Knowing this, FedEx has a laboratory to test customers' packaging and suggest improvements that will ensure safe arrival of items that are shipped. This wins FedEx support among a number of internal players and helps business customers satisfy their own customers.[17]

Depending on the organization and its structure, other internal players may wield some type of influence, such as insisting on compatibility with existing goods or services or controlling access to buyers. Not every player will participate in every purchase, so marketers must understand the decision process that takes place inside key customer organizations and plan appropriate marketing activities to reach the right players at the right time with the right message.

Finally, learn about the organization's current relations with competing suppliers, including long-term contracts, evaluations, requirements, and other elements. Campbell's and many other companies have long-term buying relationships with suppliers who meet preset quality and performance standards. Likewise, Apple depends on its suppliers for critical components such as the chips and software that make the hit iPod music player operate. However, Apple also has a strict policy against suppliers publicly revealing anything about the business relationship, a restriction that potential suppliers must bear in mind.[18] Researching a business customer's supplier connections and requirements is a good first step toward getting on the short list of approved suppliers and making the sale.

Organizational Considerations

Organizational considerations include the company's size and industry, share and growth, competitive situation, buying policies and procedures, financial constraints, and the timing of purchases. In researching these factors, marketers need to find out, for example, whether a corporation buys centrally or allows each unit to buy on its own; whether companies participate in online marketplaces; and what funding and scheduling issues affect the purchase. Internal priorities are another organizational consideration. At General Electric, units are classified as either "growth businesses" or "cash generators." To achieve long-term growth, GE plans to invest more heavily in the growth businesses than in the cash generators—a prime consideration for suppliers that market parts, components, or services needed by the designated growth units.[19]

Business buying is also affected by **derived demand,** the principle that demand for business products in an industry is based on demand for related consumer products. As an example, demand for emollients, silicones, and other chemicals is based, in part, on consumer demand for shampoo, sunscreens, and skin-care products. Recently, Dow Amerchol introduced a new line of lubricating emollients to "meet the demand for enhanced conditioning performance in hair and skin care products to overcome the damaging effects of repeated coloring, heat styling, and sun exposure," according to the global marketing manager. And Dow Corning's silicones are in higher demand because of growing sales of disposable wipes for face care, sun care, and moisturizing.[20]

Derived demand requires that B2B marketers be aware of emerging trends and needs in consumer markets and be ready to help customers serve *their* customers. If suppliers are unprepared to deliver on time and within budget, marketers that serve consumers will have difficulty providing the value that their customers demand when and where needed. When Emirates Airline, for example, projected much higher demand for international air travel, it ordered 45 jumbo jets from Airbus. However, unexpected production problems delayed delivery of the planes for six months, forcing the airline to revise its expansion plans. "We would be very unhappy to see another delay," the CEO of Emirates Airline stated. "The cost to us is very high."[21]

PLANNING MARKETING RESEARCH

This chapter has covered a wide range of issues that should be researched to give organizations a better understanding of markets and customers during the marketing-planning process. Often the best way to start is with **secondary research**—information

Planning Tip

Summarize research findings, identify key needs and influences, and plan for new research.

already collected for another purpose, such as data that the U.S. government gathers during each census. Secondary research is more readily available and less expensive than **primary research,** research conducted to address a specific situation.

Secondary Research

Exhibit 3.4 shows selected sources of secondary research for business and consumer markets and customers, as starting points for more extensive research. Before relying on any secondary research, check the dates and sources. Some sources offer new or updated statistics and profiles on a regular basis; others provide a snapshot covering a specific period, which can be useful but may be quickly outdated. Also consider the source's credibility to be sure the information is from an unbiased and reputable source. If a source reports data but did not actually conduct the research, find out where the information came from and whether it was changed from the original. Also try to verify the information as a double-check on accuracy.

Secondary research can help marketers construct a good overview of the market, but this may be too general to answer detailed questions about particular markets and types of customers. That's where primary marketing research comes in. Marketers who are qualified to do so can conduct primary research on their own, work with internal research specialists, or hire outside specialists to collect and interpret data through surveys and other methods.

Primary Research

Primary research starts with a definition of what the marketer needs to know about a specific market. For example, a printer manufacturer might want to find out how many small businesses use or want to use color laser printers and whether it will be profitable to be active in this market. It is important to detail what exactly the company wants to find out and how that knowledge will be used in developing and implementing a more practical or effective marketing plan. As an example, one specific research objective might be to identify the unmet (sometimes unstated) needs of customers in this market— needs that are currently not being satisfied by existing offerings—in preparation for developing a new product with the benefits that satisfy those needs.

EXHIBIT 3.4   Selected Sources of Secondary Research

Market	*Source*
Consumer	• U.S. Census Bureau (www.census.gov)
	• Conference Board Consumer Research Center (www.crc-conquest.org)
	• Intute: Social Sciences (www.intute.ac.uk/socialsciences/services.html)
	• ClickZ Web usage (www.clickz.com)
	• United Nations statistics (http://unstats.un.org/unsd/default.htm)
	• GeoHive world statistics (www.xist.org)
Business	• NAICS industry data (www.census.gov/naics)
	• *Industry Week* magazine (www.industryweek.com)
	• CEO Express portal (www.ceoexpress.com)
	• *E-Commerce Times* (www.ecommercetimes.com)
	• *The Economist* (www.economist.com/business)

The next step is to plan for collecting data through observation, surveys (online, by phone, by mail), experiments, and other research methods. Many companies use **focus group** research, gathering a small group of customers/prospects for a guided discussion of their needs or behavior relative to a product or product category. This type of research can yield interesting insights into customers' thinking and attitudes, although the results may not be representative of the entire market.

Another technique gaining attention is **ethnographic research,** observing how customers behave in actual product purchase or usage situations and asking questions to clarify the reason for their behavior. Ethnography can help marketers come up with new product ideas, fine-tune personal selling, or plan for other marketing attention.[22]

Ethnographic Research. Marriott recently used ethnographic research to study what business travelers actually do when they're at a hotel. After observing that many travelers use the hotel lobby as a place to work quietly or meet with colleagues, the company asked travelers about their preferences and then redesigned the lobbies of its Marriott and Renaissance Hotels. Now guests who visit the lobby can sit at small tables, use the hotels' wireless Internet access, or just sip a cup of coffee while closing a deal.

OXO's experience with ethnography is another good example. Interested in designing professional tools for use by consumers, OXO's marketers observed builders using tools on the job. This research led to the development of a low-vibration hammer, which allows for more accuracy and less chance of slipping. Although consumers did not articulate a need for this benefit, OXO's research revealed that lower vibration was valuable to professionals and would likely be valued by consumers as well.[23]

More and more companies are researching customers' behavior by using sophisticated software to analyze data in their internal databases or data captured when customers visit the company's Web site. Dell did this by merging dozens of internal databases into one giant data warehouse so its marketers could tease out buying and ownership patterns. If a product's sales drift downward, Dell marketers know quickly and can make changes to improve performance (such as offering a limited-time price promotion). Just as important, having a single data warehouse ensures that all Dell decision-makers are working from the same information.[24]

Using Marketing Research

For planning purposes, if marketing research is not available or must be carried out, indicate this in the marketing plan and include the research as part of the plan's budgets and schedules. Also plan ongoing marketing research to help measure results during implementation. For instance, advertising research can be used to test messages and media as well as to study customer response; test marketing can help marketers determine customer reaction to new products. Research studies of customer satisfaction, market share changes, and customer attitudes and buying patterns are also valuable for spotting and analyzing clues to the company's effect on the market and on customers (as well as seeing how competitors are doing).

Be aware that marketers are often forced to make decisions based on incomplete data; given the fast pace of the global marketplace, marketers rarely have enough time or money to conduct exhaustive research covering every contingency. Each company, therefore, must assess the risk of waiting for more research compared with the risk of seizing an opportunity before it slips away or before competitors gain an edge.

Finally, privacy has become a major issue in marketing research. Although marketers can do a better job of targeting segments and planning marketing activities by gathering and analyzing vast amounts of data, some customers have privacy concerns.[25] Most people are aware that supermarket purchases, Web-surfing habits, and other behavior can be easily tracked. This raises questions such as: What information is being collected? Can individuals be personally identified? How is the information used? Can individuals opt out? How are individuals protected by privacy laws and companies' privacy policies? Given such concerns, both the legal and the ethical dimensions of privacy must be considered when planning marketing research.

SUMMARY

When analyzing markets, companies start by broadly defining the general market and the needs of customers in that market. Markets are always changing, as consumers or business customers enter or leave and start or stop buying a product. For this reason, marketers should project market changes and demand prior to selecting a specific segment to target. Many companies track their market share over time, compared with that of competitors, to understand market dynamics and establish a standard for measuring marketing results.

Research is important for analyzing consumers and business customers. In consumer markets, cultural considerations, social connections, and personal factors help shape needs, wants, and behavior patterns. Marketers also must research how consumers think and act in each stage of the buying decision process. Business buyers are influenced by both organizational considerations and organizational connections. Companies can use secondary research and primary research to gain a better understanding of their markets and customers. However, marketers may be forced to plan marketing activities based on incomplete data in order to keep up with fast-moving market opportunities or to parry competitive initiatives.

4

Planning Segmentation, Targeting, and Positioning

In this chapter:

PREVIEW

For a long time, marketers could successfully follow one marketing plan to satisfy the entire market; think of the milk market, for instance. These days, however, markets are increasingly fragmented and diverse, with customers exhibiting a much wider variety of needs, attitudes, and behaviors. Companies also are under intense competitive pressure and therefore must differentiate themselves more distinctively in the markets in which they compete. The result is a move away from *mass marketing*—using one marketing mix to reach the entire market—and toward *segment marketing,* marketing to certain groups (segments) within the market. Consider milk: a huge variety of milk products are now available, including low-fat milk for weight-conscious consumers, soy milks for health-conscious consumers, and flavored milks for children.

    This chapter explains how to use segmentation, targeting, and positioning during marketing planning. The first section reviews the major steps and explores how to select the consumer or business market, how to apply segmentation variables, and how to assess and select segments for targeting. The next section discusses targeting and coverage strategies; the final section looks at positioning for competitive advantage. After reading this chapter, continue your marketing plan by summarizing your decisions and noting any issues using *Marketing Plan Pro* software or in a written marketing plan document. See this chapter's checklist for ideas about segmenting consumer and business markets.

SEGMENTING CONSUMER AND BUSINESS MARKETS

Market segmentation is the process of grouping customers within a market according to similar needs, habits, or attitudes that can be addressed through marketing. The point is to identify distinct segments, defined in Chapter 1 as sizable groupings of consumers or business customers with similarities (such as similar needs, buying preferences, or attitudes) that respond to marketing efforts.

CHAPTER 4 CHECKLIST   Identifying and Evaluating Segments

Segmenting Consumer Markets
- ✔ Can demographics be used to group consumers according to needs or responses that differ by gender, household size, family status, income, occupation, education, religion, race, nationality, and social class?
- ✔ Can geographic variables be used to group consumers according to needs or responses that differ by nation, region, state, city, postal code, climate, and distance?
- ✔ Can psychographic variables be used to group consumers according to needs or responses that differ by lifestyle, activities, and interests?
- ✔ Can behavioral and attitudinal variables be used to group consumers according to needs or responses that differ by benefits expected, usage occasion, user status, loyalty status, technological orientation, attitudes, and price sensitivity?

Segmenting Business Markets
- ✔ Can demographics be used to group business customers according to needs or responses that differ by industry, business size, business age, and ownership structure?
- ✔ Can geographic variables be used to group business customers according to needs or responses that differ by nation, region, state, city, climate, postal code, and distance?
- ✔ Can behavioral and attitudinal variables be used to group business customers according to needs or responses that differ by benefits expected, usage occasion, user status, loyalty status, technological orientation or usage, purchasing patterns, attitudes, and supplier standards and evaluation?

Evaluating Segments
- ✔ Which segments are a good fit with company resources and competencies?
- ✔ How attractive is each segment in terms of market factors like growth and profitability?
- ✔ How attractive is each segment in terms of competitive factors like threat of substitution?
- ✔ How attractive is each segment in terms of economic and technological factors like investment required?
- ✔ How attractive is each segment in terms of business environmental factors like regulation?

Planning Tip

No product can be all
things to all customers;
segmentation and target-
ing focus your marketing.

In the milk market, for instance, one segment consists of people who want to limit their fat intake and therefore want low-fat varieties; another consists of people who prefer flavored varieties; and a third consists of people who buy milk (or substitute) products for health reasons. Customers within each segment have similar needs or are seeking the same benefits, and they react differently to marketing-mix stimuli than do people in other segments. If all the people in all the segments (either consumers or business customers) reacted the same way to the same marketing mix, there would be no need for segmentation.

Even within a large segment, marketers often can identify **niches**—smaller segments with distinct needs or benefit requirements, such as people who buy low-fat milk in individual serving sizes at meal time. Over time, tiny niches can expand into small yet profitable segments. Today's technology allows marketers to tailor some parts of the marketing mix for individual customers, as postal services around the world are now doing with their stamp products.

Personalized Postage. Through arrangements with Endicia, Zazzle, and Stamps.com, the U.S. Postal Service now invites consumers and businesses to order stamps personalized with customer-supplied pictures or images. The stamps cost significantly more than ordinary first-class postage but add value, says the U.S.P.S. vice president of product development, by helping businesses, in particular, "create awareness for their products or services, build their brand, and develop strong customer relationships." Both Canada Post and the U.K.'s Royal Mail also encourage customers to submit images or logos for personalized stamps, which increases sales revenue while giving customers the opportunity to express their individuality or feature a corporate symbol.[1]

Segmentation allows marketers to focus their resources on the most promising opportunities. This improves marketing efficiency and effectiveness as the organization gets to know each segment's customers and what they want and need. Such customer intimacy also enables marketers to notice changes in the segment and respond quickly. Finally, it gives marketers the choice of entering segments in which only a limited number of competitors are active or in which their most powerful rivals are not competing.

As shown in Exhibit 4.1, segmentation lays the foundation for decisions about targeting and coverage strategy. The **target market** is the segment of the overall market that a company chooses to pursue. With these decisions, marketers are ready for positioning, giving the brand or product a distinctive and meaningful place (position) in the minds of targeted customers, as discussed later in this chapter.

Select the Market

Planning Tip

Broadly define the
market, then delete
inappropriate markets
or segments.

The first step in segmentation is to select the general market(s) in which the company will target customers, based on the market definition, situational analysis, and SWOT analysis (see Chapter 3). Eliminate markets or segments that have no need for the product or are inappropriate for other reasons, such as geographic distance, lack of purchasing power, ethical issues, or troubling environmental threats. Cosmetics giant Avon Products selects its markets carefully to manage significant financial or political risks while making the most of opportunities.

Avon. Avon's marketing plan for entering Russia was very different from its marketing plan for continuing to operate in China. The company waited to market in Russia until 1995; by that time, the country was democratic, purchasing power was rising, and capitalism was welcomed. Eyeing growing demand for beauty products, Avon built a Moscow factory, recruited thousands of independent sales representatives, and gave away samples to build awareness and trial. Today, Russia is worth more than $140 million in annual sales to Avon. Doing business in China has been more problematic, however. Avon was already active there when the government banned door-to-door selling in 1998. Until the ban was lifted in 2006, Avon had to change its marketing plan and sell through shops and kiosks. Afterward, Avon's plan focused on recruiting reps and attracting buyers in this fast-growing but challenging market in which a customer will, on average, spend $5 yearly on cosmetics. Understanding market-by-market nuances is important because 60 percent of Avon's revenues come from non-U.S. sales.[2]

Now marketers start to search for segments within the markets they have defined. People and businesses differ in many ways, but not every difference is meaningful from a marketing perspective. The purpose of segmentation is to form groups of customers that are internally similar yet sufficiently different that each group will not react in exactly the same way to the same marketing activities. If all segments were similar or responded in the same way to marketing, segmentation would not be needed—the company could simply use one marketing plan for the entire market. Therefore, marketers create segments by applying one or more variables to the chosen consumer or business market.

EXHIBIT 4.1 Segmentation, Targeting, and Positioning

Segmentation
- Select the market
- Apply segmentation variables
- Assess and select segments for targeting

Targeting
- Select number and priority of segments for entry
- Select segment coverage strategy

Positioning
- Select meaningful attributes for differentiation
- Apply positioning through marketing strategy and tactics

EXHIBIT 4.2	Segmentation Variables for Consumer Markets
Type of Variable	*Examples*
Behavioral and attitudinal	Benefits perceived/expected, occasion/rate of usage, user status, loyalty status, attitude toward product and usage, technological orientation, price sensitivity
Demographic	Age, gender, family status, household size, income, occupation, education, race, nationality, religion, social class
Geographic	Location (by country, region, state, city, neighborhood, postal code), distance, climate
Psychographic	Lifestyle, activities, interests

Apply Segmentation Variables to Consumer Markets

Marketers can isolate groupings within consumer markets using behavioral and attitudinal, demographic, geographic, and psychographic variables (see Exhibit 4.2). Consumer markets can be segmented with just about every one of these variables; the choice depends on the company's detailed marketing research profiling customers and analyzing their buying behavior. Sophisticated marketers often apply a combination of variables to create extremely well-defined segments or niches for marketing attention.

Planning Tip

Use marketing research to profile customers and identify variables for meaningful segmentation.

Common sense also plays a role: some variables simply don't lend themselves to certain markets. For example, the consumer market for paper towels might be segmented in terms of education, but will the resulting groupings reveal differing needs or responses to marketing efforts? On the other hand, income and household size are likely to be better variables for segmenting this market, since either (or both) may result in groupings that have different needs or respond differently to marketing activities. The following sections take a closer look at the main consumer segmentation variables.

Behavioral and Attitudinal Variables

Behavioral and attitudinal variables are, in many cases, the best way to identify a consumer group for marketing purposes. This is because such variables help marketers analyze the specific value that a group of consumers expects from a particular offering. Note that benefits required or expected, usage occasion and status, loyalty status, technological orientation, and attitudes toward products or usage generally cross demographic and geographic lines, yielding segments based on how consumers act or feel rather than on where they live or how old they are. For example, air travelers look for different benefits: business travelers may put more value on convenient schedules, whereas vacation travelers may put more value on affordability. Therefore, marketers will use different marketing messages for each of these segments, putting the emphasis on what people need or the benefits they seek.

Segmenting by usage occasion helps marketers group consumers based on the occasion(s) when they buy or use a product. User status—whether a consumer has ever used the product, is a first-time user, or is a regular user—is particularly important when a company wants to increase sales by selling to nonusers, first-time users, or light users. Do consumers in the market tend to be brand-loyal or do they constantly switch—and why? Companies often mount one marketing program to reinforce loyalty and another to court switchers from other brands.

Attitudes and behavior play an important role in Harley-Davidson's marketing.

Harley-Davidson. "We stand for freedom and independence," says the CEO of Harley-Davidson. Some customers sport a Harley tattoo to express their inner outlaw; most prefer to live the brand by accessorizing their Harley motorcycles and getting outfitted in Harley clothing and apparel. These attitudes and behaviors cut across demographic lines: two-thirds of Harley owners are in the 35-54 age group, for example, and most are male. Harley's marketing plan includes segmentation by gender (with special programs targeting women) and by product usage (with special programs for consumers who want to learn how to ride). The company particularly wants to reinforce loyalty because, the CEO notes, "half of our customers are people who have never owned a Harley." In the past, however, inventory was so scarce that buyers had to wait for their bikes and perhaps pay more than sticker price. Now Harley is expanding production—with close attention to quality—so first-time bikers can buy when they're ready and existing customers can trade up without delay.[3]

Demographic Variables

Demographic variables are popular for segmentation because they are common and easily identified consumer characteristics. In addition, they often point to meaningful differences in consumer needs, wants, and product consumption, as well as media usage. For instance, Beiersdorf and other skin-care marketers segment customers on the basis of gender, knowing that men and women have different needs, attitudes, and behavior patterns.

Segmenting on the basis of income can help marketers of upscale goods and services, such as Tiffany's, identify consumer segments with the means to buy. It also can help marketers of lower-priced products focus on customers who need to stretch their dollars; an example is Dollar General, which segments by income and geography.[4] In fact, discount store sales volume has grown so rapidly that Procter & Gamble and other manufacturers are creating products and brands specifically for lower-income segments.[5] Combining demographic variables can focus marketing even further; Charles Schwab looks at household income, investment assets, and several other variables when segmenting the market for brokerage services.[6]

Marketers must avoid stereotyping customers when using demographic variables such as race, nationality, and income. Adding behavioral and attitudinal variables linked to customers' underlying wants and needs will reveal customer motivations and benefits that can be addressed, segment by segment, through marketing. Sprint-Nextel has done just that.

Sprint-Nextel. This telecommunications company has segmented the market for cell phone and "push to talk" walkie-talkie services by nationality, family status, occupation, and benefits expected. One of its programs targets immigrants who live in the United States and have family or coworkers in Central or South America. Sprint-Nextel's research revealed that Hispanic executives value being able to communicate instantly with employees and colleagues, regardless of geography. In response, company marketers created a program in which these U.S. customers can call Sprint-Nextel customers in Argentina, Brazil, Peru, and Mexico for an affordable, flat monthly fee. The Spanish-language campaign promoting this program uses the tagline "ya" (meaning "now") to emphasize the benefit of instant accessibility.[7]

To research consumer demographics, check the U.S. Census pages (www.census. gov) for statistics and trends. Also see Economy.com's Free Lunch page (www.economy. com/freelunch), with links to reports and statistics covering consumer markets, economic trends, industry analyses, and other demographic issues. Many sources listed in Chapters 2 and 3 also provide demographic data.

Geographic Variables

As shown in the earlier Avon example, companies routinely use geography to segment consumer markets. The decision to use geographic variables may be based on a company's ability to sell and service products in certain areas or climates, its interest in entering promising new markets, or its reluctance to sell in certain areas because of environmental threats or unfavorable climate. For instance, Somerfield, a large U.K. grocery chain, segments on the basis of neighborhood to identify locations for its smaller Kwik Save food stores. Tesco, the dominant U.K. grocery chain and a Somerfield competitor, also segments by geography to identify neighborhoods for new Tesco Express convenience food stores.[8]

Planning Tip
Geographic segmentation may cover a single neighborhood or an entire continent.

Still, companies that segment by geography should note meaningful differences within each area or similarities that cross geographic boundaries. Waitrose, a grocery chain in Southern England, competes with Tesco, Somerfield, and other rivals by featuring organic foods and emphasizing quality and service. Because customers all over the United Kingdom are interested in organic foods, Waitrose can broaden its segmentation beyond the boundaries of current store locations, serving a wider geographic area through online shopping.[9]

Psychographic Variables

Segmenting on the basis of psychographic variables such as lifestyle, activities, and interests can help companies gain a deeper understanding of what and why consumers buy. Sometimes psychographic segmentation is the only way to identify a consumer group for special marketing attention, because activities and interests tend to cross demographic and geographic lines. People who share an interest in sports, for instance, may live anywhere in the United States—or in another country—and be of almost any age or gender.

Marketers who apply both psychographic and demographic variables may be able to create one or more segments that will respond to different marketing initiatives. The key is to identify the specific psychographic variables (and any other variables) that correspond to meaningful differences. Home Depot has done this.

Home Depot. The home-improvement retailer Home Depot is tapping a significant profit opportunity by segmenting according to gender and interest in do-it-yourself projects. Based on research showing that many women like to pick up tools and work on home renovation, the company tidied up its stores, started a gift registry program, and initiated "Do-It-Herself" workshops to teach skills such as flooring installation. It is also testing catalogs featuring home furnishings and decorative accessories that appeal to women but are not spotlighted in the stores. "Historically, we have overmarketed to men and undermarketed to women," explains a store executive. "The reality is of an increasing partnership. Women are definitely equal partners in home renovations." This segment also is a driving force behind purchases for kitchen makeovers and other projects.[10]

EXHIBIT 4.3   Segmentation Variables for Business Markets

Type of Variable	Examples
Behavioral and attitudinal	Purchasing patterns and process, user status, benefits expected, supplier requirements and evaluation, attitude toward product and usage, technological orientation, loyalty status, order size/frequency, buyer/influencer/user attitudes
Demographic	Industry, business size, business age, ownership structure
Geographic	Location (by country, region, state, city, neighborhood, postal code), distance, climate

Thus, segmentation not only identifies the segment (in this case, women do-it-yourselfers) but also provides clues to how it can be reached through marketing (through workshops, better-organized stores, and catalogs).

Apply Segmentation Variables to Business Markets

As Exhibit 4.3 shows, business marketers can segment their markets using three major categories of variables: (1) behavioral and attitudinal, (2) demographic, and (3) geographic. In many cases, marketers use a combination of variables, including industry (a demographic variable), size of business (another demographic variable), location (a geographic variable), and purchasing patterns (a behavioral variable). Again, the purpose is to create segments that are internally similar but don't have the same needs or don't respond exactly the same as other segments when exposed to the company's marketing activities.

Behavioral and Attitudinal Variables

In many ways, segmenting by behavior or attitude (such as purchasing patterns, user status, attitude toward technology, loyalty status, price sensitivity, order size/frequency, attitudes, or benefits expected) is especially effective because it helps marketers understand what specific business segments want and value, as well as how and why they buy. Purchasing patterns can vary widely; for example, companies have differing buying policies and practices and buy at different times or intervals. Understanding buying cycles and policies can help marketers design and deliver the right offer at the right time. Similarly, companies that are frequent users may require a different offer or message than first-time buyers.

Segmenting on the basis of expected or required benefits can be effective for B2B marketers. To illustrate, when 3M's sales representatives asked television manufacturers about the benefits that consumers want in the next generation of flat-screen models, they learned about two desirable benefits: a wider viewing area and a darker background color. The profit potential of this segment is so attractive that 3M immediately started refining optic films for improved television displays.[11]

Demographic Variables

The main demographic variables in business markets are industry, business size, business age, and ownership structure. Industry segmentation is a good starting point, but it doesn't necessarily result in groupings that are sufficiently different to warrant different marketing approaches. Therefore, marketers typically segment further on the basis of size (as measured by annual revenues or unit sales, number of employees, or number of branches) or even rate of growth, reasoning that businesses of different sizes or growth rates have different needs. As an example, Esselte segments the market for office supplies according to business size (demographic variable) and benefit required (behavioral/attitudinal variable). Its advertising campaigns for Pendaflex filing systems

Planning Tip
Think creatively about grouping customers using multiple variables, including behavior and attitude.

are directed at small business owners and entrepreneurs seeking solutions to the problem of organizing document storage.[12]

Marketers that segment according to business age are looking for differing needs or purchasing patterns that relate to how long the business has been in existence. Businesses in the formation stage often have a higher need for office or factory space, computers and equipment, accounting and legal services, and other offerings needed for starting a new business. In contrast, older businesses may need repair services, upgraded computers and equipment, and other goods and services related to maintaining an existing business. Segmenting by ownership structure also can reveal meaningful differences. For instance, the insurance and accounting needs of sole proprietorships are not the same as those of corporations. Only by segmenting the market can marketers identify these differences for appropriate marketing attention.

Geographic Variables

Business marketers, like their consumer counterparts, can use geographic variables such as nation, region, state, city, and climate to segment their markets. This allows grouping of business customers according to concentration of outlets, location of headquarters, and geography-related needs or responses. Consider the experience of WebEx Communications.

WebEx. This provider of services for online meetings segments the business market by geographic distance. Multinational firms like Texas Instruments, with offices spread over vast distances, need a cost-effective way of enabling far-flung personnel to meet and exchange information. That's where WebEx comes in: Customers simply log on to a secure site for private teleconferences or other types of meetings, complete with shared documents and multimedia information, plus instant messaging and other communication extras. Because online meetings are less expensive than flying staff members to one location, WebEx has attracted a solid customer base and holds a large share of the online conferencing market.[13]

Assess and Select Segments for Targeting

Planning Tip
Determine criteria for assessing the attractiveness of segments under consideration.

Once the company has applied segmentation variables, it must evaluate each segment based on attractiveness and fit with the firm's resources and core competencies, goals and objectives, and offerings (identified during the analysis of the current situation). Segments that require a different set of specialized skills or resources that are beyond the company's reach will be less attractive, for instance. The point is to screen out unattractive or unsuitable segments and gauge the attractiveness of the remaining segments. France's Alpha M.O.S. is a good example.

Alpha M.O.S. Alpha M.O.S., which makes electronic odor and taste sensors, eliminates segments of business customers that require customized "noses" or "tongues," because of the additional research and development cost. Instead, Alpha segments by benefit required and industry to put its marketing emphasis on larger segments, such as wineries, food manufacturers, and breweries. This segmentation strategy allows Alpha to identify and respond to the needs of businesses seeking a cost-effective electronic nose to test for consistent product quality and to determine how well packaging is protecting their products. Thanks to focused marketing, Alpha has captured roughly 70 percent of the worldwide market for electronic noses.[14]

34%
of people who plan on working out
come up with better plans in the process.

Ok, nobody's perfect. Good thing there's a snack that's perfect for you.

New! Quaker® Multigrain Snacks.
60 calories and a cinnamon toasty crunch.
Made with whole grain so your heart will be happy, too.

Get back to goodness.

Health-conscious consumers are the target market for Quaker Multigrain Snacks.

EXHIBIT 4.4   Assessing Segment Attractiveness

Fit with company resources and competencies

Market factors Size; growth rate; life cycle stage; predictability; price elasticity; bargaining power of buyers; cyclicality of demand	**Economic & technological factors** Barriers to entry and exit; bargaining power of suppliers; technology utilization; investment required; margins
Competitive factors Intensity; quality; threat of substitution; degree of differentiation	**Business environment factors** Economic fluctuations; political and legal; regulation; social; physical environment

Identify most promising segments and order of entry

Exhibit 4.4 shows factors used to evaluate segments and identify the most promising for marketing attention. As this exhibit indicates, one key measure of attractiveness is the market segment itself, including current and future opportunity for sales and profits. Large, more profitable, or faster-growing segments are generally more attractive than smaller, less profitable, or slower-growing segments. In assessing opportunity, marketers also look at how each segment would affect the company's ability to reach its overall goals, such as growth or profitability.

A second factor is the potential for competitive superiority. Can the company effectively compete or lead in the segment? How intense is the competitive pressure in each segment? How well differentiated are competing products and companies that are already targeting each segment? A third factor is the extent of environmental threats. Based on the environmental scanning and analysis, what macroenvironmental threats, such as more restrictive regulatory guidelines, exist now or could emerge to hamper the company's performance in the segment? Economic and technological factors are the fourth category; these include investment required for entry, expected profit margins, and barriers to entry/exit in the segment.

TARGETING AND COVERAGE STRATEGIES

Planning Tip
Summarize your ranking and targeting decisions in the marketing plan.

Through segmentation, the company has identified various segments within the larger consumer or business market and screened out segments it will not enter. Now it selects and ranks the remaining segments in order of priority for entry. Some marketers do this by weighing the evaluation criteria to come up with a composite score for each segment. This shows which segments are more attractive and allows comparisons based on higher profit potential, faster projected growth, lower competitive pressure, or other criteria. Different marketers plan for different ranking systems and weighing criteria, based on their mission and objectives, resources, core competencies, and other considerations. As shown in the simplified ranking in Exhibit 4.5, some segments may score higher for competitive superiority but lower for fit with organizational resources, for instance. The

EXHIBIT 4.5 Sample Segment Ranking

Segment	Score for segment growth, potential	Score for competitive superiority	Score for fit with resources, core competencies	Score for economic, technological factors	Score for environmental threats	Overall score
A	3	5	2	4	3	17
B	5	4	4	3	4	20
C	4	2	3	2	5	16

Scoring key: 5 = highly attractive, 4 = moderately attractive, 3 = average, 2 = moderately unattractive, 1 = highly unattractive

overall score generally determines which segments are entered first; here, segment B has the highest overall score and will be the top priority for marketing attention.

Other marketers, such as Harrah's, prefer to rank segments according to similar customer needs or product usage.

> **Harrah's Entertainment.** Harrah's Entertainment, which operates casinos and hotels in Las Vegas and elsewhere, has a sophisticated system for tracking what its 40 million customers spend in Harrah's properties so marketers can analyze their behavior and demographics. Which customers visit during a business trip and which visit on vacation? How often do customers come to a Harrah's property, and what are their spending patterns? Answering these questions has led Harrah's to segment the consumer market by frequency of usage and loyalty, among other variables. Its main marketing focus is on the segment of people who visit casinos most frequently; these customers receive free or discounted transportation to Harrah's casinos, plus communications and gifts to reinforce loyalty. In contrast, competitors generally segment according to the amount of money spent in the casino and rank the biggest spenders as the top priority.[15]

Concentrated, Undifferentiated, and Differentiated Marketing

After ranking, the company is ready to determine which segments to enter and what coverage strategy to use. Many companies use **concentrated marketing,** identifying the most attractive segment and concentrating marketing attention on only that one. The advantage is that the company can focus all its marketing activities on a single customer grouping. However, if the segment stops growing, attracts more competition, or changes in other ways, it might become unattractive almost overnight.

At the other extreme, a company may decide to target all segments with the same marketing strategy, which is **undifferentiated marketing.** This mass-marketing approach ignores any segment differences and is based on the assumption that one marketing strategy for the entire market will yield results in all segments. Although undifferentiated marketing requires less investment in product development, advertising, and other tactics, it is rarely used today because it doesn't adequately address the needs of fragmented, diverse markets.

Instead, companies that target multiple segments generally use **differentiated marketing** to create a separate marketing strategy for each segment. Colgate, which once used mass marketing to target everyone who needed toothpaste—one product for all, one benefit for all, one campaign for all—has become expert at differentiated marketing. It targets an immensely diverse group of segments with individual marketing mixes: people who want whiter teeth, people who want less tooth tartar, people who have sensitive teeth, and so on.

Banks are also embracing differentiated marketing. KeyCorp, a Cleveland-based bank, has segmented its customer base according to attitudes, aspirations, and demographics (creating consumer segments like "Young Transactor" and "Family Asset Builder"). Now when a customer calls the service center, the segmentation "tag" on that account prompts the bank's representative to ask particular questions related to that segment's needs and then suggest appropriate bank products. This program has boosted KeyCorp's sales by 150 percent in just three years.[16]

Differentiated marketing entails considerable research to understand each segment's needs and results in higher costs for different products, different advertising campaigns, and so on. These costs must be taken into account when preparing the marketing plan and related budgets. If the company's resources won't stretch to cover all the targeted segments, a rollout strategy may be needed for entering one segment at a time, in order of priority.

Personas for Targeted Segments

A growing number of companies are gaining customer insights by developing **personas,** detailed but fictitious profiles representing how individual customers in a company's targeted segments behave, live, and buy. As preparation for target marketing, personas give marketers a deeper understanding of what shapes each segment's needs, preferences, buying behavior, and consumption patterns.

A persona brings the segment's customers into sharper focus and, says Jackie Yeaney, chief marketing officer of HomeBanc Mortgage, helps all employees "relate to the actual people they're serving." HomeBanc developed 11 personas representing the behavior of specific targeted segments, then confirmed the details of these personas through focus-group research. For example, Christina and Lee Gillespie are personas representing a Generation Y couple with a growing income, a growing family, and the desire for a larger house in a better community. HomeBanc redesigned its Web site based on the behavior of customers represented by the Gillespies, making changes such as featuring mortgage information more prominently on the home page.[17]

Chrysler and its advertising agency, Organic, have decorated rooms to reflect the personas of customer segments being targeted for the Jeep Compass and Dodge Caliber models. The rooms reflect what each targeted customer might read, eat, buy, and do for fun. "We are finding persona rooms to be very useful in developing marketing campaigns for our new product launches," says a Chrysler executive, who adds that the goal is to "create more targeted, lifestyle-appropriate communications and to identify the right media opportunities to reach potential buyers."[18]

POSITIONING FOR COMPETITIVE ADVANTAGE

Planning Tip

Your positioning must tap into what customers value and effectively differentiate the offering.

After selecting segments for entry and determining the coverage strategy, the next step is to decide on a positioning strategy to differentiate the brand or product on the basis of attributes that customers find meaningful. Marketing research can uncover customers' views of the brand and its competitors, revealing key attributes that influence customer buying decisions. Then the marketer must determine which attribute (or combination of attributes) supports the most meaningful differentiation and conveys a competitive advantage that will lead to achieving sales, market share, or other objectives.

Meaningful Differentiation

Companies can differentiate their brands and products by physical attributes such as product features, service attributes such as convenient installation, channel attributes such as wide availability, and pricing attributes such as bargain pricing. The choice depends on what customers value and how competitors are perceived. If customers value wide availability of a product, that point of differentiation is a potentially meaningful basis for positioning. However, it won't be a powerful point of differentiation if a competitor has already used that attribute to differentiate its product or brand. Also, a positioning will not work if it conflicts with the company's mission, goals, or resources.

Here are some examples of positioning based on meaningful differentiation:

- FedEx: fast, reliable, on-time delivery
- Rolex: status-symbol fashion accessory
- Southwest Airlines: affordable, no-frills air travel

In each case, the positioning conveys the value that the brand provides and sets the brand apart from competitors in a sustainable way. FedEx's positioning on the attribute of on-time delivery—backed up by day-in, day-out performance—has given the company a distinct image and competitive edge. What about two competitors that share a meaningful attribute such as low pricing, the way Southwest and JetBlue do?

> **JetBlue and Southwest.** JetBlue Airways' positioning stresses low fares but the in-flight amenities of leather seats and personal video screens add a dimension of comfort that sets that airline apart. Southwest Airline's positioning on the attribute of affordable air travel—backed up by low fares and few frills—has given it a distinct image and helped it build market share in a turbulent industry. Southwest is known for its friendly humor, JetBlue for its style and efficiency. Even when higher costs for fuel and other expenses prompt both airlines to hike fares, the affordability positioning clearly differentiates them from competitors like American and Delta, which are not looking for a "budget" image.[19]

Positioning and Marketing Leverage

Positioning alone won't build competitive advantage, although it can act as the driving force for marketing strategies and programs, setting the tone for the rest of the marketing plan. Thus, to leverage the company's investment in marketing, all marketing programs should support and reinforce the differentiation expressed in the positioning. Consider how Agfa Graphics, an Agfa division, positions itself as a B2B problem-solving supplier.

> **Agfa Graphics** Recognizing that publishers and printers need to both improve efficiency and achieve growth, Agfa Graphics has developed high-tech ways of automating many preproduction and postproduction tasks. The company's Web site supports its positioning as a "problem solver" in several ways. First, prospects can click to see demonstrations of Agfa Graphic's software applied to specific problems commonly experienced by commercial printers, packaging printers, and other printing businesses. Second, prospects can click to read case studies of businesses that have used Agfa Graphics software to solve particular problems and better serve their customers. Third, Agfa Graphics posts white papers filled with

technical details and cutting-edge information to help prospects and customers make informed decisions about choosing among alternative solutions. Finally, the company invites visitors to subscribe to e-newsletters so they can stay updated on new technology and products.[20]

All marketers should reevaluate the basis of their product's or brand's differentiation as the environment changes or customer perceptions change. This applies to countries and states marketing themselves to attract investment; tourist areas and attractions seeking to bring in travelers; and communities seeking to build pride and retain residents. The high school in Manchester, Connecticut, decided to reposition itself after the school's image suffered because of reports of crowding, student fights, and other problems. The head of the local parent–teacher association said the new marketing plan would communicate the school's positive qualities without camouflaging its problems. The school adopted a new motto, "Manchester High School—Our Future, Taught Today," to convey "the far-reaching impact the high school has on this community," a parent-teacher official explained. Other marketing actions included opening the school for senior citizen events and arranging for students to speak with civic groups.[21]

SUMMARY

Market segmentation is the process of grouping customers within a market according to similar needs, habits, or attitudes that can be addressed through marketing. The purpose is to form groupings that are internally similar yet sufficiently different so that each grouping will not react in exactly the same way to the same marketing activities. Segmentation is the basis for targeting decisions about which market segments to enter and the segment coverage strategy to use. Once segments have been chosen, the company creates a positioning strategy for effective differentiation.

The market segmentation process consists of three main steps: (1) select the market, (2) apply segmentation variables, and (3) assess and select segments for targeting. Consumer markets can be segmented using behavioral/attitudinal, demographic, geographic, and psychographic variables. Business markets can be segmented using behavioral/attitudinal, demographic, and geographic variables. Next, each segment is evaluated, unsuitable segments are screened out, and remaining segments are ranked in order of entry, using concentrated marketing, undifferentiated marketing, or differentiated marketing for targeting coverage. For deeper understanding, some marketers use personas, detailed but fictitious profiles representing how targeted customers behave, buy, and live. Finally, the company must create a positioning strategy to differentiate the brand or product on the basis of attributes that are meaningful to customers, supported by the company's marketing mix.

CHAPTER

5

Planning Direction, Objectives, and Marketing Support

In this chapter:

PREVIEW

The ultimate purpose of the marketing plan is to help the organization achieve a number of *objectives*—short-term performance targets—that will, in turn, bring it closer to achieving its *goals,* long-term performance targets tied to the purpose described by the mission. The planning process started with a thorough examination of environmental factors, strengths and weaknesses, markets, and customers, followed by targeting and positioning decisions about reaching selected consumer or business segments.

    As discussed first in this chapter, marketers are now ready to determine the overall direction for the marketing plan. Whether or not growth is chosen, the direction has to be consistent with the organization's priorities and strengths. Next, the chapter explains how to set effective marketing, financial, and societal objectives for the coming year or whatever period the plan covers. The final section in the chapter discusses how customer service and internal marketing provide marketing support for decisions about product, place, price, and promotion. After reading this chapter, document your chosen direction, objectives, and marketing support decisions using *Marketing Plan Pro* software or in a written plan. Consult this chapter's checklist for questions to ask when developing objectives for your marketing plan.

DETERMINING MARKETING PLAN DIRECTION

The natural foods supermarket Whole Foods Market and the insurance firm Progressive both want to expand within the United States; the soft drink giant Coca-Cola wants to expand globally. These firms, like many businesses and nonprofit organizations, have marketing plans for growth.

CHAPTER 5 CHECKLIST   Do Your Objectives Measure Up?

✔ Is the objective specific, time-defined, and measurable?
✔ Is the objective realistic yet challenging?
✔ Is the objective consistent with the organization's mission and overall goals?
✔ Does the objective support the strategic direction of the marketing plan?
✔ Is the objective consistent with resources and core competencies?
✔ Is the objective appropriate, given environmental opportunities and threats?
✔ Does the objective conflict with other objectives?

Planning Tip

Be guided by the mission, goals, and situational analysis when planning your direction.

Growth is not always an appropriate direction, however; to deal with constant and inevitable change, some companies may strive to maintain current sales or revenue levels during certain years and others may choose retrenchment (see Exhibit 5.1). Radio Shack recently closed more than 450 U.S. stores that were not meeting sales expectations, as part of a turnaround aimed at boosting profits and slashing costs.[1]

What are the choices for growth strategies and nongrowth strategies? The next two sections explain what each choice entails and the implications for marketing planning.

Growth Strategies

If an organization wants to pursue growth, marketers can develop plans for one of these four broad strategies:[2]

Market penetration is a growth strategy in which the company sells more of its existing products to customers in existing markets or segments. It is especially viable for companies that can build on established customer relationships and positive value perceptions, as the multinational financial services firm HSBC has found.

EXHIBIT 5.1   Options for Marketing Plan Direction

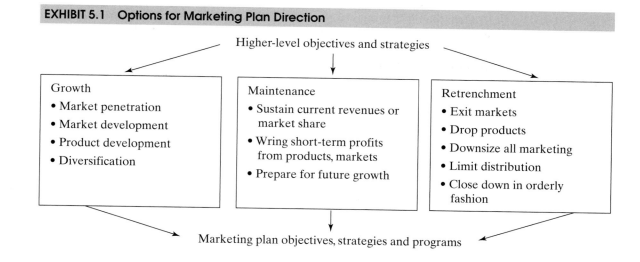

HSBC Group. London-based HSBC sees significant growth opportunity in cross-selling additional services to its consumer and commercial banking customers around the world. Its new megabranches, located in major North American and European cities, are customer-friendly and heavy on personalized service—a comfortable environment for discussing customers' current needs and long-term financial goals. Many HSBC branches in the United States and elsewhere have weekend hours to accommodate time-pressured customers interested in financial services beyond checking or savings transactions. Some of HSBC's Hong Kong branches remain open both Saturday and Sunday because "people prefer to discuss their retirement planning at the weekends, when they can take more time to consider a decision which can affect their whole life," notes Teresa Au Pui-yi, HSBC's Asia-Pacific head of service and sales.[3]

Market development involves identifying and reaching new segments or markets for existing products. The Daryl Roth Theatre in New York City has grown by attracting audiences drawn from a new segment: local college students. The theater offers discounted tickets to students at New York University and other nearby colleges who have signed up to receive text-message promotions via cell phone. "We are constantly looking for ways to tap into new markets," notes the theater's general manager.[4]

Product development is a growth strategy in which the company sells new products to customers in existing markets or segments. Toymaker Mattel, for instance, is targeting its Hyperscan game console to preteen boys, a market it already serves. Hyperscan's play experience combines a CD game and trading cards based on Marvel's X-Men heroes and other superhero characters. "Video games are at the top of the list of what boys are interested in, and it piqued our interest in creating video games in a way that meshes with our core strengths," explains Mattel's vice president for games and interactive.[5]

Diversification is a growth strategy of offering new products in new markets to take advantage of new opportunities, through internal product-development capabilities or by starting or buying a business for diversification purposes. Diversification can help an organization avoid overreliance on a small number of products and markets; on the other hand, too much diversification can dilute available resources and open the organization to competitive attacks on multiple fronts. Is this what happened at Dell?

Dell. Dell is well known for its PCs, which make up a large part of its $56 billion yearly revenue. But diversifying into consumer electronics (like TVs) and printers (including printer cartridges) has not helped Dell achieve the significant profit growth it anticipated. Despite introducing numerous non-PC products, Dell couldn't keep rival Hewlett-Packard from strengthening its market share in PCs. Dell's image was also hurt by a massive laptop battery recall and customer service problems. In all, it has spent more than $300 million on the battery recall and improving service for higher customer satisfaction. Can Dell make its diversification strategy pay off?[6]

Nongrowth Strategies

Growth is not always desirable or even possible. In tough economic times, for instance, organizations often marshal their resources and strive to simply maintain current sales or market share. Another maintenance strategy is to seek the highest possible profits from current products and current customers without trying for growth. At times, companies can be forced into a period of retrenchment because of rising costs, slower sales, lower profits, or a combination of these three. Consider the situation of Rallis India. After suffering losses for more than a year because of lower purchasing power in its main market, the company divested itself of seeds and other products to concentrate on marketing its top-selling pesticides for farmers.[7]

With sufficient time, management attention, and judicious investment, the most drastic change of direction—bankruptcy—sometimes leads to successful turnarounds. Less drastic decisions include withdrawing from certain markets, deleting particular products, cutting back on marketing, limiting distribution, or closing a division. Clearly, nongrowth strategies call for different marketing plans than those used for growth. Kellwood Corp., once known for mid-priced clothing that is "on trend but not trendy," has been in this position.

Kellwood. Consolidation in the retailing industry took a $75 million bite out of Kellwood's sales not long ago. Macy's, part of the Federated Department Store group, dropped Kellwood's Sag Harbor line of ladies' apparel as part of a move toward more exclusive clothing and lifestyle brands following Federated's acquisition of May's Department Stores. Kellwood, meanwhile, looked for growth by licensing the Calvin Klein and Oscar de la Renta brands for mid-priced women's apparel—with disappointing sales results. Finally Kellwood sold off several unprofitable businesses, including some men's apparel lines, and redesigned both the Calvin Klein and Oscar de la Renta collections for a new start. After posting lower revenue and profits, the company began experimenting with retail stores under the Sag Harbor, Koret, and Phat Fashions names. Kellwood's CEO says: "We recognize we are in the early stages of a turnaround."[8]

SETTING MARKETING PLAN OBJECTIVES

Planning Tip
Review the SWOT analysis to identify potential problems and sources of strength for achieving objectives.

After choosing a direction for the marketing plan, marketers must set objectives as short-term destinations along the path toward longer-term organizational goals. Step by step, the achievement of each objective will bring the organization closer to fulfilling its purpose. The exact objectives set will depend on the marketer's knowledge of the current situation, environmental issues and keys to success, customers in targeted segments, the organization's mission and goals, and the chosen positioning.

As summarized in this chapter's checklist, objectives will be effective for guiding marketing progress only if they are:

- *Specific, time-defined, and measurable.*   Objectives must be specific and include both deadlines and quantitative measures so marketers can plan the timing of activities and evaluate interim results. Marketers also should be able to measure progress by looking at sales figures, customer counts, satisfaction surveys, or other indicators. USAA, an insurance company based in Texas, makes customer relationships its highest priority and monitors results by counting how many customers defect during each period. Its marketers carefully analyze customer data to identify new needs and provide information and offers timed to life-stage changes. Not surprisingly, USAA has one of the best records for customer retention of any insurance firm anywhere.[9]
- *Realistic but challenging.*   Marketing plan objectives should be rooted in reality yet be sufficiently challenging to inspire high performance. Eclipse Aviation, based in New Mexico, recently set an aggressive marketing

sold out in the United States even before the cars were produced. As a result, Bentley is using marketing to maintain good relations with customers who will not get their cars for 12 to 18 months. Parent VW is also delighted: savvy marketing helped Bentley achieve the break-even point and start generating profits one year earlier than called for in the marketing plan.[16]

Financial Objectives

Planning Tip
Be sure your objectives are achievable, given your resources, competencies, and marketing tools.

Although the exact financial objectives will vary from organization to organization, businesses generally quantify sales volume and product targets; profitability targets such as margin or pretax profit; return on investment (ROI) targets for marketing; and break-even targets (see the discussion of pricing in Chapter 7). Not-for-profit organizations might set targets for fund-raising, among other financial objectives. To be effective, financial and marketing objectives must be consistent. On the other hand, key financial objectives may have to give way if a company is to achieve a particularly coveted marketing objective.

Some sample financial objectives might be:

- *Sales revenue.* Achieve $150,000 yearly sales revenue by December 31.
- *Product sales revenue.* Sell $3,000 worth of Product A every month.
- *Channel sales revenue.* Increase monthly Internet sales to $50,000 by end of year.
- *Profitability.* Increase the gross profit margin to 25 percent by end of year.
- *Return on investment.* Achieve 17 percent ROI on funds invested in direct marketing activities.
- *Break-even.* Reach the break-even point on the new service offering by June 30.

Consider Air Deccan's break-even objective.

Air Deccan. Start-up airlines require considerable investment in airplanes, facilities, employee recruitment and training, ticketing systems, and marketing activities. Air Deccan, a discount airline based in India, is no exception. It was founded in 2003 and has grown rapidly, carrying 4 million passengers in its first three years alone. Air Deccan's target market is middle-class families seeking affordable air travel to destinations within India—a market expected to expand very fast as incomes rise in the coming years. Despite a market share of 16 percent and flights that leave with no or very few empty seats, Air Deccan's objective is to break even by 2008. Breaking even sooner would be challenging because of continuing investments in equipment, facilities, and training.[17]

Societal Objectives

These days, customers, suppliers, employees, civic leaders, and other stakeholders are looking more closely at what companies do for society; as a result, more organizations are including societal objectives in their marketing plans. As shown in Exhibit 5.2, some societal objectives may call for cleaner operations or "greener" (more ecologically friendly) products, charitable donations, volunteerism or other involvement with community projects, energy conservation, and other socially responsible actions. For

The Ad Council sets specific societal objectives for its public service announcements.

example, DuPont set a long-term goal of cutting greenhouse-gas emissions by 65 percent by 2010—then surpassed that goal four years early.[18]

Fulfilling societal objectives polishes company or brand image and shows that the organization is doing something constructive about important issues. Setting objectives is not enough; stakeholders often follow the company's progress. For this reason, a growing number of firms are posting social responsibility reports on their Web sites or producing printed versions for customers and employees. Find out more about corporate social responsibility on the Business for Social Responsibility site (www.bsr.org) and the Corporate Social Responsibility Newswire site (www.csrwire.com).

Cause-related marketing falls under the umbrella of social responsibility because it links the marketing of a brand, good, or service to a particular charitable cause. Although the charity benefits, this is not outright philanthropy because of the explicit marketing connection. For example, the Red Lobster restaurant chain operates an annual cause-related program called Cobs and Lobsters, in which a portion of sales revenue is donated to Special Olympics. Olive Garden restaurants also run an annual cause-related marketing program, Pasta for Pennies; since 1990, this program has raised $15 million for leukemia and lymphoma research and treatment. According to Olive Garden's media relations director, "An emotional something happens when your restaurant develops a relationship with its community in this way. It lets people know and feel your dedication and concern—that there's more than profit on your mind."[19]

Planning Tip

Choose a cause that makes sense for your organization, your customers, and your employees.

Some sample societal objectives might include:

- *Conservation.*   Reduce each store's use of electricity by at least 5 percent annually.
- *Reduce waste.*   Increase the proportion of recyclable product parts to 50 percent by the end of next year.
- *Issue awareness.*   Inform customers about substance abuse prevention by printing flyers for distribution with the February direct-mail campaign.
- *Community involvement.*   Encourage employees to volunteer for local projects on company time, receiving pay for up to 40 hours of volunteerism per year.

Putting resources toward social responsibility can be controversial, as in the case of Petróleos de Venezuela.

Petróleos de Venezuela. This state-run oil company, known as Pdvsa, puts profits toward social responsibility. "Pdvsa used to function as a transnational company only interested in maximizing oil sales," says the president. "Now, Pdvsa is working with other state institutions to reduce Venezuela's exceedingly high rate of poverty." It pays for agricultural development programs, low-income housing, and basics such as digging new wells. Critics say that Pdvsa's social responsibility budget diverts resources that should be used to increase oil output. However, the managing director says Pdvsa is channeling profits to social projects the way other companies channel profits to shareholders. As a result, many residents see the company in a new light. "I'm so happy that we're finally going to have water in the house," comments one. "This is the first time the company has ever done anything for us."[20]

PLANNING MARKETING SUPPORT

Before marketers plunge into the details of planning the marketing mix, they need to set objectives for two aspects of marketing support: customer service and internal marketing (see Exhibit 5.3). Customer service is important in any business because it offers opportunities to reinforce competitive differentiation and start or strengthen customer relationships. **Internal marketing**—marketing to managers and employees inside the organization—is equally important for building internal relationships as a foundation for implementing the marketing plan and satisfying customers. Decisions to be made in setting objectives for these two areas of marketing support are discussed in the following sections.

Customer Service

From the customer's perspective, service is part of the product or brand experience, and thus has a major influence on customers' perceptions and responses. When setting customer service objectives, then, marketers must understand what customers need and expect, what they consider satisfactory, and how service reflects on the brand or product. Although good customer service cannot make up for a bad product or spotty distribution, it can enhance the brand's image and may even allow management to raise prices despite intense competitive pressure or other challenges.

EXHIBIT 5.3   Customer Service and Internal Marketing Objectives

Internal Marketing Objectives
- Keep employees focused on customers
- Keep employees involved in marketing
- Keep employees informed about marketing
- Improve employee performance and satisfaction

← Support marketing objectives and the marketing mix →

Customer Service Objectives
- Meet targeted segment's needs, expectations
- Attract, retain, satisfy customers
- Reinforce the product or brand positioning
- Allocate service resources appropriately

In general, customers have different customer service needs and expectations at different points in the buying process:

- ***Customer service before the sale.***   Before they buy, customers often need assistance obtaining information about the product and its usage, features, benefits, and warranty; matching the right product to the right situation or need; researching add-ons like availability and pricing of replacement parts; and understanding how installation, training, or other postsale services operate.
- ***Customer service at the moment or point of sale.***   When they are about to buy, customers may need help choosing a specific model; scheduling delivery, pickup, or use; choosing among payment options or preparing purchase orders; arranging trade-ins or taking advantage of promotional offers; completing paperwork for warranty registration; or handling other sale-related issues.
- ***Customer service after the sale.***   After the purchase has been completed, customers sometimes need assistance installing a product; ordering refills or spare parts; scheduling maintenance or repair services; training users; or dealing with other postsale needs. Bank of America calls new customers a few weeks after they open accounts to answer questions and follow up on problems or needs. "It's low-tech, but it can have a tremendous impact on the quality of new customer relationships," says a marketing official.[21]

Planning Tip
Because they are interconnected, coordinate service objectives with internal marketing objectives.

The marketing plan also should set objectives for allocating service resources to deliver the appropriate level of customer service for each segment. Some marketers offer a lower level of customer service to less profitable segments while providing more profitable segments with a higher level of customer service, the way Merrill Lynch has done. This customer service strategy, along with aggressive internal cost-cutting, boosted Merrill Lynch's profit margin and enabled Merrill Lynch to invest in marketing to wealthier customers who need (and can pay for) multiple investment services.[22]

Knowing that customer service is rarely perfect every time, marketers should include objectives for **service recovery,** how the organization will recover from a service lapse and satisfy its customers. Research shows that if customers are satisfied with the way their complaints are resolved, 70 percent will continue the relationship. In fact, those who are pleased will be more likely to tell others about their experience, bringing the company new customers through positive word of mouth.[23] In setting service recovery objectives, companies should think about the process (such as what customers must do to register a complaint and what employees are supposed to do in response) and the results (such as measuring satisfaction with customer service).

Internal Marketing

Internal marketing objectives are used to focus the entire organization on the customer and generate support for the marketing plan. At the very least, internal marketing should ensure the proper staffing levels across functions and within the organization structure to carry out the marketing plan. It should also help marketers secure cooperation and involvement from other departments involved in implementation, such as research and development, and keep employees informed about marketing activities so they can communicate knowledgeably with customers and each other. Another objective is to increase employee performance and satisfaction in a job well done.

Depending on the company's resources and priorities, internal marketing communication can take place through internal newsletters and Web pages; training and marketing or sales meetings; and other techniques. Here's how the U.K. electronics and appliance retailer Comet uses internal marketing.

Comet. Through its "Comet Vision" internal marketing project, this 250-store chain has reinforced four employee behaviors that support better customer service: product knowledge, detail orientation, passion for service, and positive attitude. In addition to training sessions and ongoing communications, Comet Vision includes a recognition program in which employees nominate coworkers who have achieved excellence in one of the four behaviors. The retailer also changed its logo and employee uniforms to communicate the new customer service orientation to shoppers. Thanks to Comet Vision, customer complaints have plummeted, employee turnover has dropped dramatically, and both sales and market share have gone up.[24]

Upward communication is also vital, because it gives senior managers a feel for what the market wants and how marketing is meeting customers' needs. Executives of Walt Disney, for example, periodically suit up as Mickey or another Disney character and walk through Disney World or Disneyland to see what is happening firsthand. The company stresses internal cooperation and commitment to delivering quality service at every contact point. "Our goal is to treat one another the way we treat our guests," says the manager of performance and training.[25]

SHAPING THE MARKETING MIX

Planning Tip
The strategy pyramid shows how marketing programs are driven by strategic decisions.

As shown in Exhibit 5.4, the organization's mission, direction, goals, and objectives (at the top of the pyramid) are the guiding force behind decisions about the marketing mix, marketing support, and specific marketing programs. Managers look to the priorities reflected at the top of the pyramid as they determine action steps and allocate resources. All the tactics and programs developed during the remainder of the marketing planning process must not only be consistent with the mission, direction, goals, and objectives in the marketing plan; they must actually support them.

Thus, by properly implementing the programs in the marketing plan and measuring the results periodically against preset standards, the organization should be able to move in the chosen direction and progress toward accomplishing its financial, marketing, and societal objectives. Understanding this essential link between strategy, goals, objectives, tactics, and programs can help marketers make appropriate, effective, and productive marketing-mix decisions.

EXHIBIT 5.4 Strategy Pyramid

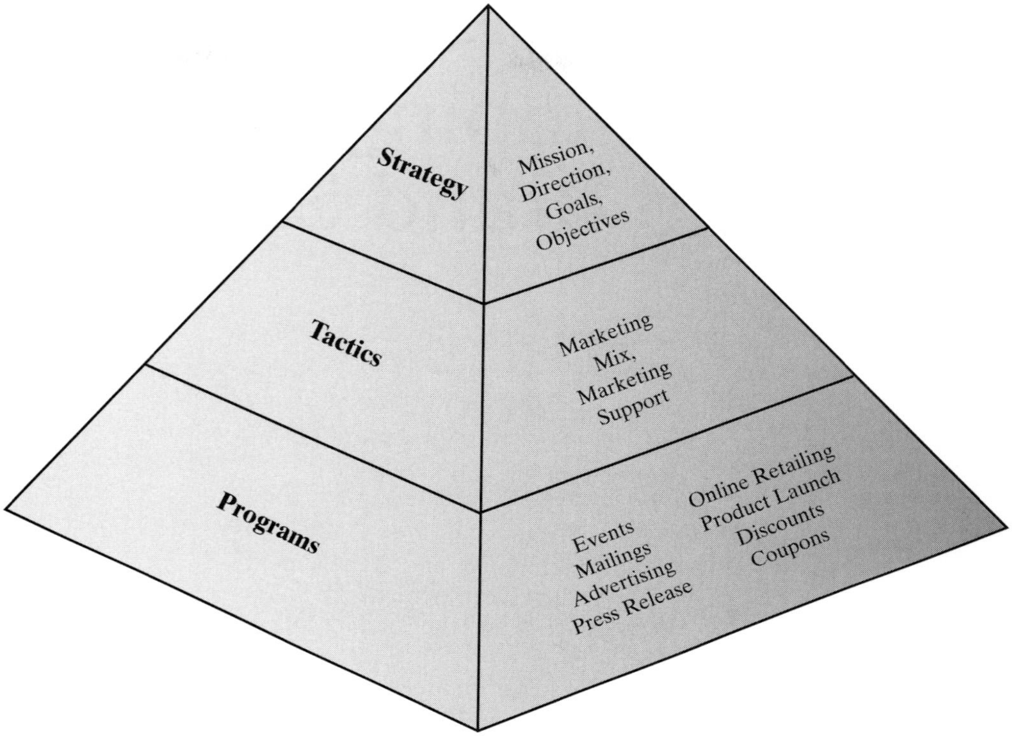

Strategy — Mission, Direction, Goals, Objectives

Tactics — Marketing Mix, Marketing Support

Programs — Events, Mailings, Advertising, Press Release, Online Retailing, Product Launch, Discounts, Coupons

SUMMARY

A marketing plan may point the way toward growth (including market penetration, market development, product development, and diversification), maintenance of current sales levels, or retrenchment. Once the direction has been set, marketers establish objectives for the marketing plan that are specific, time-defined, and measurable; realistic but challenging; consistent with the organization's mission and goals; consistent with resources and core competencies; and appropriate for the external environment. Marketing objectives are short-term targets for managing marketing relationships and activities; financial objectives are short-term targets for managing financial results; societal objectives are short-term targets for managing social responsibility results.

For marketing support, marketers need to set objectives for customer service and for internal marketing. Customer service can be provided before, during, and after the sale, with service geared to customer segments and marketing plan objectives and with appropriate objectives for service recovery. Internal marketing involves marketing to people inside the organization, necessary for building external relationships and implementing the marketing plan. The strategy pyramid illustrates the principle that marketing tactics and programs must support the mission, direction, goals, and objectives.

Developing Product and Brand Strategy

In this chapter:

PREVIEW

Some of the 33,000 new food, beverage, personal care, household, and pet products launched in any given year will succeed—but many will not.[1] Meticulous marketing research, in-depth customer knowledge, careful planning, and good implementation make all the difference. Even expensive failures can yield lessons to help marketers do a better job of planning for new products; for example, General Electric routinely picks the brains of managers whose much-anticipated new products did not perform well.[2]

In formulating product strategy, marketers must determine how existing and proposed products fit with the chosen direction and objectives and how each can contribute to building relationships with targeted customers. Branding plays a vital role in positioning and relationship-building as well. Strong brands, such as Nike, John Deere, and Starbucks, can create sufficient customer value to enhance the effectiveness of the entire marketing mix.

This chapter opens with an exploration of the main decisions in planning product strategy, the first of the four Ps in the marketing mix. These decisions cover tangible and intangible products; features, benefits, and supplementary services; quality and design; packaging and labeling; and product development and management. The second part of the chapter explores the basics of branding, including how branding works with positioning and how brand equity affects customer loyalty and lifetime value. Once you have finished this chapter, document your decisions and observations using *Marketing Plan Pro* software or in a written plan. This chapter's checklist suggests questions for analyzing offerings and developing product strategy.

PLANNING PRODUCT STRATEGY

Planning Tip

For existing products, review your strategy and research market changes to plan for adjustments.

What value can each product (existing and proposed) provide by satisfying the needs of specific customer segments? How can each product help the organization capture value by attaining one or more of its objectives? These are two key questions underlying the development of product strategy. From the customer's perspective, a product's value derives from the benefits delivered by its features and supplementary services, quality and design, packaging and labeling, and branding (see Exhibit 6.1). The marketer must therefore make decisions about each of these elements to formulate a strategy for offering goods, services, and other products that suit the organization's unique situation and satisfy or exceed targeted customers' needs and expectations.

CHAPTER 6 CHECKLIST   Analyzing and Planning Product Strategy

Current Offerings

✔ What products are being offered, at what price points, and for what customer segments?

✔ What are the unit sales, revenues, and profit trends of each product over the years?

✔ What is the age of each product? How are newer products faring in relation to older products?

✔ What is the market share of each product or line and how does each support line sales?

✔ How does each product contribute to the company's performance and goals?

✔ Which product accounts for the largest proportion of sales and profits?

✔ How do product sales vary according to geography?

✔ How do product sales vary according to channel?

✔ What are the strengths and weaknesses of the current offerings?

Product Plans

✔ How does each product support the organization's objectives and strategic direction?

✔ What opportunities for adding value through product modifications or introductions exist?

✔ What strengths and core competencies apply to product strategy?

✔ What weaknesses and threats pose risks to product strategy? How can these be minimized or overcome?

✔ How do each product's features and benefits, quality, packaging, services, and branding provide value for customers? What enhancements would add value and help the company achieve its goals?

✔ How do each product's features and benefits, quality, packaging, services, and branding compare with competitive offerings?

✔ Where is each product in the life cycle? How can each be aligned with plan objectives?

✔ How can product introductions be managed to minimize cannibalization?

✔ What changes to product lines and product mixes will help the company pursue its goals?

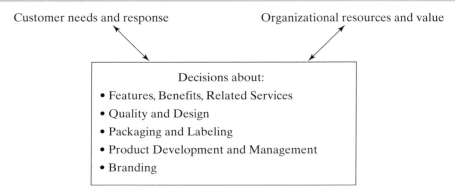

EXHIBIT 6.1   Elements of Product and Brand Strategy

Customer needs and response · · · · · · Organizational resources and value

Decisions about:
* Features, Benefits, Related Services
* Quality and Design
* Packaging and Labeling
* Product Development and Management
* Branding

Goods, Services, and Other Products

During planning, organizations must determine what, exactly, constitutes the product to be offered. Products can be:

* *Tangible goods* such as ice cream sandwiches and filing cabinets, which customers can buy, lease, rent, or use.
* *Services* such as Internet search engines or cell phone services, which are primarily intangible but may involve physical items (computer or cell phone).
* *Places* such as geographic regions courting tourists, states vying for business investment, or cities seeking to host activities such as the Olympic games.
* *Ideas* such as eating healthy or supporting human rights, with the objective of shaping the targeted segment's attitudes and behavior.
* *Organizations* such as a corporation or a government agency, with the objective of affecting the targeted segment's attitudes and behavior.
* *People* such as Daniel Ewing of the Los Angeles Clippers basketball team or the rock star Madonna, with the objective of affecting the targeted segment's attitudes and behavior.

In designing a service, marketers should think about who or what is being processed and whether the service activity is tangible or intangible (see Exhibit 6.2). Remember that the processing experience is as important as the end results, because customers are present during many service operations. Therefore, when planning services, marketers must focus on delivering benefits through the appropriate combination of activities, people, facilities, and information.

EXHIBIT 6.2   Designing a Service

Tangible activities	*People Processing*	*Item Processing*
	• Health care	• Package delivery
	• Hotel accommodations	• Janitorial service
	• Mass transit	• Parking garage
Intangible activities	*Mental Processing*	*Information Processing*
	• Entertainment programs	• Banking
	• Management consulting	• Legal services
	• Local phone service	• Accounting services

Features, Benefits, and Services

Features are specific attributes that enable a product to perform its function. In physical goods such as backpacks, features include padded shoulder straps and strong zippers; in intangible services such as online banking, features include integrated display of all account information and one-click funds transfer. Companies incorporate features to deliver **benefits,** the need-satisfaction outcomes that customers want from a product. For example, customers who buy cordless drills are seeking the benefit of creating holes for nails and screws, although some may seek additional benefits such as convenience or status. Thus, consumers and business customers buy products not for the features alone but for the value in providing benefits that fulfill needs or solve problems (which marketers can uncover through market and customer analysis).

To illustrate, Microsoft has enhanced its Office software suite to help PC users understand the benefits delivered by the programs' many features. When a user moves the cursor over one of the Excel spreadsheet icons, a brief demonstration pops up and shows what that feature does. "We're doing some amazing reinventions of our product to get people to see that there's a lot of new value we can deliver," explains a Microsoft executive.[3]

Exhibit 6.3 shows some sample needs, features, and benefits for two tangible products and one service. Each product targets a different consumer or business segment that is described according to behavior (do-it-yourselfers) or demographics (first-time home buyers, small business owners). In each case, note how the benefit interprets the feature in relation to each segment's specific need. Taking the analysis down to this level, feature by feature, helps marketers understand the value that each product offers to satisfy customer needs—at a given time. Needs and environmental influences can change at any point, so marketers must factor this into their analyses and plans.

A product will be at a competitive disadvantage if its features deliver benefits not valued by the targeted segment. Even if these customers value the benefits, the features must also be of value to the organization, consistent with the marketing plan's objectives. If a feature supports an objective such as capturing higher market share, it is valuable to the organization. However, if a feature does not contribute to achieving an objective (because it is too expensive to be profitable, for instance), it is not valuable to the organization—even if it is highly valuable to customers. Some experts warn of "feature bloat," adding so many features that customers become confused, frustrated, or dissatisfied. Mercedes recently removed hundreds of features from its cars, features

EXHIBIT 6.3 Sample Needs, Features, and Benefits

Product	Targeted Segment	Need	Feature	Benefit
Cordless drill (tangible)	Do-it-yourselfers (behavioral description)	Drill holes without electricity	Extra battery pack included	Drill can be used for long periods
Mortgage loan (intangible)	First-time home buyers (demographic description)	Obtain money to buy a home	Low down payment	Less money needed up front to buy a home
Laser printer (tangible)	Small business owners (demographic description)	Print documents economically	Draft-quality printing mode uses less toner	Saves money by making toner cartridge last longer

that "no one really needed and no one knew how to use," according to a Mercedes vice president.[4]

More companies are building customer loyalty and profits through a product strategy calling for **mass customization,** creating products, on a large scale, with features tailored to the needs of individual customers. General Electric does this with industrial plastics formulated to meet the specific needs of corporate customers. Some customers need unusually strong plastics, some need especially flexible plastics, and some require multiple benefits that are delivered by a variety of features. Now more than 70,000 customers order custom-developed plastics from the GE Plastics Web site. Because customers use the site to configure their plastics formulas and submit orders, GE can respond to needs more quickly.[5] Mass customization is available for consumers as well.

Myjones.com. Jones Soda, a premium soft drink brand distributed through Starbucks, Panera Bread, and other outlets, invites customers to order personalized 12-packs for delivery to home or office. First, the customer visits www.myjones.com, uploads a digital image for the front of the label, and writes a personalized paragraph for the back. Next, the customer chooses a flavor (such as Blue Bubble Gum or FuFu Berry) and enters shipping and payment information. Before the order is finalized, the automated ordering system shows how the photo will look on the front label. After buying, the customer gets an e-mail saying when the soda will be shipped.[6]

Planning Tip
Seek ways to add value while achieving societal and marketing objectives, not just financial objectives.

Although many customers are willing to pay for personalized soda, not all customers value the entire bundle of features and benefits inherent in a particular product. Marketing research is therefore a critical element in planning features. For instance, Ducati uses online research, listing the features of motorcycles in development on a page of its Web site and asking for customer comments before deciding which to actually include when production begins.[7] Studying sales trends of current offerings and researching customer reactions to those products also yields clues as to how well features satisfy customers' needs.

In planning product strategy, marketers should consider how the supplementary services related to a product can deliver valued benefits to satisfy customer needs, now and in the future. Some supplementary services may supply information for better use of the product, as in training; some may offer consultation for problem solving or customization of the product; some may involve safety or security, as in storage of products or data. IBM exemplifies this range, which has helped it achieve higher profit margins.

IBM. Big Blue markets stand-alone computer hardware and software but puts its main marketing emphasis on product-service bundles that more precisely address business customers' problems and needs in specific industry groups, including banking, telecommunications, and retailing. Consider FinnAir airlines, which once bought mainframe computers from IBM. Still an IBM customer, FinnAir now buys some hardware, some services (such as outsourced data-center operations), and some product-service combinations (such as specialized software with services tailored to FinnAir's requirements). The changes in purchasing reflect changes in FinnAir's needs and IBM's marketing of product-service bundles to meet those changing needs.[8]

Quality and Design

Planning Tip
Determine how customers perceive your product's quality compared with that of competing products.

Often defined in terms of performance capabilities, the most important definition of **quality** is how well the product satisfies customers. By this definition, a high-quality product is one that does a competitively superior job of fulfilling customer needs. Savvy marketers know that the basic functionality of acceptable quality is the price of entry in the contemporary global marketplace. Word of mouth (or online, word of mouse) can quickly sink a product with inferior quality—and just as quickly generate interest in a product with excellent quality. Good quality is no guarantee of success, but it can help companies attract new customers, retain current customers, capture market share, charge higher prices, earn higher profits, or meet other objectives.

The marketing plan should take into account customers' tendency to switch to a competing product if they believe its quality is superior (meeting their needs more consistently or more quickly). Quality is a major concern among cell phone users, for example, which is part of the reason for the higher **customer churn** (turnover in customers) at some phone service carriers. Verizon Wireless and Sprint-Nextel watch customer churn rates very closely because when customers leave, they are defecting to a competitor. Customers cite quality of call services, inaccurate billing, and unhelpful customer service representatives as reasons for defecting.[9]

Another focus of product strategy is design, inextricably linked to quality. A good design means more than style; it means that the product can perform as it should, can be repaired easily, is aesthetically pleasing, and meets other needs. Services are affected by design as well: New York's Long Island College Hospital has redone its emergency room design to add efficiency as well as comfort, cutting in half the waiting time for medical attention.[10]

Design is at the forefront of many product categories, from computers and entertainment electronics to home appliances and workshop tools. When good quality is the minimum that customers will accept, the "emotional quality" of design is the marketing battleground that more companies are choosing for differentiation. "A car can't exist in the future if it doesn't show passion," says Volkswagen's head designer.[11] Ford is steering in that direction as well.

Ford. Peter Horbury, who oversees design for the company's Ford, Lincoln, and Mercury brands, views design as a critical marketing element: "When cars start to become equally reliable and equally competent in other aspects, then the differentiator between brands has to be the way it looks." Ford's latest designs follow "the golden rules of touch," how a car's features feel to the driver. "Everyone has discovered the importance of craftsmanship and quality in the interior," says a Ford design executive. "Now it's an all-out war" around such features as dashboards and turn-signal levers. As one example, Ford's newest Mustangs allow customers to choose among 125 different color combinations for dashboard gauge displays. And to attract price-conscious Generation Y consumers, Ford is designing new subcompact cars that will be "sleek and sporty, but not quirky," says the head of product development.[12]

Packaging and Labeling

From the customer's perspective, packaging adds value by keeping tangible products safe and in convenient containers until they are used; labeling adds value by communicating product contents, uses, and warnings. Thus, Post breakfast cereals stay fresh and uncrushed in the plastic-lined cardboard packaging, and Advil pain reliever tablets are kept out of tiny hands by child-resistant containers; both packages bear labels with

Planning Tip
Consider the needs of channel members as well as customers when planning packaging and labeling.

information about product ingredients and consumption. When planning for labels, check on compliance with regional, national, and local laws and requirements mandating warnings (such as about the health hazards of cigarettes or alcohol), allowable use of certain phrases (such as "low fat"), and even the size or type of words (for warnings or other details).

Packaging can help companies burnish brand image by communicating and delivering benefits that customers value. Look at Nestlé's packaging initiative.

> **Nestlé.** After research showed that consumers dislike hard-to-open packaging, Nestlé's global head of packaging assigned a team of engineers and designers to a new packaging initiative. One of the first products to be introduced in new packaging was Country Creamery ice cream, which now comes in a carton with ribbed corners. The ribbing allows customers to get a firmer grip on the carton as they scoop out ice cream. Not all packaging changes receive rave reviews from customers, however. After marketers developed a new push-button lid for jars of Nestlé's Taster's Choice coffee, thousands of customers called to complain that the lid was not easy to open. The company listened and responded: it not only redesigned the lid; it sent a new jar to each customer who had complained.[13]

Packaging and labeling play an important marketing role by highlighting points of differentiation, explaining the product's features and benefits, reinforcing what the brand stands for, and attracting attention among customers and channel partners. In certain product categories, marketers plan innovative packaging as an effective point of differentiation. To illustrate, shelf-stable aseptic containers are gaining popularity for beverages, soups, and other foods, because they preserve taste and require no refrigeration until opened. Baby foods in aseptic packaging instead of glass jars? An executive at Gerber Products says: "We looked at a lot of [packaging] technologies, but aseptic was the most appropriate in terms of cost effectiveness and making parents' lives easier by providing lighter containers that won't break as well as providing a good-tasting, shelf-stable product."[14]

Marketers should plan packaging and labeling to "sell" from the shelf, because more than 70 percent of shoppers make their buying decisions while in the store. One reason that Listerine's PocketPak breath strips became a hit is that the package looked "cool and functional," notes an executive with Listerine's parent company. Research confirmed that customers found the package attractive and consistent with the brand. Even before Listerine kicked off its advertising campaign, shoppers noticed PocketPaks and bought them on impulse, giving the new product considerable sales momentum.[15]

Product Development and Management

Planning Tip
Aim to have different products in different stages of the life cycle at any one time.

The fourth major element of product strategy is managing movement through the **product life cycle** of introduction, growth, maturity, and decline. Even experts have difficulty predicting the exact length and shape of a product's life cycle, which limits the practical application of this theory. However, marketers can look at sales trends for clues to a particular product's life-cycle stage: new products with low but growing sales are in the introduction stage; young products with rapidly increasing sales are in the growth stage; existing products with relatively level sales are in maturity; and older products with decreasing sales are in decline.

These stages can be influenced by factors such as competition and societal attitudes, which are constantly changing. Therefore, marketers should carefully monitor the environment as they plan to manage their products throughout the life cycle (see Exhibit 6.4).

EXHIBIT 6.4   Product Strategy from Development through the Life Cycle

Idea Generation and Screening	*Initial Concept Testing*	*Business Analysis*	*Design Prototype*	*Market Testing*	*Commercialization*
• Based on customer needs and wants, identify new product ideas	• Research customer value of product concepts	• Estimate development, production, and marketing-mix costs	• Design and produce working prototypes	• Test customer reaction through limited market trials or simulated testing	• Plan targeting and timing of launch
• Screen out unprofitable or unsuitable ideas	• Refine concept based on research	• Compare costs with potential share, sales, profitability to identify good candidates	• Test prototype functionality, customer appeal	• Test different marketing-mix combinations for support	• Plan production and marketing-mix support for launch

Introduction	*Growth*	*Maturity*	*Decline*
• Launch the new product	• Enhance product (new features, improved quality, added services, new packaging)	• Add brand or line extensions	• Reposition, reformulate, or cut struggling products
• Support launch with marketing-mix programs to build customer awareness, make product available, and encourage trial	• Support rising sales with expanded channel coverage, pricing for market penetration, and communications to start and reinforce customer relationships	• Defend market share through competitive pricing, channel expansion, communicating differentiation, and promotion to reinforce customer loyalty	• Manage profitability through careful pricing, pruning channel outlets, and minimal or highly targeted communications

Deciding to cut older products in decline is not an easy decision, as in the case of Konica Minolta.

Konica Minolta. The rapid rise of digital photography prompted this Japanese company to divest all of its camera and film products not long ago. Konica Minolta had built a worldwide reputation for quality cameras, photo film, and photo paper. As more amateurs and professionals moved to digital photography, however, sales slowed and profits evaporated. Konica Minolta announced it would cut back on these products, then sold its high-end camera line to Sony and set a firm deadline for closing down film and paper production. This has allowed the company to re-focus on its more profitable product lines, including photocopiers, medical equipment, and optical devices.[16]

New Product Development

Although Konica Minolta has discontinued some product lines, it continues to move ahead with new products. Its marketing planners, like their counterparts in other firms, look closely at potential opportunities for providing value in each segment, build on internal strengths and core competencies to create competitively superior products, and think about how to deal with any weaknesses and external threats. Planning for new product development covers these basic steps:

- *Idea generation.* Collect ideas from customers, managers and employees, suppliers, distributors, and other sources. Procter & Gamble, for instance, heard about a professor who had perfected a method for putting edible images on baked goods. This led to the idea of printing jokes and pictures on Pringles potato chips—an idea that significantly boosted the brand's sales.[17] Kraft Foods solicits ideas from customers through a link on its Web site.[18]
- *Screening of new ideas.* Eliminate inappropriate or impractical ideas early in the process to avoid wasting time and resources later.
- *Initial concept testing.* Test to discover whether customers in the targeted segment understand and like the most promising new product ideas; refine or drop concepts that test poorly.
- *Business analysis.* Assess the business prospects of the remaining ideas and eliminate any that could be too expensive or will not contribute to the marketing plan's objectives. W. L. Gore, which makes Gore-Tex and other products, analyzes the business case by researching the size of the market segment, the product's value to customers, the potential profitability, and the ability to maintain a competitive advantage.[19]
- *Prototype design.* Design and produce a prototype to determine the practicality and cost. If different technology or skills are needed, making a prototype will bring such issues into focus before full production.
- *Market testing.* Test the new product and various introductory marketing activities to gauge demand and competitive strength. Amazon.com tested a limited line of gourmet foods to gain experience with customers and suppliers, then expanded its offerings little by little. More than two years later, the company launched an online grocery store featuring a wide variety of nonperishable foods.[20]
- *Commercialization.* Introduce the new product in some areas or across the entire market, with the support of channel, pricing, and promotion strategies.

- *Monitoring of customer reaction.* Monitor customer reaction; if a new product does not fare as well as expected, the company faces decisions about changing the marketing mix (including the product), repositioning the product, or pulling it from the market. U.K.-based Virgin, which has introduced products in many categories and many countries, got in and out of the consumer electronics market in less than one year after selling fewer digital music players than expected in the first six months.[21]

In many cases, companies make decisions about new products and life-cycle movement to avoid or minimize **cannibalization**—allowing a new product to eat into sales of one or more existing products. Some cannibalization is inevitable in high-tech markets, where life cycles are relatively short because competitors race to launch the next breakthrough product. Companies often believe that if they don't cannibalize their own products, rivals will seize the opportunity to grab both sales and customer relationships.

Rather than completely cannibalize a product, however, the firm may prefer to reposition it for other uses or segments. For example, expensive computer chips that were state-of-the-art last year may be priced lower than today's top-performing chips and repositioned for use in computers designed for segments where speed or power is less of a priority and customers are more price-sensitive. Intel routinely does this when it introduces speedy new chips and lowers prices on existing chips to make them more attractive to different segments.[22]

Product Lines and the Product Mix

Product strategy also covers the management of each **product line** (products that are related in some way) and the overall **product mix** (the assortment of all product lines offered). The existing mix is analyzed as part of the current situation; after examining each product and line individually, marketers plan product decisions that will affect the length and width of lines and mixes (see Exhibit 6.5). One way to grow is by putting an established brand on a new product added to the existing product line, creating a **line extension.** Another is to plan a **brand (or category) extension,** putting an established brand on a new product in a different category for a new customer segment.

Longer product lines and wider product mixes typically require more resources to develop and sustain, but they help companies grow and pursue ambitious objectives. In contrast, shortening or narrowing lines and mixes can help the firm concentrate its resources on the most promising products and segments for survival, maintenance, or growth. When Konica Minolta deleted its cameras, film, and paper product lines, it narrowed its product mix and freed up resources for more profitable lines and new product development, with the overall aim of growth. Clearly, decisions about the product mix and individual product lines must fit with the organization's situation, direction, and objectives.

EXHIBIT 6.5 Product Line and Mix Decisions

Decision	Result
New product	Lengthens product line
Line extension	Lengthens product line
New line	Widens product mix
Brand extension	Widens product mix
Product deletion	Shortens product line
Line deletion	Narrows product mix

One way customers judge quality is by looking for the logo of Underwriters Laboratories.

Kellogg's acquisition of Keebler helped expand its mix and inspired new product lines.

> **Kellogg.** This big name in breakfast cereals has introduced many line and brand extensions since acquiring Keebler, known for its cookies and crackers. Leveraging more of its established brands has resulted in longer product lines through the introduction of snacks like Fudge Stripe Chips Deluxe cookies and Cheez-It Crisps. Kellogg has also widened its mix by putting its famous brands on products in different categories; one example is Special K Snack Bites in controlled-portion packages for consumers who want a treat without wrecking their diet plans. By launching products targeted to potentially lucrative segments, Kellogg is achieving its sales and profit objectives despite intense competition.[23]

PLANNING BRANDING

Planning Tip
Pay attention to brand symbols because they can become as recognizable as brand names.

Branding is the use of words, designs, and symbols to give a product a distinct identity and differentiate it from competitive products. After customers learn to associate a brand with the value created by a particular set of product elements (such as features, benefits, and quality), they simplify the decision-making process by routinely buying that brand rather than stopping to evaluate every alternative on every shopping occasion. Strong brands can help marketers in a number of ways (see Exhibit 6.6).

In terms of branding, a product may carry:

- *Company name and individual brand,* such as Courtyard by Marriott, Marriott Marquis.
- *Individual name* for a product, a category, or targeting a segment; Gap and Old Navy are separate brands, under the same ownership, geared toward different segments.
- *Private-label brand,* used by one retailer or wholesaler, such as Wal-Mart's George brand.
- *Multiple brands,* by *cobranding,* in which two or more organizations put their brands on one product; or by *ingredient branding,* in which an ingredient's brand is featured along with the product's brand, as when Dell PCs showcase Intel computer chips).

EXHIBIT 6.6   Marketing Advantages of Strong Brands

- Improved perceptions of product performance
- Greater loyalty
- Less vulnerability to competitive marketing actions
- Less vulnerability to marketing crises
- Larger margins
- More inelastic consumer response to price increases
- More elastic consumer response to price decreases
- Greater trade cooperation and support
- Increased marketing communications effectiveness
- Possible licensing opportunities
- Additional brand extension opportunities

Brands should be recognizable and memorable, capable of being legally protected, and suitable for international markets if and when the company expands globally. They should also have some meaning for the target market and be appealing (whether expressed in words, images, or sounds).[24] Online brands are not immune to these basic branding guidelines. Amazon.com, eBay, and Yahoo! have become strong and distinctive brands through constant, consistent marketing-mix support, whereas online brands without clear differentiation or marketing reinforcement have struggled or been acquired by other companies. For brands with physical presence, aroma can be an integral element that enhances appeal and emotional response, not just for personal fragrance products but also for retail and restaurant locations.[25]

Branding decisions made during the planning process are closely tied to product positioning and other marketing activities for building customer relationships through brand equity, as the next two sections explain.

Branding and Positioning

Every consumer or business product faces some competition in the marketplace, from direct competitors (Huggies disposable diapers compete with Pampers disposables), substitutes (Huggies disposables compete with cloth diapers), or both. In this context, the brand not only identifies a particular product; it reminds customers of the value that sets the product apart from all others—what makes the product both distinctive and competitively superior. The brand name should trigger associations with those points of differentiation, the way the hair-growth treatment Rogaine triggers associations with the word "regain."[26]

The Google brand, for example, is reminiscent of the mathematical term *googol* (1 followed by 100 zeroes). The positioning relates to the benefit of speedy searching for a high number of relevant result listings. The brand thus stands for what customers perceive and believe about this product compared with competitors (which the company can influence but cannot control), as well as the features, benefits, design, and other points of differentiation that the company can control. Consistency counts: if a marketing-mix strategy or implementation conflicts with the positioning, customers can become confused about what the brand stands for.

What if a company wants to change the value that its brand stands for? Haier Group, based in China, is facing that challenge in the U.S. market.

Haier America. A market leader in its home country of China, Haier entered the U.S. market in 1999 with an array of home appliances like compact refrigerators and freezers. Originally, Haier's products were priced low to build volume and economies of scale. "We used all our resources to get into the market at the low end, then we creeped into the midrange," explains the president of Haier's U.S. operations. "Now we are entering a new strategic phase." In this phase, Haier America is putting its brand on more expensive, high-tech appliances with "green" benefits, such as water-miser washing machines and dishwashers with sensors to monitor dirt removal. Can the brand cover a higher-end positioning after entering the market with low-end products? The company is about to find out, even as competitors like General Electric move upmarket with flashy appliances for affluent households.[27]

The Power of Brand Equity

The stronger the brand, the more it encourages customer loyalty and boosts **customer lifetime value,** the total amount a customer spends on a brand or with that company

EXHIBIT 6.7   Pyramid of Brand Equity

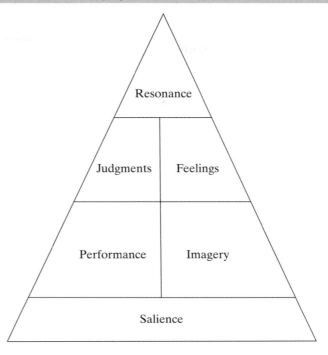

Planning Tip
High brand equity can help defend share when a product is mature or faces fierce competition.

during the entire relationship. As one example, the Louis Vuitton brand has developed such a loyal long-term following among the status-conscious that sales have continued to rise year after year, even under unfavorable economic conditions.

Vuitton also illustrates the power of **brand equity,** the extra value customers perceive that enhances their long-term loyalty to the brand. Customers are extremely aware of the Vuitton brand, understand the image and performance that it stands for, respond positively to it, and want an ongoing relationship with it—all hallmarks of high brand equity (see Exhibit 6.7). As a result of high brand equity, Vuitton's profit margins continue to be strong and are generally higher than the industry average for high-end fashion accessories.[28]

And although LVMH is the parent company, it is the Vuitton name that brings the value of brand equity to customers and to the organization, not the corporate name. This is also the case with a number of consumer product giants such as Procter & Gamble (well known for individual brands such as Pampers and Tide) and B2B marketers, including the U.K.-based manufacturer Tomkins, which offers industrial, automotive, and other business products under individual brands such as Fedco and Trico. In contrast, Sony and Honda build the equity of their corporate brands by showcasing them on diverse product lines and in marketing communications across targeted markets (think Sony PlayStation and Honda Accord).[29]

Brand equity should be addressed in the marketing plan because it can insulate a company against competitive threats and, just as important, become a driver for growth. Thanks to brand equity, consumer packaged goods manufacturer Unilever says that 75 percent of its revenues come from 20 global brands. When it lavished extra marketing attention on six personal-care brands, they achieved double-digit revenue growth—despite ongoing competition and sluggish economic conditions—plus higher profits.[30]

In addition, brand and line extensions can help a new product achieve customer acceptance, if marketing research shows that the brand has a positive image consistent with the segment's needs, expectations, and perceptions. Giorgio Armani is a good example: its luxury brand appears on a wide variety of products, from clothing and fragrances to a new chain of 30 upscale hotels and resorts to be designed by Armani and managed by professionals.[31] Yet extending a brand too far from its roots can dilute the image, especially if the new line or product does not completely deliver on the brand's promises of quality, status, need satisfaction, or another point of differentiation.

SUMMARY

Product strategy covers decisions about features, benefits, and supplementary services; quality and design; packaging and labeling; product development and management; and branding strategy. Products can be tangible goods, services, places, ideas, organizations, or people. Features are the attributes that enable the good or service to perform its intended function and deliver benefits—the need-satisfaction outcomes customers want from a product. Product-related supplementary services deliver valued benefits to satisfy customer needs as part of the product strategy.

Product quality means how well the product satisfies customers, and it is closely linked to design. Packaging and labeling deliver value to customers (storing products, keeping them safe, explaining ingredients and usage) and to organizations (polishing brand image, communicating product features and benefits, attracting interest). Product strategy includes planning for the four stages of the product life cycle (introduction, growth, maturity, and decline) and for new-product development. It also covers the management of each product line and the overall product mix. Branding gives a product a distinct identity and differentiates it from competitive products. Moreover, it supports the chosen positioning for a product in a targeted segment and helps build customer relationships for long-term loyalty and brand equity.

CHAPTER

7

Developing Pricing Strategy

In this chapter:

PREVIEW

Pricing strategy, the second major component of the marketing mix, is vital because it directly produces revenue, whereas other marketing functions require investments of money, time, and effort. Most pricing decisions can be implemented relatively quickly, whereas product, promotion, and place (distribution) changes usually take longer and cost more to complete. For many products and markets, marketers rely on **fixed pricing,** in which customers in the targeted segment pay the price set (fixed) by the marketer—the figure on the price tag; in other cases, marketers use **dynamic pricing,** varying prices from customer to customer or situation to situation.

This chapter opens by exploring customers' perceptions of value, how demand operates, and the role of pricing. The following section examines pricing objectives and the various internal and external influences on pricing decisions. Finally, the chapter concludes with a look at how and why marketers should plan to adapt prices. Once you have completed this chapter and made your pricing decisions, take a few minutes to document them using *Marketing Plan Pro* software or in a written plan. This chapter's checklist covers three key areas to be considered when formulating pricing strategy.

UNDERSTANDING VALUE AND PRICING

Planning Tip

Research the key benefits that customers value to satisfy needs or solve problems.

As noted in Chapter 1, customers assess the *value* of a product according to the difference between the total perceived benefits they receive and the total perceived price they pay. Exhibit 7.1 shows the components of total benefits and total price that customers take into account when evaluating value. The more weight customers give to benefits in relation to perceived price, the higher the value they perceive in that product. In addition, customers in different segments may perceive an offering's value in different ways. Thus, during the planning process, marketers must research and analyze value from the customers' perspective, including perceptions of the total price—initial cost plus shipping, maintenance, and any later costs—as well as perceptions of the product's benefits. When making pricing decisions, marketers also must consider how the product's value will be communicated to customers.[1]

CHAPTER 7 CHECKLIST   Planning Pricing Strategy

Internal Factors

✔ What does the organization want its pricing strategy to achieve?

✔ How can pricing be used to support positioning and targeting decisions?

✔ How can pricing be used to manage the product life cycle and product line objectives?

✔ How can pricing support the marketing and financial objectives?

✔ How do channel and promotion decisions affect pricing?

✔ Will the emphasis be on price or nonprice competition?

✔ What are the product's costs, and how do they affect the price floor?

✔ How are different prices likely to affect revenues, volume, and break-even?

External Factors

✔ How do industry customs affect pricing?

✔ How do customers perceive the product's value?

✔ What is the price sensitivity of customers in the targeted segment versus other segments?

✔ What are the prices and costs of competing products, and how do they affect the price ceiling?

✔ What nonprice alternatives exist for reacting to competitive price changes?

Price Adaptation

✔ Are discounts or allowances appropriate for achieving pricing objectives?

✔ Is bundling an appropriate tactic for achieving pricing objectives?

✔ Is product enhancement an appropriate tactic for achieving pricing objectives?

✔ Is loss-leader pricing an appropriate tactic for achieving pricing objectives?

✔ Is it necessary or advisable to raise prices, and if so, how?

✔ How do resources, capabilities, goals, and direction affect pricing and price adjustments?

In practice, the value of a product is not considered in isolation; customers look at value in the context of the benefits and prices of competing or substitute products. Where and when a purchase is made can enter into the value equation as well. Even if customers perceive all products as being priced the same (whether or not their

EXHIBIT 7.1 Perceptions of Total Benefits and Total Price

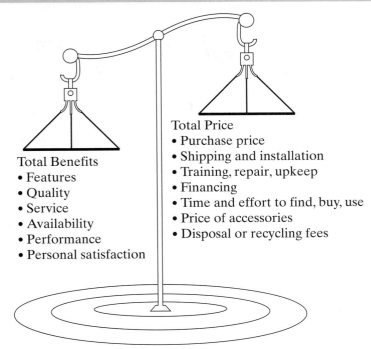

Total Benefits
• Features
• Quality
• Service
• Availability
• Performance
• Personal satisfaction

Total Price
• Purchase price
• Shipping and installation
• Training, repair, upkeep
• Financing
• Time and effort to find, buy, use
• Price of accessories
• Disposal or recycling fees

perceptions match reality), no two customers are likely to place exactly the same value on the total perceived benefits. To enhance value, the marketer must either add to the perceived benefits (e.g., by improving quality or introducing new features) or reduce the perceived price (e.g., by lowering the purchase price or offering more affordable financing).

Generic drugs made by Mylan, for example, provide value because their lower-price formulations are as effective as the brand-name versions.

> **Mylan Laboratories.** After a branded drug's patent expires, any company can apply for FDA approval to market it in generic form. As generic versions of a drug come on the market, prices and margins tend to drop; according to one study, the average branded drug price is $76.29, compared with an average generic drug cost of $22.79. Mylan Laboratories earns higher margins with generics that are more difficult to manufacture, such as drugs delivered through adhesive skin patches. There is less competition in these segments, Mylan can charge a bit more because its products are differentiated, and customers still save money. The company also offers some proprietary branded drug products, which carry higher margins, as well.[2]

Customer Perceptions and Demand

Planning Tip
Understand how customers view value and know the value your organization wants to achieve.

When customers act on the basis of their perceptions of price and benefits, their purchases create demand for a product. If customers perceive the price to be too high in relation to the benefits, they simply won't buy, which lowers demand; if they perceive the price to be too low for the expected benefits or quality, demand also will suffer. On the other hand, if the total perceived benefits outweigh the total perceived price, customers are more likely to buy, raising demand.

EXHIBIT 7.2 How Pricing Affects Demand

Change in Price	Under Inelastic Demand	Under Elastic Demand
Small increase	Demand drops slightly	Demand drops significantly
Small reduction	Demand rises slightly	Demand rises significantly

For example, when Procter & Gamble introduced Swiffer, a lightweight mop to be used with disposable cleaning wipes, customers quickly recognized the new product's value. The immediate surge of demand helped P&G capture 25 percent of the broom and mop market within four months of Swiffer's launch. Over time, so many customers switched to wipe-type products (higher demand) that rival Rubbermaid saw sales of its traditional brooms and mops drop by 20 percent (lower demand).[3]

Research can help marketers determine customers' sensitivity to pricing and the level of demand for a product at different price points. This sensitivity is shown by the **price elasticity of demand,** calculated by dividing the percentage change in unit sales demanded by the percentage change in price. When a small price change significantly increases or decreases the number of units demanded, demand is *elastic;* when a price change does not significantly change the number of units demanded, demand is *inelastic.* Exhibit 7.2 indicates how different price changes affect demand under elastic and inelastic demand conditions.

In general, customers tend to be less sensitive to a product's price when they[4]:

- are considering a relatively small amount or
- are unaware of or can't easily compare substitutes and prices;
- would incur costs or difficulties in switching products;
- perceive that the product's quality, status, or another benefit justifies the price;
- are spending a relatively small amount or are sharing the cost;
- perceive the price as fair;
- are buying products bundled rather than separately.

Customers' price sensitivity and perceptions of value also can be used to deal with imbalances of supply and demand. U.S. steel mills recently experienced unusually strong demand while simultaneously coping with a shortage of raw materials; in response to the imbalance, some added surcharges to the price per ton. Construction companies with firm deadlines saw no alternative to paying the higher prices and even then, some had to wait longer than usual for their orders.[5] As another example, many airlines price flights lower during off-peak periods to stimulate demand. The idea of managing rush-hour traffic through pricing is catching on in some municipalities.

Pricing Roadway Access. To minimize highway congestion, Orange County and San Diego charge drivers $6 or more for access to express lanes. Drivers who perceive value in the benefit of arriving at their destinations more quickly will pay the express-lane charge; those who believe the price outweighs the benefit will not. As another example, London charges drivers the equivalent of more than $10 to enter certain parts of the city during peak periods. Pricing helps balance supply and demand during busy periods, which in turn prevents traffic tie-ups, moves vehicles along, and minimizes air pollution. London has not only reduced downtown traffic by 20 percent, its pricing has generated revenue for public transportation projects. And to avoid massive traffic jams during the 2012 Summer Olympics in London, athletes, officials, and corporate sponsors will drive in special lanes, but unauthorized drivers will pay very stiff fines if they are caught using those lanes.[6]

Value-Based Pricing

Planning Tip

Research customers' perceptions so you can use target costing to best advantage.

Researching and analyzing how customers perceive the value of a product should be the first step in formulating an appropriate pricing strategy to build demand and meet internal objectives. Nagle and Hogan[7] note that this is not the typical approach to pricing. The most common way is to start with the product and its cost, set a price that covers the cost, and then communicate the value to customers.

In contrast, the starting point for **value-based pricing** is research about customers' perceptions of value and the price they are willing to pay. Then the company finds ways of making the product at a reasonable cost (**target costing**) to return a reasonable profit or achieve other marketing plan objectives based on the value price. Exhibit 7.3 contrasts cost-based with value-based pricing.

Consider the situation of Dollar General.

Dollar General. With more than 8,000 stores, Dollar General caters to lower-income customers in smaller communities who seek bargain prices and convenience when shopping for household basics. On the shelves are manufacturer-branded and private-label products, with many (but not all) items priced at $1. The Treasure Hunt section is a microcosm of Dollar General's value-based pricing approach: The company arranges special deals on national brands such as Barbie and Conair and features them at unusually low prices. Dollar General is also working closely with manufacturers to create products especially for its stores. During the first season that Dollar General stocked an exclusive Fisher-Price line of toddler's clothing, with items priced from $6 to $10, shoppers responded so positively that the apparel sold out more quickly than expected.[8]

From a strategic perspective, Nagle and Hogan emphasize that price decisions must be value-based, profit-driven, and proactive. In other words, simply reacting to the market is not an effective approach; marketers must proactively develop appropriate pricing strategies based on how customers perceive value and how the company can profitably achieve its objectives through pricing.[9]

EXHIBIT 7.3   Cost-Based versus Value-Based Pricing

Cost-Based Pricing

PRODUCT ⟶ COST ⟶ PRICE ⟶ VALUE ⟶ CUSTOMERS

Value-Based Pricing

CUSTOMERS ⟶ VALUE ⟶ PRICE ⟶ COST ⟶ PRODUCT

PLANNING PRICING DECISIONS

When planning pricing, marketers first must determine what this strategy is intended to achieve, given the marketing, financial, and societal objectives they have set. They also need to investigate the various external influences (customers; competitors; channel members; legal, regulatory, and ethical concerns) and internal influences (costs and break-even; targeting and positioning strategy; product strategy; and other marketing decisions) that can affect pricing decisions.

Pricing Objectives

Because a product's price is the organization's source of revenue, marketers should establish specific objectives for all pricing decisions. These objectives must be consistent with each other and with the overall mission, direction, goals, and marketing plan objectives. Due to market realities, organizations may have to trade off one pricing objective for another. Rarely can a company boost profitability while simultaneously raising its market share to a much higher level, for example. This is why American Airlines, among other carriers, has switched from pricing for market share to pricing for profitability, cutting routes and flights that fail to meet profitability objectives.[10]

Verizon Wireless, one of the largest U.S. cell phone carriers, is using pricing for customer retention as well as for financial objectives.

Verizon Wireless. Like most cell phone carriers, Verizon Wireless minimizes customer churn by charging a hefty early-termination fee if a contract is canceled. Because of complaints, however, Verizon Wireless recently reduced its termination fee. The CEO noted that current customers are generally loyal and unlikely to terminate their contracts early. Therefore, reducing the fee will not hurt revenue and should, in fact, bring in new customers. In another change, the company is pricing downloadable music as a separate service rather than as part of a larger (and more expensive) multimedia package. The idea is to encourage customers to subscribe to the specific services they value most.[11]

In some industries, one additional percentage point of market share can translate into millions of dollars in higher sales, which is why certain companies put share ahead of profit when setting pricing objectives. Over the long term, however, companies cannot survive without profits. Exhibit 7.4 shows a number of pricing objectives that firms may set.

EXHIBIT 7.4 Sample Pricing Objectives

Type of Objective	Sample Pricing Objectives
Financial	• For profitability: Set prices to achieve gross profit margin of 40 percent on this year's sales. • For return on investment: Set prices to achieve full-year ROI of 18 percent.
Marketing	• For higher market share: Set prices to achieve a market share increase of 5 percent within 6 months. • For customer acquisition: Set prices to attract 1,500 new customers from January to June.
Societal	• For philanthropy: Set prices to raise $10,000 for charity during second quarter of year. • For energy conservation: Set prices to sell 500 alternative-fuel vehicles nationwide during August.

External Pricing Influences

Planning Tip
Analyze these influences for each geographic region if you plan to price market by market.

Many factors outside the organization—and outside its control—come into play when marketers make decisions about pricing. In addition to customers, pricing can be influenced by competitors, channel members (as in the Dollar General example), and legal, regulatory, and ethical considerations. Because not every external influence is equally important for each product, targeted segment, or market, marketers should analyze each within the context of other marketing plan decisions and the organization's situation.

Customers

Perceptions of value, behavior, and attitudes all affect a customer's reaction to pricing. In consumer markets, research shows that customers are willing to buy a good or service if the price falls within a range they view as acceptable for that type of product.[12] This suggests that consumer marketers have some pricing latitude if they stay within the accepted range or change the product to change its perceived value. However, it is important to remember that today's price is a big factor in customers' decisions to continue the relationship and buy again tomorrow, as the auto repair chain Monro Muffler knows.

Monro Muffler Brake & Service. Seeing customer loyalty as a vital ingredient in long-term profitability, Monro Muffler is using pricing to encourage repeat purchasing, rather than pricing for short-term gain. The CEO explains: "We're lower priced on oil changes, but we're not lower priced on everything. Once you build up trust with the customer, price becomes less important in the equation." In fact, Monro Muffler's results show that new customers satisfied with the cheap oil changes are returning for different repairs, lifting both sales and profits. Because of customer trust and loyalty, the company has been able to increase prices on many services and improve operating profit margins to a level above that of most competitors.[13]

In business markets, customers frequently search for the lowest price to minimize their organizational costs, and some switch suppliers constantly to pay less for parts, materials, components, or services. Globalization has only increased customers' choices and opportunities to obtain better prices. Consider the situation of ArvinMeritor, which feels intense pressure to price its car and truck parts as low as possible for automakers that, in turn, feel pressure to keep vehicle prices low. Thus, "when DaimlerChrysler or Volvo negotiates a 5- to 7-year deal, you don't want to lose, because when you do, you're out for 5 to 7 years," notes one of its executives. With this behavior in mind, ArvinMeritor uses continuous improvement to increase efficiency so it can keep prices low, offer new products, and win multiyear contracts.[14] Rather than emphasizing low prices, many B2B marketers build relationships by communicating benefits such as how the product saves customers money in the long run or how it enhances quality.

Even where free alternatives are available—as on the Internet—savvy marketers have been able to build relationships with paying customers. Consider the *Wall Street Journal* Online, which has tens of thousands of subscribers paying $99 per year ($49 for those who also subscribe to the print version). Why pay for news that can be found elsewhere for free? Customers trust the *Wall Street Journal* brand and value the exclusive columns and intraday updates, the customizable home page, and the industry-specific news pages.[15]

Competitors

Customer behavior is one external clue to an acceptable price range (the ceiling, in particular). The competitive situation provides another external clue. By analyzing the prices, special deals, and probable costs of competing products, a company can get a better sense of the alternatives that are available to customers and competitors' pricing objectives and strategies. Home Depot, for instance, electronically compares the prices of key products to the prices charged by competitors. Its marketing managers look at these comparisons, plus internal records, sales trends, and other information, when setting prices by product, by store, and by market.[16]

Pricing is a highly visible competitive tool in many industries, often exerting downward pressure on profits and limiting pricing options. Hewlett-Packard, for example, lost money for a time on its PC business because of price competition with Dell. When HP decided to compete by differentiating its notebook computers more distinctly, it was able to boost both sales and profit margins.[17] Price wars can erupt when competitors battle over market share.

Intel and AMD. These two competitors, which make chips for PCs, laptops, and other computers, are constantly introducing chips that speed up processing without drawing more power. Intel has dominated the market for years, but AMD's products have steadily made inroads on the basis of high performance and lower price. In cutting prices to counter AMD's competitive initiatives, Intel has hurt its profit margins, but it continues investing in new-product development. Meanwhile, a spokesperson says AMD expects "to continue taking market share away from Intel, in some parts of the market more than others." Despite the push for market share, AMD's chief financial officer remains focused on the bottom line and has rejected sales opportunities when the deals were not financially sound.[18]

Because no two companies have exactly the same objectives, resources, costs, and situations, competitors cannot simply copy each other's pricing. To illustrate, because of strong and direct competition in the United States, Coca-Cola and Pepsi-Cola soft drinks remain close in price—nor have their prices risen much in two decades.[19] Marketers need not always match or beat competitors' prices but they do have to ensure that their product's price fits into the value equation as perceived by customers and makes economic sense for the company.

Channel Members

Companies that reach customers through wholesalers or retailers must take into account these intermediaries' pricing expectations and marketing objectives. As an example, more than half of the shoppers who buy at Family Dollar and Dollar General stores have household income below $30,000, so those retailers aim to keep most prices at or below $10. Thus, to achieve their profit and market share objectives, dollar store retailers must keep merchandise costs and prices within strict limits.[20] In turn, manufacturers that sell to dollar stores must set wholesale prices that accommodate both channel and customer expectations.

A sample progression of how a consumer product might be priced by the producer, wholesaler, and retailer is in Exhibit 7.5. In this sample, the producer charges the wholesaler $20 for the product and the wholesaler sells it to the retailer for $24, twenty percent above the producer's price. The retailer sells the product to the consumer for $36, which is 50 percent above the price paid by the retailer and 80 percent above the price paid by the wholesaler. Of course, the actual number of participants in the outbound side of the value chain will vary according to product, industry, market, and segment, affecting the

EXHIBIT 7.5 Sample of Consumer Pricing in the Retail Channel

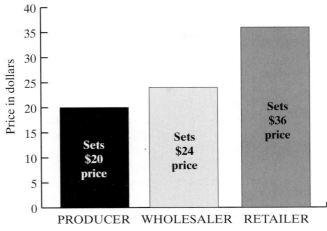

Outbound movement in value chain

prices paid by intermediaries and the ultimate customer. Note that when a participant performs more functions or enhances the product in a unique way, it may be able to set a higher price (and make more profit) because its immediate customers perceive more value in the offering.

In pricing a product, also consider that the Internet is bringing wholesale and retail prices down in many categories, thanks to more efficient transaction capabilities, convenient price comparisons, and higher competition—sometimes from unexpected sources. For instance, Amazon.com, which started out as an online book retailer, now markets fine jewelry. Its transactional technology is already in place, so it can easily offer a wider range of products to the millions of shoppers who browse the site. Amazon can buy a pair of gem-studded earrings at wholesale for $850 and retail them for $1,000. In contrast, a traditional jewelry store might price the same earrings at $1,700. Amazon is counting on price-sensitive customers to compare jewelry prices and value before buying. "We believe over time, customers figure these things out," observes its chief financial officer.[21]

Legal, Regulatory, and Ethical Concerns

Whether planning for domestic or international marketing, all companies need to comply with a variety of pricing laws and regulations. Some of these include:

- *No price collusion.* In the United States, the European Union, and many other areas, competing firms are not allowed to collaborate in setting prices and cannot take other pricing actions that reduce competition.
- *No minimum retail price.* In the United States, United Kingdom, and some other countries, companies are not permitted to enforce a minimum retail price among channel members (although in some cases, a "suggested" retail price may appear on the package or price tag).
- *No price discrimination.* In the United States, a company usually cannot charge different prices for essentially the same product at the same time in the same market unless the lower price(s) are available through discounts or allowances that are open to all. However, there are exceptions; for example, different prices may be allowed if the company has different costs, is responding to competition, or is clearing outdated merchandise.[22]

- *No predatory pricing.* The United States outlaws the aggressive use of low pricing to damage a competitor or reduce competition.
- *Price limits.* Some nations set an upper limit on the price that can be charged for certain products, as Canada does with prescription drugs.

Planning Tip

Be sure your pricing strategy complies with your company's ethical code.

Apart from applicable laws and regulations, marketers must make decisions about ethic dilemmas in pricing. Is it ethical for a company to raise prices during an emergency, when products may be scarce or especially valuable? Should a company set a high price for an indispensable product knowing that certain customers will be unable to pay? What are a company's ethical responsibilities regarding full disclosure of prices for upkeep, updates, or replacement parts? How far in advance should customers be notified of planned price increases, and what form should notification take? The chief information officer of Hyundai Motor America has complained about technology companies that attempt to "slip in surprise increases for maintenance, licensing, or other services."[23] As difficult as the ethical aspects of pricing may be, marketers must carefully think through the consequences on customer relationships and company image.

Internal Pricing Influences

Within the organization, costs and break-even are critical influences on pricing. Targeting and positioning strategy, product strategy, and other marketing decisions must also be factored into pricing plans.

Costs and Break-Even

Costs typically establish the theoretical floor of the pricing range, the lowest price at which the organization will avoid losing money. Even the largest company cannot afford to price products below cost for an extended period, although (where legal) it may do so to combat a competitive threat or achieve another objective over a limited period. Therefore, companies need to understand their costs and the **break-even point**—the sales level at which revenue covers costs. Costs and break-even are more easily calculated for existing products in existing market segments, because marketers can use historical results as a basis for future projections. For new products and segments, marketers must rely on research-based forecasts and expert estimates of costs and sales volume (see Chapter 10). When detailed or timely information is unavailable, marketers often make educated guesses about costs for planning purposes.

The total cost of a product consists of *fixed costs*—overhead expenses such as rent and payroll, which do not vary with volume—plus *variable costs*—expenses such as raw materials, which do vary with volume. As one example, corporate rent is a fixed cost and jet fuel is a variable cost for airlines; to keep ticket prices low and avoid unexpected cost spikes, Southwest uses "hedging" techniques that lock in low fuel costs for months. When fuel costs jumped 60 percent in a year, however, Southwest decided on higher fares; some competitors facing similar or higher fuel costs tacked fuel surcharges onto ticket prices.[24]

Planning Tip

If you don't know your costs, estimate for now and start tracking costs for next year's plan.

Once marketers know a product's total costs, they can calculate the average cost of producing a single item (total costs divided by production) at various output levels, corresponding to different assumptions about demand. This reveals cost changes at a number of output levels and indicates how low the company might price the product at each level to at least cover its costs. Next, the marketer calculates the break-even point to see how a price will affect revenues and profits at different sales levels.[25] The break-even formula is:

$$\text{Break-even volume} = \frac{\text{fixed cost}}{\text{price} - \text{variable cost}}$$

Exhibit 7.6 illustrates a sample break-even analysis for a company that manufactures specialized software for dentists. In this example, the price (unit revenue) is $995, the variable cost is $45 per unit, and the fixed cost totals $40,550. Thus, the calculation is:

$$\text{Break-even volume} = \frac{40{,}550}{995 - 45} = \frac{40{,}550}{950} = 42.6 \text{ units (rounded up to 43)}$$

Cost containment is a high priority for many companies today, not just to achieve quarterly profit targets but to prepare for future market conditions. Deluxe, the U.S. market leader in printing checks for consumers and businesses, is a good example.

Deluxe. Checks are a mature industry: usage is declining 3 to 5 percent yearly as electronic transactions become more commonplace. Yet the majority of Deluxe's revenue comes from printing checks, which explains its determination to defend against other check printers and electronic payment methods. Meanwhile, mergers are giving big banks more power to negotiate lower prices with Deluxe. To prevent significant deterioration of profit margins, Deluxe has cut costs by closing some facilities and improving efficiency. Recognizing that it will sell fewer checks in the future, its strategy is to emphasize more lucrative customized checks and diversify into other products.[26]

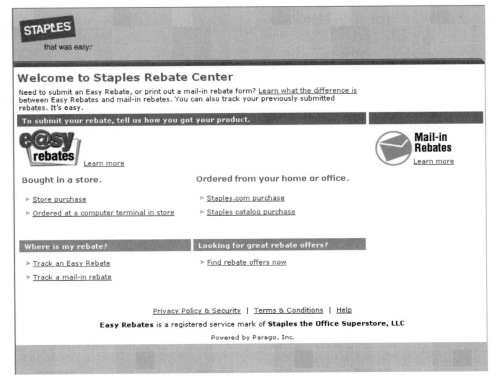

The office supply retailer Staples offers rebates on a variety of selected products.

EXHIBIT 7.6 Break-Even Analysis

Fixed Costs		
Creation of printed material graphics and text	$	3,200
Creation of CD-ROM graphics	$	750
Initial set up fee for CD	$	1,600
Initial set up fee for printed materials	$	1,250
Production of 2,000 demo units	$	33,750
Estimated Fixed Costs	$	40,550
Per-unit variable costs (to fulfill orders sold)	$	45
Per-unit revenue	$	995
Break-even (in Units)		43

Break-Even Analysis:		
Assumptions:		
Average Per-Unit Revenue	$	995
Average Per-Unit Variable Cost	$	45
Estimated Fixed Costs	$	40,550
Units Break-even		43
Sales Break-even	$	42,471

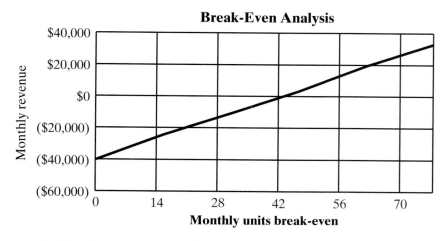

Break-Even Analysis

Units break-even point = where line intersects with $0

Targeting and Positioning Strategy

A product's price must be appropriate for the organization's targeting and positioning strategy. To illustrate, because Southwest Airlines targets the segment of price-sensitive travelers and positions itself as affordable and no-frills, charging high fares would be inconsistent (and would confuse customers). Conversely, if the luxury goods manufacturer Louis Vuitton put low price tags on its handbags and accessories, the target segment of affluent consumers would question the products' positioning as symbols of status, style, and quality. In fact, Vuitton refuses to mark down its handbags for clearance, on the basis that low pricing would conflict with the positioning.[27]

Product Strategy

Marketers should not only examine every pricing decision in the context of costs, targeting, and positioning, they should set prices in line with their product strategy. In particular, pricing can be used to manage the product's movement through the life cycle:

- *Introduction.* Some companies use **skimming pricing,** pricing a new product high to establish a top-quality image or highlight unique value and more quickly recover development costs in line with profitability objectives. Intel does this with its "good, better, best" pricing tiers. A new computer chip, which customers value for speed and other benefits, is positioned as the "best" at a premium price; existing chips are positioned as "good" and "better" with correspondingly lower prices.[28] Other marketers prefer **penetration pricing,** pricing products relatively low to penetrate the market more quickly. Toyota did this to build sales of its feature-packed Yaris subcompact car in Europe.[29] These two approaches are compared in Exhibit 7.7.
- *Growth.* Pricing is important for competitive strategy during the growth stage, when rival products challenge the new product. During growth, companies also use pricing to stimulate demand while moving toward the break-even point.
- *Maturity.* With sales growth slowing, companies can use pricing to defend market share, retain customers, pursue profitability, or expand into additional channels. For instance, McDonald's has used its Dollar Menu to compete with fast-food rivals—with such success that Wendy's and Burger King also began promoting menu items priced at $1 or less.[30] Procter & Gamble is also doing

EXHIBIT 7.7   Skim Pricing and Penetration Pricing Compared

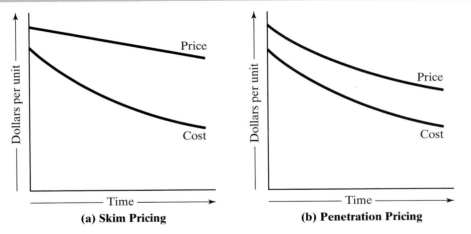

(a) Skim Pricing   (b) Penetration Pricing

this in mature categories by introducing lower-priced "basic" versions of its branded products, such as Bounty Basic paper towels.[31]

- *Decline.*   Pricing can help clear older or outdated products to make way for new ones, stimulate sales to prevent or at least slow a product's decline, or maximize profits. To illustrate, makers of cell phones and other technology products often cut prices to sell off older models when they introduce new models. Yet prices do not necessarily drop during decline: scarcity may make a product more valuable to certain customers and therefore justify a higher price.

Planning Tip
Price multiple products in the context of achieving your plan's overall objectives.

Moreover, pricing is vital for managing the strategy of products in a single line and in the overall mix. After researching customers' perceptions, marketers may set different prices to signal the value of the features and benefits of different products and to differentiate among multiple lines and brands in the product portfolio. When Apple introduced its MacBook laptops, the company charged a little more for the black version than for the white version. Both laptops had the same computing capabilities, but customers who valued cutting-edge styling were willing to pay a small premium to buy the black version.[32]

Sometimes marketers plan to price one product in order to encourage purchases of other products in the line or mix, as Gillette does with razors and blades. Every eight years, the company introduces an entirely new type of razor, priced higher than current models. Then, over time, it gradually increases the price of blades that fit older razor models to encourage customers to trade up to the new model.[33]

Other Marketing Decisions

The marketing plan's direction will strongly influence the organization's pricing strategy. For survival, the organization's prices should cover costs at the very least; for bankruptcy, organizations can use pricing to liquidate stock and raise money quickly. For aggressive growth, the company may decide to set prices that return slim or no profit margins in the short run.

In addition to the influence of channel members, pricing is influenced by decisions about suppliers and logistics. In terms of promotion strategy, higher-priced products aimed at higher-income customer segments are often promoted in different media and with different messages than lower-priced products aimed at lower-income segments. Pricing is a big challenge for companies that market through personal selling—especially when customers expect to negotiate prices with salespeople. For this reason, the Swiss pharmaceutical firm Roche has equipped its salespeople with software to check the profitability of different prices before finalizing sales to medical institutions or other customers.[34]

Adapting Prices

Planning Tip
Consider which adaptations are traditional—and nontraditional—in your industry or channel.

If internal factors suggest the price floor and external factors suggest the price ceiling, price adaptation helps companies modify and fine-tune prices within an acceptable range—or even beyond. Marketers may use price adaptation to make changes in support of their objectives:

- *Discounts.*   Many companies offer quantity discounts for buying in volume and seasonal discounts for buying out of season. Business customers also may earn a cash discount for prompt payment; intermediaries may earn a functional discount when they perform specific channel functions for a producer.
- *Allowances.*   Wholesalers and retailers may receive discounts, extra payments, or extra product allocations for participating in special promotions. Some companies offer trade-in allowances for businesses or consumers who bring in older products and buy newer ones.

- *Bundling or unbundling.* The company may enhance customer perceptions of value by bundling one product with one or more goods or services at a single price. McDonald's meal deals, for example, are priced lower than the sum of the individual menu items but help the firm sell more soft drinks and fries, boosting overall profit margin. Unbundling can be used if the bundle price is perceived as too high and individual products will sell well on their own.
- *Product enhancement.* Enhancing the product to raise its perceived value can help the company maintain the current price or perhaps increase the price.
- *Segment pricing.* Pricing may be adapted for certain customer segments, such as a children's menu (segmenting by family composition), a senior discount (segmenting by age), or a delivery charge (segmenting by need for service). To illustrate, the New York City drug store chain Duane Reade prices disposable diapers for newborns to yield a higher profit margin than pull-up disposables for toddlers. Why? Its research shows that the new-parent segment is less price-sensitive than the toddler-parent segment.[35]

Changes in consumer behavior may also prompt price adaptation, as the team-buying phenomenon is doing in China.

Team Buying. Chinese shoppers are increasingly shopping together so they can bargain as a group for better prices, a practice known as *tuangou* (team buying). The trend started when online chatters found that they were planning purchases of similar products and decided to strengthen their buying power by visiting stores together. Now several Web sites have sprung up to help consumers coordinate their buying trips. "Sometimes we call the shop," says one participant, "but often we just surprise them. Shopkeepers argue, but in the end they want the business." When 500 consumers converged on an electronics superstore, the retailer turned away other shoppers, agreed to cut its prices by 10 to 30 percent on TVs, DVD players, and other goods, and even gave the team buyers a goody bag when they left.[36]

Specific pricing tactics can help marketers achieve specific marketing or financial objectives. Loss-leader pricing, for instance, with popular or new items priced near cost, is a common way to build store or Web-site traffic. Objectives for customer acquisition might be supported by short-term pricing cuts or tactics that temporarily enhance value, such as low interest rates during select periods. The chosen adaptation depends on the company's resources and capabilities, its goals and strategic direction, and its marketing plan objectives.

Marketers also should plan for the short-term and long-term effects of price competition. If every company matches or beats the price of its rivals and a price war ensues, customers will soon perceive few if any differences and be less brand-loyal. In fact, research shows that in more than two dozen product categories, customers give more weight to price than to brand because they perceive few differences among the brands. In contrast, they give more weight to brand than to price when buying automobiles and alcoholic beverages, which have more perceived differences.[37] See Exhibit 7.8 for some alternative reactions to competitive price cuts. Stressing product, promotion, or channel differentiation, along with value-based pricing, will confer the strongest advantage, given that prices are easily matched but non-price-related points of difference are not.

EXHIBIT 7.8   Alternative Reactions to Competitive Price Cuts

Strategic Options	Reasoning	Consequences
1. Maintain price and perceived quality. Engage in selective customer pruning.	Firm has higher customer loyalty. It is willing to lose poorer customers to competitors.	Smaller market share Lowered profitability
2. Raise price and perceived quality.	Raise price to cover rising costs. Improve quality to justify higher prices.	Smaller market share Maintained profitability
3. Maintain price and raise perceived quality.	It is cheaper to maintain price and raise perceived quality.	Smaller market share Short-term decline in profitability Long-term increase in profitability
4. Cut price partly and raise perceived quality.	Must give customers some price reduction but stress higher value of offer.	Maintained market share Short-term decline in profitability Long-term maintained profitability
5. Cut price fully and maintain perceived quality.	Discipline and discourage price competition.	Maintained market share Short-term decline in profitability
6. Cut price fully and reduce perceived quality.	Discipline and discourage price competition and maintain profit margin.	Maintained market share Maintained margin Reduced long-term profitability
7. Maintain price and reduce perceived quality.	Cut marketing expense to combat rising costs.	Smaller market share Maintained margin Reduced long-term profitability
8. Introduce an economy model.	Give the market what it wants.	Some cannibalization but higher total volume

SUMMARY

From a customer's perspective, value is the difference between the total perceived benefits and the total perceived price of a product. Marketers care about customers' price perceptions because they influence the number of units demanded. Price elasticity, which indicates customers' price sensitivity, is calculated by dividing the percentage change in unit sales demanded by the percentage change in price. Marketers should use value-based pricing rather than cost-based pricing to formulate a strategy that will drive demand and satisfy company objectives.

As they plan pricing strategy, marketers first must determine what they want to achieve in the context of the marketing plan's marketing, financial, and societal objectives. Next, they need to factor in key external influences (customers; competitors; channel members; and legal, regulatory, and ethical concerns) and key internal influences (costs and break-even; targeting and positioning strategy; product strategy; and other marketing decisions) when making pricing decisions. Finally, marketers have to consider when and how to adapt prices as appropriate.

Developing Channel and Logistics Strategy

In this chapter:

PREVIEW

The third major component of the marketing mix is channel (place) strategy, covering decisions about how, when, and where to make goods and services available to customers. Because of the complexities of channel strategy, decisions about it must be carefully coordinated with other marketing decisions. Channel strategy also must be based on a thorough understanding of the targeted segment (including how customers expect or prefer to gain access to the product), the environment (the effect of competition, legal and regulatory considerations, geography, technology, costs, and other realities), the product's characteristics (such as price or perishability), and its life cycle (appropriate channels for introduction, growth, maturity, and decline).

This chapter opens by exploring the connections and flows in the value chain and how various participants add value to the product offering that customers buy. The next section explains the major influences on channel strategy and the decisions to be made about channel functions, levels, and members. The closing section looks at logistics strategy, including decisions about transportation, storage, inventory management, and other functions. After reading this chapter, document your marketing decisions using *Marketing Plan Pro* software or in a written plan. See this chapter's checklist for issues to consider when working on the channel and logistics section of your marketing plan.

PLANNING FOR THE VALUE CHAIN

Planning Tip
Think ahead: altering channel arrangements can be difficult and time-consuming.

Every good or service is made and marketed as part of a **value chain,** also known as a *supply chain,* a series of interrelated, value-added functions plus the structure of organizations performing them to get the right product to the right markets and customers at the right time, place, and price. The marketer (shown as "producer" in Exhibit 8.1) manages supplier relationships and logistics on the inbound side to obtain the inputs (such as parts, shipment dates, and cost figures) needed for creating goods and services. On the outbound or demand side, the marketer manages logistics and **channels** (also called *distribution channels*), the functions that must be completed to meet demand by making a product available to the customers in each market.

CHAPTER 8 CHECKLIST   Channel and Logistical Issues

Channel Issues

✔ How do product, data, and money flow through the value chain, and how can participants add more value?

✔ How do goals and objectives, resources and competencies, direction, need for control, and marketing mix decisions affect channel choices?

✔ How do current channel arrangements contribute to current objectives?

✔ Which channels and members perform the best, and at what cost to the organization?

✔ How do product characteristics and life cycle, positioning, targeting, market issues, and competitive factors affect channel choices and costs?

✔ How do customers expect or prefer to gain access to the product, and what is the impact on channel decisions?

✔ How many levels/members are needed/desirable to make products available to targeted segments?

Logistical Issues

✔ What logistical functions must be performed and by which channel members?

✔ Who will transport and store supplies, parts, and finished products—how, where, and when?

✔ Who will manage inventory, orders, billing, shipping, payment—and how?

✔ How do production- and sales-related objectives affect logistical plans?

✔ How are logistics affected by customer needs/preferences, channel/company capabilities, product plans, and marketing plan objectives?

EXHIBIT 8.1   Major Links in the Value Chain

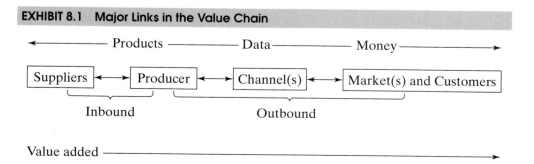

During the planning process, marketers analyze how value is added at each connection in this chain of functions, from inputs on the inbound side to finished products moving outbound to meet customer demand. Here is how Procter & Gamble manages outbound links in its value chain.

> **Procter & Gamble.** P&G collaborates with channel members for what it calls "joint value creation"—getting Bounty towels, Gillette razors, and other products onto store shelves for purchase by consumers around the world. One key is sharing sales information so P&G and its retailers can plan inventory levels to meet demand. Another key is being able to track product movement so P&G and its retail partners know exactly when and where shipments will arrive. In one test, P&G put radio frequency identification (RFID) tags on cartons of Gillette razors shipped for a special promotion. Its marketers were surprised to find that some stores displayed the razors before the campaign actually began and a few stores never even unpacked the cartons. On the other hand, they were pleased to find that Gillette sales rose by 61 percent in stores where the products were displayed during the campaign.[1]

Why is P&G so particular about when its products are displayed? If products are unpacked too soon, they may sell out before the promotion begins; if unpacked too late, consumers who come to the store in search of the advertised products won't find them. In fact, when P&G launched the Gillette Fusion razor, its marketers worked closely with CVS's logistics experts to get the product to every one of the chain's 5,400 U.S. drug stores on the same day. As a result, CVS's displays were in place when the Fusion's introductory ad campaign kicked off.[2]

Flows in the Value Chain

Channel and logistics strategy involves managing the three value-chain flows shown in Exhibit 8.1. The flow of products refers to physical items such as raw materials and product packaging (on the inbound side) and finished products (on the outbound side) plus other items that move from outbound to inbound (such as products returned for repair). The flow of data refers to information such as the number of items ordered (moving inbound or outbound); customer requirements and feedback (passed along from channel members or directly from customer to producer); and other information that adds value through effectiveness and efficiency. The flow of money refers to payments for supplies (on the inbound side); reseller or customer payments for finished goods (on the outbound side); and other money movements between participants.

Clearly, a marketing plan should take into account the movement of all three flows in both directions. Some plans will cover flows between noncontiguous links in the value chain, such as the flow of a rebate check from a producer directly to a customer who has purchased a product from a retailer. Note that the inbound side of the value chain is always B2B. For example, P&G is a business customer to suppliers or industrial distributors that sell it raw materials, components, and other inputs. After manufacturing its diapers, paper towels, and other merchandise, P&G gets the products to its targeted consumer markets through retailers like CVS in the outbound channel.

Adding Value through the Chain

Each participant adds value to satisfy the needs of the next link (the immediate customer) as well as the needs of the customer at the end of the value chain. Thus, the retailers that market P&G's products must have the items on display and in stock so

Planning Tip

Diagram the value chain to see where value is added and find areas for improvement.

customers can take their purchases with them or arrange for home delivery. The price paid by each successive participant reflects the value added by the previous link; customers at the end of the chain ultimately pay for the combined value added by all participants, an element of pricing strategy that was discussed in Chapter 7.

Increasingly, producers and wholesalers, retailers, industrial distributors, and other channel members are teaming up for competitive advantage by adding value in unique ways. For instance, LG and its channel partner, Verizon, have forged a close relationship to add value for cell phone users.

LG Electronics and Verizon Wireless. The Korean cell phone maker LG Electronics works closely with the U.S. phone service provider Verizon to provide handsets that meet the needs of the carrier as well as its subscribers. Because Verizon Wireless (like its competitors) has direct customer contact through stores, service representatives, and other methods, the carrier hears firsthand what the market wants—and uses the information to shape its services and the offerings of cell phone manufacturers. Verizon Wireless's marketing experts collaborate with LG's engineers to develop phones with features tailored for and marketed only to Verizon customers. Everyone benefits: LG gets its products into the hands of U.S. customers, building sales and market share; Verizon Wireless gives customers what they want and ensures that the phones support profitable services such as downloading music and video clips.[3]

Services and the Value Chain

Marketers planning for restaurants, financial services, or other intangible products need to map all the flows within their value chain. The inbound flows relate to ordering, paying for, and receiving shipments of supplies that support service delivery (such as office supplies or food). The outbound flows help customers arrange to receive the service (such as making airline reservations). Because services are usually produced and used simultaneously, marketers must plan flows to match supply and demand. KFC needs timely shipments of chicken and other ingredients to meet daily and weekly sales objectives for chicken meals; Citibank must stock each ATM with sufficient $20 bills and receipt paper for the anticipated daily usage.

Value for services, like tangible products, is added inbound through the chain as the producer incorporates a variety of inputs. Outbound, channel members add value by promoting the service, communicating with the customers, making appointments or selling tickets, managing payments and paperwork, and handling other functions to give customers access to the service at an appropriate price, place, and time. Consider the channel for medical services. MinuteClinic, which offers walk-in medical care for minor illnesses, operates small clinics inside retail stores like CVS; InterFit Health, a competitor, operates small clinics in some Wal-Mart outlets and in other chains. The clinics benefit from access to the retailers' customer base and store location. Customers value the convenience of quick medical attention, without an appointment, at an accessible location. The retailers put clinics inside their stores because they attract customers who may buy merchandise before or after getting medical care.[4]

Channel strategy should satisfy customers' needs in such a way that the organization's objectives can be met as well. The travel Web site Travelocity, for example, serves as a channel for services such as cruise lines, rental cars, airlines, and hotels. The site sports a distinctive look and simple navigation so travelers can find what they want quickly and easily. "We did a lot of consumer research, and [consumers] told us all the Web sites look alike," the chief marketing officer explains. "They're all visually cluttered."

By adding value through easy navigation, convenience, and speed, Travelocity attracts customers and builds sales.[5]

PLANNING CHANNEL STRATEGY

Although many aspects of channel strategy are invisible to customers, this part of the marketing mix is both visible and a vital ingredient in any product's success. Channel strategy made *The Da Vinci Code* a best-selling book. Doubleday originally planned to print 60,000 copies of Dan Brown's thriller. Then a buyer for the Barnes & Noble chain read an advance copy and ordered 15,000 copies but quickly raised the order to 80,000 copies. Doubleday increased its print run and kicked off a promotional campaign with store posters and shelf tags, online contests, and e-mailed notes to opinion leaders. Barnes & Noble prominently displayed the novel, posted sales ideas on its intranet, and had employees talk up the book to shoppers. Propelled by channel attention and media coverage, the novel became the fastest-selling novel ever for the adult market.[6]

Planning Tip

Ideally, ask each channel partner to prepare a plan showing how it will market your product.

In the course of developing channel strategy, each organization has to decide which channel functions must be covered; who will handle each function; how many channel levels to use; and how many and what type of channel members to choose. (In addition, marketers face decisions about logistics, as discussed later in the chapter.)

Channel Functions

What channel functions are needed for the product, market, or targeted customer segment, and who will handle each? The channel as a whole must perform a variety of value-added outbound functions such as matching the volume, amount, or offer to customer needs; providing intermediaries and customers with product and market information; contacting and negotiating with customers to maintain relationships and complete sales; and transporting and storing products prior to purchase.

During planning, producers must identify the channel functions needed for each product, determine which functions intermediaries should handle, and estimate the compensation each channel member should receive for the value it adds. Some producers prefer to assume many or all of the functions themselves because they want more control over customer contacts, pricing, or other elements; others delegate selected functions to reduce costs and focus resources on other tasks. Even within the same industry, a channel strategy that works for one company may not be suitable for its competitors. Contrast Dell's channel choices with those of Apple.

Dell and Apple. Known for its PCs and related products, Dell mainly handles its own channel functions. By Web and by phone, it takes orders for products, processes payments, arranges shipping, and provides technical support. By marketing directly to customers, the company can continually upgrade features without making store inventory obsolete; custom-build PCs to order; and adapt prices instantly for competitive reasons. Dell also maintains 160 kiosks in shopping centers and is testing small stores where customers can get a hands-on feel for its PCs and place orders. However, Dell's stores and kiosks do not actually sell merchandise, which keeps costs low and eliminates inventory investment. In contrast, competitor Apple operates 150 full-sized, fully stocked stores where shoppers can buy on the spot; it also sells through its own Web site and selected retailers and catalogs.[7]

Channel Levels

How many channel levels are needed or desirable? The higher the number of channel levels, the more intermediaries are involved in making the product available (see Exhibit 8.2). Each channel level adds value in some way by having the product in a convenient place for purchase, for instance, or providing information and demonstrations. In exchange, each level expects to profit from the sale to the next level or to the final customer, costs that must be factored into the ultimate selling price.

A *zero-level channel* refers to a direct channel linking seller and buyer. Dell uses this approach, marketing directly to consumers and business customers and bypassing wholesalers and retailers. However, Dell entered the market during the growth stage of the product life cycle, so customers knew enough about such products to risk ordering without a demonstration. In contrast, new products often need considerable support from channel members, which may mean using a one-level, two-level, or even three-level channel for certain markets or segments.

In a *one-level channel*, the seller works with a single type of intermediary, such as Doubleday working with book stores like Barnes & Noble to reach consumer markets. Many producers choose a one-level channel so they can build strong channel relations and facilitate product, data, and financial flows through the value chain. Some products, such as automotive parts, are customarily distributed through two- or three-level channels. Apple uses multiple channel levels, marketing through selected retailers and catalog merchants as well as through its own stores. Kandy Kastle, maker of Lightning Bugs and other candies, relies on sales brokers and wholesalers to get its merchandise into youth-oriented stores like Hot Topic.[8] Often producers with something new must find ways of breaking into certain channels to reach targeted segments, which is not always easy with an unproven product or brand.

Reverse Channels

In some industries or countries, a company's marketing plan also must allow for reverse channels to return products for exchange, repair, or recycling. Reverse channels can even be used to build relationships with customers and the community. To illustrate, the office supply retailer Staples maintains a community-oriented "Recycle for Education" program. After a school registers for the program, it receives prepaid

EXHIBIT 8.2 Channel Levels

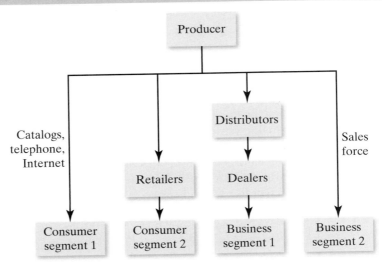

shipping labels to send recyclable ink and toner cartridges to Staples, which pays the school $3 for each cartridge.[9] Marketers must investigate applicable laws or regulations, such as the European Union's strict rules mandating recycling of certain products and materials, when planning channels in various markets.

Reverse channels present profit opportunities for enterprising companies. ReCellular, based in Michigan, has built its business on recycling old cell phones. Of the 15,000 handsets it receives every day, 9,000 can be cleaned and refurbished for sale to U.S. customers of prepaid phone services or to customers in other countries. The remaining units are stripped of hazardous materials, with the plastic and metal parts recycled for use in other products. ReCellular holds 53 percent of the cell phone recycling market, and its annual revenue is growing at more than 50 percent.[10]

Channel Members

How many and what type of channel members will be needed at each channel level? Customers' needs and habits are important clues to appropriate channel choices and to identifying creative new channel opportunities for competitive advantage. Financial considerations are another key factor. Channel members have certain profit expectations and customers have their own perceptions of a product's value; both affect the marketer's pricing strategy and profit potential. In addition, the choice of channel members depends on the product's life cycle, the positioning, and the targeted segment (see Exhibit 8.3).

At introduction, an innovative new product may be offered in a very limited number of outlets (*exclusive distribution*) to reinforce its novelty and enable store staff to learn all about features and benefits. In maturity, the company may try to keep sales going by getting the product into as many outlets as possible (*intensive distribution*). In decline, companies may sell through fewer channel members (*selective distribution*) to keep shipping costs down. Consider how Redbox Automated Retail gives movie studios more intensive distribution for their DVDs.

> **Redbox.** Launched by McDonald's in 2004, Redbox is just what it sounds like: a red box-like vending machine that rents DVDs for $1 per night. Catering to impulse rentals and customers seeking convenience, Redbox machines have been installed in hundreds of McDonald's restaurants as well as in grocery chains such as Stop & Shop and Giant Food. Each Redbox holds about 500 DVDs (representing 60 different movie titles) ready to be dispensed after the customer swipes a credit or debit card through the reader. Using Redbox "is as easy or easier than [using] an ATM," notes the head of marketing. Redbox competes with other channel choices, including: video chains like Blockbuster; online movie services like Netflix; electronics chains like Best Buy; and movies-on-demand available through cable TV providers.[11]

Relations with channel members should be reexamined periodically to be sure the organization is achieving its objectives and to determine whether channel members and customers are being satisfied. IBM, for example, sets sales and fulfillment targets for its own sales force and for channel members, monitors weekly progress, and has a structured process to get channel members the leads, products, education, and support they need to achieve objectives. Its marketers calculate return on investment to assess the financial payback of the channel strategy and to consider changes. They also hire researchers to survey thousands of channel members twice a year in each market. The purpose is to solicit feedback about IBM's support and training, reseller margins, and responsiveness as a business partner—in short, to find out whether channel members are satisfied with value-chain flows and if not, what can be done to increase satisfaction and loyalty.[12]

	Value to Marketer	*Value to Customer*	*Planning Considerations*
Intensive Distribution (in many outlets for maximum market coverage)	Increase unit sales; market impulse items; cover more of each market; reduce channel costs per unit sold.	Convenient, wide access to frequently used or impulse products; price may be lower due to competition.	• Will service be adequate? • Will product be displayed and sold properly? • Will conflict arise between outlets?
Selective Distribution (in a number of selected outlets)	Cover specific areas in each market; reduce dependence on only a few outlets; supervise some channel activities; control some channel costs.	See product and receive sales help in more outlets within each market; obtain some services as needed.	• What is the optimal balance of costs, control, and benefits? • Will outlets be convenient for customers? • Do sales reps understand the product and customers' needs?
Exclusive Distribution (in few outlets for exclusivity within each market)	Choose specific outlets to introduce an innovative product; support product or brand positioning; build closer channel relationships; better supervise service, etc.	Receive personalized attention; access to delivery, alterations, customization, and other services.	• Will channel costs be too high? • Will product be available in all targeted areas? • Will price be too high, given channel profit requirements? • Will outlets be committed as marketing partners?

EXHIBIT 8.3   Intensive, Selective, and Exclusive Distribution

Influences on Channel Strategy

All the channel decisions discussed above are influenced by a number of internal and external factors, summarized in Exhibit 8.4. The major internal factors for marketers to consider during this part of the planning process include:

- *Direction, goals, and objectives.*   The channel strategy must be consistent with the organization's chosen direction, its higher-level goals, and its marketing plan objectives. Companies with green marketing objectives need to plan reverse channels for reclaiming recyclable products or parts.
- *Resources and core competencies.*   If the company has the resources and competencies to handle certain channel functions, it may do so while keeping costs in line by hiring others for different functions. Companhia Brasileira de Distribuiçã, the largest retail firm in Brazil, has the resources to manage quality and inventory by storing seafood products in one specialized distribution center and flowers and plants in another.[13]
- *Marketing mix.*   Channel decisions must work with the organization's product, pricing, and promotion strategies. Unusual or unexpected combinations (like marketing fine art through Costco's Web site or marketing crab

EXHIBIT 8.4   Influences on Channel Strategy

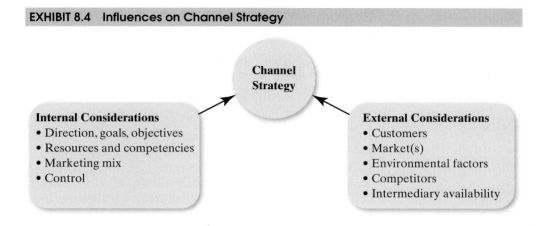

Internal Considerations
- Direction, goals, objectives
- Resources and competencies
- Marketing mix
- Control

Channel Strategy

External Considerations
- Customers
- Market(s)
- Environmental factors
- Competitors
- Intermediary availability

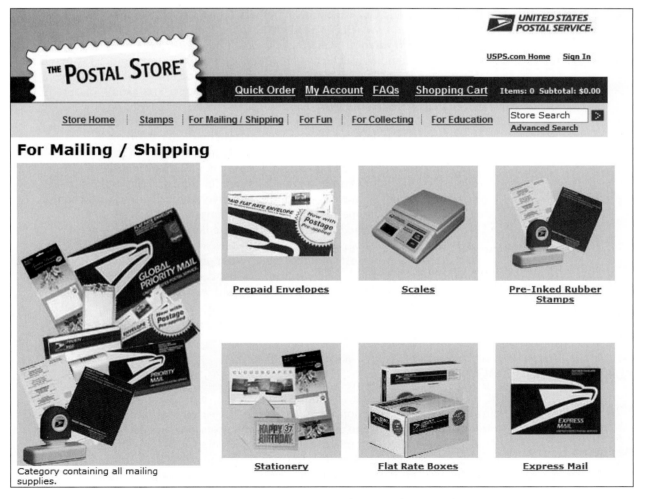

Helping marketers ship goods to customers is big business for the U.S. Postal Service.

cakes through QVC) can be successful, but require careful planning and top-notch implementation.[14]

- *Control.* Does the company want or need tight control over channel functions for quality or image reasons? Can the company afford this kind of control or must it give up some control in exchange for other benefits, such as lower costs or wider coverage in certain areas?

The major external factors influencing decisions about channel strategy are:

- *Customers.* Channel choices should be consistent with what customers want, prefer, expect, or will accept. John Deere sells riding lawnmowers through Home Depot and other retail chains because "that's where our customers are going," says its head of worldwide sales. Yet Stihl advertises to tell customers that its chain saws and other power tools are available through 8,000 independent dealers but not giant home-improvement chains like Home Depot. "Sometimes telling someone where you're not available is more effective than telling where you are," notes the marketing manager.[15]
- *Market(s).* Companies are finding new ways to reach far-flung markets. For example, the Piaggio Group, based in Italy, now sells its popular Vespa motor scooters through the North American and European dealership network of U.S.-based Arctic Cat, which makes snowmobiles and all-terrain vehicles. In turn, Arctic Cat now sells its products through Piaggio's dealers.[16]
- *Environmental factors.* Channel choices should reflect the marketer's analysis of technological, legal-regulatory, social-cultural, and other factors in the environment. This is especially important with offerings that cannot be sold to certain segments, may become obsolete quickly, are fashion oriented, or are heavily regulated. For example, QuickHealth, which operates walk-in clinics inside retail stores, must comply with California's strict regulations requiring that a doctor be present to supervise medical treatment.[17]
- *Competitors.* How can the company use channel strategy to gain a competitive edge? Philips Lighting did this by negotiating exclusivity with Home Depot, a major competitive advantage for Philips.[18] Sometimes going outside the usual channels can be more effective than using the same channel members as most competitors, if customer behavior and costs allow.
- *Availability of intermediaries.* What intermediaries are available in each market, what are their strengths and weaknesses, and what is their reach? Marketers with frequently purchased consumer products often seek distribution through large retail chains, for instance, but each chain has its own locations, strategy, and so on. Organic food companies had relatively limited choices just a few years ago; now chains such as Whole Foods Market are expanding and Wal-Mart has begun stocking organic foods, increasing distribution opportunities.

PLANNING FOR LOGISTICS

The mechanics of managing the flows through the value chain from point of origin to point of sale or consumption are addressed by **logistics.** Marketers aim for a logistics strategy that is responsive to customer needs yet meets internal financial targets. This is a delicate balancing act: Companies do not want to overspend to get supplies and products, information, and payments where and when they should be. On the other hand, they risk losing customers if they take too long to fill orders; have too few units or the wrong assortment on hand to fill orders; have a confusing or complex ordering process; cannot easily track orders and shipments; or make it difficult for customers to return products.[19]

Planning Tip
Estimate the total cost of logistics for different service levels before making a final decision.

Still, responding to customers' needs entails some costs (for delivery, inventory, order confirmation, etc.). Thus, when planning for logistics, it is important to weigh the total cost of logistics against the level of customer responsiveness that is appropriate to meet the organization's marketing plan objectives.

For example, Wal-Mart, the world's largest retailer (a major player in the outbound section of many manufacturers' value chains), keeps logistics costs low so it can keep prices low for competitive advantage.

Wal-Mart. Wal-Mart has the best logistics in the business. Even as it unpacks 4.7 billion cartons of merchandise to stock the shelves and serve 175 million shoppers worldwide every week, it cuts prices and boosts margins. Buying from manufacturers rather than from wholesalers when possible saves time and money. Also, by forecasting demand months in advance, sharing forecasts with suppliers, and calculating and customizing inventory levels for each store, the retailer ensures enough time to plan timely, cost-effective transportation and delivery. Because Wal-Mart never wants to run out of fast-selling products like toothpaste, it warehouses and transports high-turnover goods separately from slower-selling merchandise. The logistics are so smooth that more than two-thirds of the products are in shopping carts and through the checkout before Wal-Mart pays its suppliers.[20]

Logistical Functions

Wal-Mart minimizes the total cost of logistics and operates self-service stores, a balance that supports its market share and profit objectives. Like Wal-Mart, every marketer must consider four main logistical functions when preparing a marketing plan (see Exhibit 8.5):

- *Storage.*   Where will supplies, parts, and finished products be stored, for how long, and under what conditions? Sometimes suppliers agree to warehouse goods; sometimes the marketer warehouses goods until needed to fill customer orders. More storage facilities means higher costs, but faster response times. Wal-Mart locates its huge distribution centers no more than one day's drive from each cluster of stores so it can replenish shelf stock quickly. In addition, each outlet has refrigerated storage and other special storage arrangements for perishable, tiny, outsized, or fragile products.

EXHIBIT 8.5   Logistics Decisions

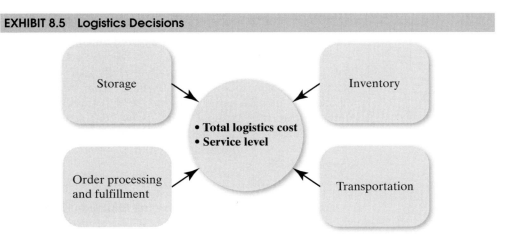

- *Inventory.*   How many parts, components, and supplies must be available inbound for production? How many finished goods are needed on the outbound side to meet customer demand and organizational objectives? How do projected inventory levels affect storage and transportation decisions? Lower inventory means lower costs but may cause delays in filling customers' orders if products are out of stock. Weyerhaeuser, which makes wood and paper products, researches customers' future needs and revises sales forecasts every month so it can plan inventory levels for the coming 6 to 24 months. During a recent slowdown in housing construction, Weyerhaeuser had about a week's worth of softwood lumber on hand; if not for its precise forecasting, the company would have had up to a three weeks' supply on hand.[21]

- *Order processing and fulfillment.*   Who will be responsible for taking orders, confirming product availability, packing products for shipment, tracking orders in transit, preparing invoices or receipts, and handling errors or returns? How will these tasks be accomplished and relevant information be tracked, and in what time frame? Such tasks are as vital to companies offering services as to companies offering tangible products. The Royal Mile Pub in Maryland is one of many restaurants where staffers use wireless handheld computers to record orders and transmit them to the kitchen, reducing errors and expediting service. The system also calculates the bill for each table and allows management to track demand and responsiveness.[22]

- *Transportation.*   How will supplies, parts, and finished products be transported inbound and outbound? Who will pay? Where and when will goods or materials be picked up and delivered? For door-to-door pickup and delivery, marketers often use truck transport. When schedules are flexible and products are heavy or bulky, they may choose less-costly rail or water transport; when deadlines are short and products are perishable or precious, marketers may use fast (but expensive) air transport. Corky's BBQ, a Memphis restaurant, uses FedEx overnight delivery for food ordered as holiday gifts. Corky's electronically creates labels, arranges for pickup, and tracks packages in transit. "We cook it, freeze it, label it, but then we don't worry about it anymore," says the chief financial officer.[23]

Planning Tip
Benchmark against best practices in several industries to improve your logistics.

Influences on Logistics Decisions

One factor that can influence logistics decisions is the organization's approach to social responsibility.

> **Clif Bar.** Clif Bar, which makes energy and nutrition bars for snacking on the go, is a $150 million business built on organic ingredients. The company also wants its logistics strategy to be environmentally friendly, so it conducted an "eco-assessment" of its value chain, looking at everything "from the field where the ingredient is planted to our packaging," says the CEO. It found that having some ingredients shipped from international suppliers by boat actually resulted in lower carbon dioxide emissions than having those ingredients trucked in from U.S. suppliers. The company's Eco Posse also identifies opportunities for handling logistics in a greener way.[24]

Cost constraints are another factor. Online businesses often provide a choice of delivery options with associated prices, allowing customers to decide how much they're willing to spend for faster delivery. In some cases, businesses simply build delivery costs into the price of their products. Netflix, which rents DVDs by mail, charges a flat monthly subscription fee that covers postage for shipments to and from customers. The company maintains 40 U.S. shipping plants, each located near a U.S. Postal Service mail-sorting center. Because Netflix mails 1.4 million movies every day, its marketing plan indicates how it will take advantage of postal discounts to keep costs low without delaying deliveries to customers.[25]

Finally, marketers should be prepared to justify the company's logistics budget. Few companies spend as much for logistics as General Mills, which annually spends $400 million just for shipping goods in volume from factories to distribution centers to stores. The cereal maker's approach to logistics management shows how attention to transportation can boost the bottom line. General Mills' shipping costs account for a whopping 60 percent of the expense of getting its products to supermarkets. Seeking higher profitability, its marketers found they could save $24 million by sharing truck space with other consumer products manufacturers.[26]

Even on a smaller scale, logistics decisions can make a real difference in any marketing plan. Note that the marketing plan need not contain every detail of the logistics strategy, but it should contain a general outline, explain the balance of total costs versus responsiveness, and indicate how logistics functions will support other marketing decisions.

SUMMARY

Products reach markets at the right time, place, and price through the value chain, a series of interrelated, value-added functions and the structure of organizations performing them. Each organization adds value to satisfy the needs of the next link (the immediate customer) as well as customers at the end of the chain. The marketer manages suppliers and logistics on the inbound side to obtain inputs, then manages channels and logistics to meet demand on the outbound side. Marketers must plan for the movement of products, information, and money in both directions along the value chain. Service marketers also need to understand all the flows in the chain, determine how value is added and by which participant, and manage flows to balance supply and demand.

Channel strategy covers decisions about which channel functions must be performed and by which participant; how many channel levels to use; how many and what type of channel members to choose. In a zero-level channel, the marketer deals directly with customers; in a one-level channel, the marketer works through one type of intermediary. Influences on channel strategy include direction, goal, and objectives; resources and core competencies; other marketing-mix decisions; control issues; customers' needs and preferences; market factors; environmental factors; competitors; and intermediary availability. Logistics involves managing the mechanics of products, data, and information flows through the value chain from point of origin to point of sale or consumption, based on objectives that balance total costs with customer responsiveness levels. The four main logistics functions are storage, inventory, order processing and fulfillment, and transportation.

9

Developing Integrated Marketing Communication Strategy

In this chapter:

PREVIEW

Every marketing plan anticipates the use of marketing messages, whether as commercials or coupons, personal selling or public relations—perhaps all of these and more. This chapter discusses planning for the five primary communication tools, starting with the concept of integrated marketing communication (IMC) to coordinate messages and media. Next, the chapter explores how to choose the target audience, set the objectives and budget, examine relevant issues, select one or more tools, and prepare for research before and after a promotion or campaign. The chapter closes with a closer look at planning for the five tools that marketers use to communicate with their audiences.

Once you have completed this chapter and made your IMC choices, record them with *Marketing Plan Pro* software or in a written plan. See the checklist in this chapter for a summary of key questions to ask when planning IMC strategy.

PLANNING FOR INTEGRATED MARKETING COMMUNICATION

The fourth component of the marketing mix is integrated marketing communication (promotion) strategy, which covers five basic tools: advertising, sales promotion, public relations, direct marketing, and personal selling. Although promotion was traditionally

Planning Tip

Maintain a dialogue with customers for feedback and open communication.

a monologue initiated by the organization, today marketers are encouraging dialogues through messages and media that invite interaction.

For maximum effect, marketers should coordinate the content and delivery of all marketing communications for a particular product and brand (and for the organization) to ensure consistency and support the positioning and direction. This approach is known as **integrated marketing communication.**

CHAPTER 9 CHECKLIST   Planning IMC Strategy

Audience Analysis
- ✔ What is the profile of a typical audience member?
- ✔ How do the audience's behavior, characteristics, and media usage affect media and message choices?
- ✔ Which IMC tools are most appropriate for the target audience?

Objectives and Budget
- ✔ What is the IMC strategy intended to achieve?
- ✔ How do the IMC objectives support the marketing plan's objectives?
- ✔ Is the budget sufficient to achieve the objectives with the chosen tools and media?

Issues
- ✔ What legal, regulatory, and ethical issues affect the audience, geographic region, or IMC tool?
- ✔ What social, cultural, competitive, and technological issues must be considered?

Research
- ✔ What does research reveal about the market, audience, and communication preferences?
- ✔ How can research be used to pretest messages and media?
- ✔ How can research be used to evaluate audience awareness and response?

Consider the level of integration in Nike's marketing communications strategy.

Nike. This athletic shoe, apparel, and gear manufacturer has a multimillion-dollar budget for advertising, sponsorships, public relations, and other programs that it carefully coordinates with sports events, product introductions, and seasonal purchasing patterns. Nike also hosts numerous Web sites (*microsites*) for specific audiences, geographic areas, and product categories. For instance, its Joga.com site invites soccer fans to play games, chat, view videos, and interact. The company is always experimenting with new media and messages, such as video ads delivered by cell phone and showing its "swoosh" logo in comic books. The head of Nike's global brand management says: "Gone are the days of the one big ad, the one big shoe, and the hope that when we put it all together, it makes a big impact."[1]

Nike knows the importance of controlling the look, content, and timing of every message to convey the right impression of its products for each target audience. Integration not only avoids confusion about the brand and the benefits, it reinforces the connection with the sports or lifestyle activities and sparks instant recognition when people in the target audience are exposed to the logo or a Nike product name. The total effect of all its IMC activities makes an impact by differentiating Nike products and communicating their value in a crowded competitive arena.

Several factors make IMC even more crucial to marketing success.[2] These include maturing markets, a decline in the effectiveness of mass-media advertising, consumers' perceptions of brand parity, increase in consumers' choices and information sources, global competition, and changes in channel power.

IMC strategy involves defining the target audience, establishing objectives and a budget, analyzing pertinent issues, selecting appropriate IMC tools, and planning pre- and post-implementation research to evaluate effectiveness. These decisions draw on the SWOT analysis conducted earlier in the planning process and are closely related to the product's movement through the life cycle.

Choose the Target Audience

The target audience might consist of customers and prospects or, when image-building is part of the marketing plan, it may consist of employees, community leaders, local officials, and a number of other key stakeholders. Some IMC strategies used to achieve market share and sales objectives can be characterized in terms of "push" or "pull" (see Exhibit 9.1). In a **push strategy,** the company targets intermediaries, encouraging them to carry and promote (push) the product to business customers or consumers. In a **pull strategy,** the company encourages consumers or business customers to ask intermediaries for the product, building demand to pull the product through the channel. Most of the marketing communications budget is devoted to pull activities.[3] However, the decision to use push or pull must fit with channel decisions and be appropriate for the product, its pricing, and its positioning.

Many companies combine push and pull. Carnival Cruise Lines uses a wide variety of consumer ads and promotions to attract vacationers interested in cruising the Caribbean and other areas (pull). It also targets travel agents and travel Web sites with sales materials and other communications to educate and inform (push). This combination has helped Carnival defend its market share while competing with Royal Caribbean International and other industry rivals.[4]

Marketers need to look beyond generalities and develop a profile of the typical member of the target audience in as much detail as possible, including gender; age;

EXHIBIT 9.1   Push and Pull Strategies

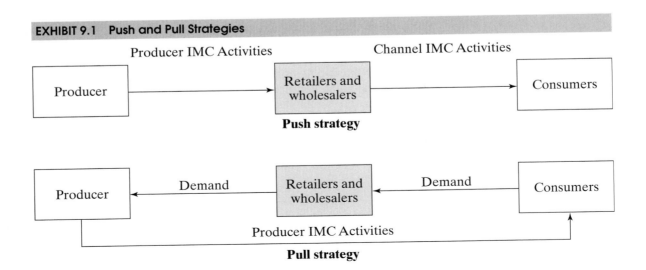

Planning Tip
Review market and customer analyses for clues to communicating with your audience.

lifestyle; media, product, and payment preferences; attitudes; timing of buying decisions; and so on. Digging for such details reveals nuances to help shape what the communication should say and how, when, and where to say it.

The marketers of BMW's Mini Cooper car know that its customers appreciate the brand's quirky image, which is why the company recently launched an unusual IMC program to reinforce customer loyalty.

BMW Mini Cooper. Current BMW Mini Cooper owners are the primary target audience for a recent campaign that includes print advertising, direct mail, and online communications. Owners receive a package containing tinted glasses and a "super-secret decoder" so they can decipher the hidden messages in certain Mini Cooper magazine ads. These hidden messages send owners to special Web sites offering free prizes and invitations to owners-only events like a cross-country car rally. Why target owners? According to the company's ad agency, "It's a covert and an overt campaign almost simultaneously. If you get the kit, you're rewarded. If not, you get the gist that owning a Mini is like being in a club."[5]

Set Objectives and Budget

IMC can be used to move the target audience through a series of responses corresponding to beliefs, behavior, and feelings about the product or brand. As Exhibit 9.2 shows, marketers of low-involvement products such as inexpensive items first want to influence the audience's beliefs, then the audience's actions, and, finally, its feelings. If a consumer sees value in a certain beverage (beliefs), she may buy a bottle and try it (behavior) and then decide whether she likes the taste (feelings). Marketers of high-involvement products such as cars also start by influencing the audience's beliefs; then they strive to influence feelings and behavior. In contrast, marketers who emphasize the consumption experience initially try to influence the audience's feelings, followed by the audience's actions and then its beliefs.

Clearly, these are simplified response models; in reality, target audiences are exposed to multiple messages in multiple media—often simultaneously, as when someone listens to the radio while surfing the Web.[6] Thus, marketers should understand the response model for a given product or category when setting objectives tied to the marketing plan's objectives.

If a company wants to acquire new customers, it must ensure that the audience knows about the offer (influencing beliefs). One IMC objective might be to "achieve 25 percent awareness of Product A among the target audience within 4 months," with the exact percentage and timing dependent on the marketing objective, the promotion investment, and knowledge of the customer's buying process. Related objectives might

---

EXHIBIT 9.2   Models for Audience Response to IMC

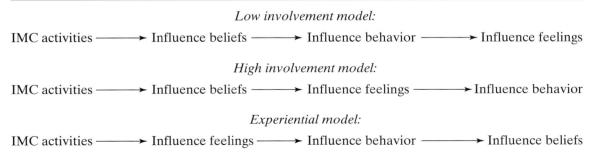

Low involvement model:

IMC activities ⟶ Influence beliefs ⟶ Influence behavior ⟶ Influence feelings

High involvement model:

IMC activities ⟶ Influence beliefs ⟶ Influence feelings ⟶ Influence behavior

Experiential model:

IMC activities ⟶ Influence feelings ⟶ Influence behavior ⟶ Influence beliefs be to "have 900 prospects request an information package about Product D before June 30" and "generate 300 qualified leads for the sales staff by March 15."

Marketing research provides critical background for setting objectives. If research shows that the segment is aware of the product but has no strong preference for it (feelings), the objective might be to "achieve 18 percent preference for Product E among the target audience within 3 months." If research indicates that customers like the product enough to try it (behavior), the aim might be to "achieve 9 percent trial of Product C among the target audience within 6 months" or "have 200 customers request samples of Product B during January." Using IMC to enhance image, the objective might be to "make 55 percent of the target audience aware of the corporation's philanthropic donations by December 31" or to "double the percentage of the target audience having positive attitudes toward the corporation within 12 months."

A number of factors should be considered when devising an IMC budget, including the overall marketing budget, the objectives to be achieved, environmental trends, choice of advertising or other tool(s), the number of markets to be covered, the competitive circumstances, the potential return on investment, and so on. Consider how marketers are handling the Oklahoma Beef Council's IMC budget.

Oklahoma Beef Council. The Oklahoma Beef Council recently boosted its annual marketing communications budget by $2 million to counter two trends: an oversupply of beef and changes in consumers' cooking habits. Because "consumers are time starved," the council participates in the national Beef Made Easy campaign, showcasing tender cuts and quick cooking methods. In addition, the yearly Summer Grilling campaign highlights beef in radio commercials, newspaper inserts, print ads, and point-of-purchase store displays and events. Targeting restaurants, the council has introduced new cuts of meat and menu ideas. Finally, the council's budget allows for promotional partnerships with complementary brands such as A1 Steak Sauce.[7]

Because organizational resources are finite, marketers need to be realistic about the situation, have definite short- and long-term objectives in mind, and budget creatively. See Chapter 10 for more about budgeting.

Examine Issues

Planning Tip
Plan ethical communications that will earn your audience's trust.

IMC strategy can be affected by a variety of legal, regulatory, technological, ethical, cultural, and competitive issues. For example, it is illegal for companies in the United States, United Kingdom, and some other nations to make false claims for a product or describe a food as "low fat" if it does not meet certain criteria.[8] Communications for products such as prescription drugs must comply with strict rules; sometimes messages must include health or product-use warnings and the company must be prepared to safeguard customer privacy in particular ways. Moreover, if companies communicate ethically and, where possible, follow voluntary industry ethics guidelines, they are more likely to build trust with target audiences and polish their image.

Although specific social issues affecting communication will vary from product to product, all marketers should understand the public's perception of promotions. In a recent U.S. survey, 60 percent of the respondents said their view of advertising was "much more negative than just a few years ago," and 54 percent said they "avoid buying products that overwhelm them with advertising and marketing."[9] In addition, ethical concerns arise when messages appear to reach inappropriate audiences, as in a recent controversy over beer advertising.

Beer Advertising. Brewers are investing heavily in ads targeting Hispanic audiences. For example, Miller Brewing has a $100 million multi-year Spanish-television advertising deal and Anheuser-Busch spends $60 million annually on ads aimed at Hispanic consumers. However, questions have been raised about whether these ads encourage underage drinking. An official with the National Latino Council on Alcohol and Tobacco Prevention states: "Latino youth are drinking more than black or white youth, with all the concurrent negative health and social consequences. We believe this is a result of beer companies aggressively targeting Latino youth." An Anheuser-Busch executive responds: "We would disagree with anyone who suggests beer billboards increase abuse among Latino or other minority communities," adding: "It would be poor business for us in today's world to ignore what is the fastest-growing segment of our population."[10]

Marketers should consider competitive issues as well. How can the company use IMC to play up a meaningful point of difference setting its product apart from rival products? How are competitors using IMC? How can the company counter campaigns from competitors with much larger budgets and better-established brands or products? Are new technologies available to pinpoint target audiences more accurately regardless of competitive campaigns? How can the company use IMC to attract attention despite a cluttered marketing environment?

Planning Tip

Consider new ways to convey your message and stimulate the desired response.

Choose IMC Tools

Marketers can choose among a wide variety of techniques in the five basic categories of IMC tools. Here is a brief overview; highlights of planning for each will be examined later in the chapter:

- *Advertising.*   Advertising is cost-effective for communicating with a large audience, with the marketer in complete control of message and media. Marketers often use advertising to introduce and differentiate a product, build a brand, polish the organization's image, communicate competitive superiority, or convey an idea.
- *Sales promotion.*   This marketer-controlled tool can be used to target consumers, businesses, or channel members and sales representatives. It is particularly useful for accelerating short-term sales results; combating competitive pressure; provoking product trial; building awareness and reinforcing other IMC activities; encouraging continued buying and usage; and increasing the offer's perceived value.
- *Public relations.*   Public relations (PR) has more credibility than other promotion tools because the audience receives the message through media channels perceived to be more objective than sources controlled by the organization. However, the outcome is unpredictable: marketers can neither control what the media will report nor guarantee that the company or product will actually get any media coverage at all. Marketers use public relations when they want to present the product and company in a positive light; build goodwill and trust; and inform customers, channel members, and other stakeholders about the product and its benefits.
- *Direct marketing.*   A highly focused, organization-controlled tool, direct marketing facilitates two-way interaction with a specific audience, allows for pinpoint targeting, and accommodates offers tailored to individual needs and

behavior. Marketers can easily measure the outcome and compare it with objectives to determine effectiveness and efficiency. Direct marketing helps organizations start, strengthen, or renew customer relationships; increase sales of particular products; test the appeal of new or repositioned products; or test alternate marketing tactics such as different prices.

- *Personal selling.* Personal selling is an excellent organization-controlled tool for reaching business customers and consumers on a personal basis to open a dialogue, learn more about needs, present complex or customized information, or obtain feedback. Companies selling expensive goods or services or customizing products for individual customers frequently rely on personal selling. However, it is labor-intensive and expensive, which is why many products are not marketed in this way. On the other hand, a number of consumer products are being successfully marketed through personal selling at home parties. Southern Living at Home, owned by the publisher of *Southern Living* magazine, has 25,000 independent representatives selling its cookbooks, candles, and home decor items in U.S. homes.[11]

Exhibit 9.3 summarizes these major promotion tools.

When possible, marketers want to spark positive **word-of-mouth (WOM) communication,** encouraging people to tell other people about a company, a product, a brand, or some clever marketing they noticed. Information spread by WOM (or *word-of-mouse* online) has more credibility because it comes from a personal source rather than being controlled by the organization. The outcome of WOM is unpredictable and often cannot even be accurately measured. With **buzz marketing,** the company seeks to generate more intense WOM, knowing that the buzz may fade as quickly as it starts; it may provide communicators with samples or coupons (or, occasionally, payments).[12]

Buzz marketing, either face-to-face or electronic, has been used to stimulate WOM for all kinds of products, from vehicles and video games to detergent and DVDs. Nivea, owned by Beiersdorf, recently used an unusual paid buzz marketing campaign to launch a new product.

EXHIBIT 9.3　Major Promotion Tools

Tool	*Use*	*Examples*
Advertising	Efficiently get messages to large audience	Television and radio commercials; Internet, magazine, and newspaper ads; paid search engine links; product and company brochures; billboards; transit ads; ads delivered by cell phone and e-mail
Sales promotion	Stimulate immediate purchase, reward repeat purchases, motivate sales personnel	Samples; coupons; premiums; contests, games, sweepstakes; displays; demonstrations; trade shows and incentives
Public relations	Build positive image, strengthen ties with stakeholders	Event sponsorship; news releases, briefings, and podcasts; speeches and blogs; public appearances
Direct marketing	Reach targeted audiences, encourage direct response	Mail, e-mail, telemarketing campaigns; printed and online catalogs; direct response television and radio
Personal selling	Reach customers one-to-one to make sales, strengthen relationships	Sales appointments; sales meetings and presentations; online chat sales help

> **Nivea.** Nivea used PR and paid buzz marketing to introduce its line of Sunkissed Skin tanning moisturizer in England. First, it advertised a series of celebrity-judged auditions to identify eight consumers who are good at gossiping and telling stories. Then the eight winners, working in teams of two, were assigned to promote the products in a specific part of the country. Nivea paid each team member and added a bonus for the team that generated the most media coverage of the new product during the month-long buzz campaign. Commenting on the campaign, the category marketing manager said Nivea was "putting the success of the launch into the hands of consumers" and "banking on their ability to gossip."[13]

Plan Research

If time and money are available, the marketing plan should allow for pretesting and postimplementation research to evaluate IMC activities. Marketers often pretest to find out whether the target audience understands the message and retains information about the brand or product. They also want to see whether the audience responds as expected: do beliefs, attitudes, or behavior change as a result of the communication? Such results help in fine-tuning the format, content, delivery, timing, duration, and context of a communication before the bulk of the campaign is implemented.

Planning Tip
When pretesting, allow time for testing any changes before launching the campaign.

Postimplementation research will show whether the IMC strategy accomplished its objectives and which activities were particularly effective. For example, the U.S. unit of Amsterdam's ING Group conducts extensive postimplementation research of messages designed to attract new customers.

> **ING Direct.** ING Direct, which serves 4 million U.S. customers, analyzes the results of every Internet ad and direct-mail campaign so it can improve future IMC programs. The company's target audience is Web-savvy middle-class people in urban areas, aged 30 to 50 years old, who have about $12,000 in savings and want a convenient banking experience plus a high interest rate. The company boosts brand awareness with media advertising and uses Internet ads and direct-mail packages to bring in new business. Based on ING's research, the most effective of its IMC activities has been a $25 incentive paid to customers who open a new account. The company continues to test new messages as it introduces new products and fends off competition from traditional banks.[14]

USING IMC TOOLS

Marketing plans usually cover the use of various tools in one or more campaigns (with the details and explanations shown in an appendix or other documents). In line with the principle of integration, marketers should consider the overall effect when planning for any combination of advertising, sales promotion, public relations, direct marketing, and personal selling. Careful coordination of content and delivery across messages and media is essential for consistency; otherwise, the target audience could become confused and the results of the IMC strategy might easily fall short of expectations.

Advertising

For the purposes of developing a marketing plan, advertising's two basic decisions concern the message (what content will be communicated?) and the media (what vehicle or vehicles will deliver the message, and when, where, how, and how often?). These decisions must be in keeping with the target audience's characteristics, needs, behavior, and receptivity; the budget allocated for advertising; relevant issues affecting IMC strategy; and the objectives set (e.g., awareness or purchase of the product). Moreover, the message and media have to work together: If, for example, the plan calls for product demonstration, a visual medium like the Internet or television will be the best choice—but only if the budget allows and the chosen vehicle reaches the target audience.

The ad's wording, format and design, graphics, sound, and other medium-specific elements will communicate the message appeal. Some messages rely on a **rational appeal,** using facts and logic to stimulate response by showing how the product solves a problem or satisfies a need. Many B2B ads, in particular, are based on rational appeals linked to the specific benefits that business buyers seek. As an example, paper manufacturer MeadWestvaco used a rational appeal when advertising its Tango paper for commercial printers. After research revealed that printers want paper to perform the same on job after job, the company put the tagline "Always Performing" in its print ads to convey the benefit of consistency.[15]

A message with an **emotional appeal** relies on feelings (fear, love, anger, happiness, or another emotion) to motivate audience response. Kellogg's planning process suggested a combination of emotional and rational appeals for advertising Smart Start Healthy Heart cereal.

Kellogg. Research by Leo Burnett USA, Kellogg's ad agency, revealed that most women mistakenly thought cancer, not heart disease, is the top threat to women's health. To raise awareness and draw visitors to Kellogg's smartstart.com microsite, the agency created a commercial called "My Sister." A woman, speaking to the camera, speaks somberly about how her sister had yearly cancer checkups. "My sister died last summer," she continues. "She was 47 years old. She died of heart disease." The commercial states that heart disease is the number-one killer of women and suggests checking smartstart.com for more information. Leo Burnett executive Dave Reger understands that planning a commercial that involves tragedy is tricky: "The viewer asks, 'Do I fell manipulated or cheated, or do I feel rewarded in a weird way, or have I learned something?' It's a real fine line."[16]

Each medium has characteristics that convey the message in a different way; the Internet offers sight, sound, motion, and interactivity, whereas print ads can offer color, longer life, and the ability to communicate more details. To achieve IMC objectives, even the most creative message must be presented in a specific medium or vehicle (such as a certain magazine or Web site) that will reach the target audience.

In particular, in-store television is becoming a medium of choice for consumer packaged goods because the message reaches shoppers when and where they buy. Unilever, for example, has advertised on the Wal-Mart TV channel, which reaches 130 million shoppers in Wal-Mart stores each month. Target, Kroger, and other big retailers also sell advertising time on in-store television networks.[17] Procter & Gamble's Crest is testing marketing messages delivered by cell phone because, says the interactive marketing manager, mobile technology is part of the targeted consumers' daily lives.[18]

Two key decisions in planning media choices are how many people to reach during a certain period (known as **reach**) and how often to repeat the message during that period (known as **frequency**). Reaching more people is costly, as is repeating the message multiple times. Thus, the marketer must determine how to allocate the budget by

Planning Tip
Be sure the creative execution of a message will work in each medium under consideration.

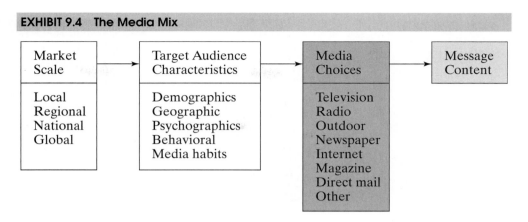

EXHIBIT 9.4   The Media Mix

balancing reach with frequency, based on knowledge of the target audience. The choice of where to advertise—in geographic terms—depends on where the product is available or will be introduced during the course of the marketing plan (see Exhibit 9.4). In terms of timing, a message or campaign might run continuously (reminding the audience of benefits or availability), during periods of seasonal or peak demand (when the audience is interested in buying), or steadily but with sporadic intensity (along with sales promotions or other marketing activities).

Sales Promotion

It takes time to build a brand, cultivate customer loyalty, or reinforce commitment among channel members, but sales promotion can help by reducing perceived price or enhancing perceived value for a limited time. Among the sales promotion techniques that marketers can plan to use when targeting customers and prospects are sampling, couponing, rebates and refunds, premiums, sweepstakes and contests, bonus packs, and loyalty programs. Among the techniques that marketers can use when targeting channel members and salespeople are allowances and incentives, sales contests, training and support, and point-of-purchase materials. Exhibit 9.5 describes the purpose of each and highlights issues to be considered during planning.

Planning Tip
Consider sales promotion for internal marketing as well as external marketing.

Objectives for sales promotion activities targeting customers and prospects may include building awareness, encouraging product trial or usage, encouraging speedy response, reinforcing loyalty, supporting advertising or other IMC activities, and defending against competitors. Objectives for sales promotion activities targeting channel members and sales representatives may include enhancing product knowledge, building commitment, reinforcing focus and loyalty, encouraging speedy response, supporting channel and other IMC activities, and defending against competitors.

A Ralph Lauren program to launch Blue fragrance shows sampling in action.

Ralph Lauren. For Ralph Lauren's launch of its Blue fragrance in the United Kingdom, the fashion firm targeted affluent, professional men aged 20 to 35. Its marketers had two objectives: to build awareness and to encourage trial of the new fragrance. During a brief and intense campaign, samplers visited 100 preselected offices in London to give away tiny trial-size tubes of Blue along with brand-emblazoned adhesive notes and postcards. The personal interaction between the target audience and Lauren's samplers added a human touch to the promotion and fostered two-way communication about the fragrance.[19]

Ragu wants parents to know that its sauce is nutritious and all-natural.

EXHIBIT 9.5	Sales Promotion Techniques

Technique and Purpose	*Issues*
Sampling—Allow prospects to examine and experience product without risk.	• Does the budget allow for sampling? • How, when, and where will samples be distributed?
Couponing—Reduce the perceived price of a product.	• Will coupons be redeemed by loyal customers rather than prospects? • Will coupons be redeemed properly?
Rebates and Refunds—Reduce the perceived price and lower the perceived risk.	• Is the organization prepared for the mechanics? • How will returning money to customers affect financial objectives?
Premiums—Offer something extra for free or for a small price to enhance product's value.	• How will the premium affect the plan's financial objectives? • Will the premium be unattractive or too attractive?
Sweepstakes, contests, and games—Attract attention and build excitement about a product or brand.	• What legal and regulatory rules apply? • Does the budget allow for prizes, operational mechanics, and IMC support?
Bonus packs—Bundle two or more products together for a special price, lowering the perceived price.	• Does the budget allow for special packaging? • Will customers perceive sufficient added value?
Allowances and incentives—Give retailer or wholesaler financial reasons to support the product.	• Will intermediaries offer their customers special prices as a result? • Will intermediaries overorder now, reducing orders in later periods?
Contests—Reward salespeople for selling a certain product.	• Will the product receive adequate attention after a contest is over? • Will the budget cover the cost of prizes and administration?
Training and support—Educate salespeople about product and support the sales effort.	• How often is training needed? • How much support does a product or channel member need?
Point-of-purchase materials—Use signs, other methods of in-store promotion.	• Will retailers use the materials? • Does the budget allow for providing different intermediaries with different materials?

Many marketers include sales promotion in their marketing plans as a way of accelerating response over a set period, with clearly measurable results (such as counting the number of coupons redeemed and the number of units sold). However, overuse can lead customers or channel members to be more price-sensitive when buying certain types of products, posing a potential threat to brand equity and profitability.[20]

Public Relations

The purpose of public relations (PR) is to open the lines of communication and develop positive relationships with one or more of the organization's stakeholder groups. Target audiences (the *public* in public relations) usually include some combination of customers and prospects, employees and job applicants, channel members, suppliers, government officials, local community groups, special interest groups, and the financial

Planning Tip
Identify the audience to be targeted for each public relations objective you set.

community. As an example, Atlanta's Home-Banc Mortgage directs PR at four target audiences. For home buyers and homeowners, it emphasizes superior customer service; for local communities, it emphasizes involvement in nearby Habitat for Humanity projects; for the financial community, it emphasizes its rapid expansion and innovation; and for job applicants, it emphasizes its attractiveness as an employer.[21]

Some of the objectives that marketers may set for PR are:

- *Understanding stakeholders' perceptions and attitudes.* PR can help take the public's pulse and identify concerns about products and operations, social responsibility, and other issues. Whether feedback comes in through letters, e-mails, phone calls, or interaction with company personnel, the organization can learn what its audiences care about and see itself through the public's eyes—then plan to respond.
- *Manage image.* Shaping and maintaining the company's or brand's positive image generates goodwill and sets the stage for strong relations with target audiences. One way to do this is by having management and employees participate in community events, charitable causes, and other local activities. PR is also used to minimize image damage if the company makes a mistake or is involved in a crisis such as suspected product contamination.
- *Communicating views and information.* Sometimes PR is used to correct public misperceptions or clarify a company's stand or action on a particular issue. After accusations that The Gap's clothing is made in overseas factories that operate like sweatshops, the company investigated and reported about conditions at its 3,000 factories. The Gap announced that it had dropped 136 factories because of violations but also candidly stated that "few factories, if any, are in full compliance all of the time" with the retailer's code of labor practices. This honesty strengthened trust among key target audiences such as investors and union officials.[22]
- *Building brand and product awareness.* Through news conferences, special events, and other techniques, PR can spotlight a brand or a product line. Germany's Siemens uses PR to demonstrate its technological savvy in B2B products such as medical diagnostic equipment. One of its PR programs involved sending a 14-car train on a world tour, filled to capacity with Siemens products, specialists, and multimedia kiosks. Thousands came aboard, increasing brand awareness, stimulating new orders, and boosting market share—returns far outweighing the $16 million cost of outfitting the train.[23]

Many companies plan to build product awareness through a combination of PR and other communications. Instead of using eye-catching ads and detail-laden news releases, Nokia introduced one of its cell phones by sending samples to 50 tech-savvy *bloggers* (people who write Web logs). The tactic created tremendous interest and sales. "So many blogs picked it up that it blew out our server twice," says the manager of Nokia's blogging program. Fox promoted the DVD release of the series *Family Guy* by sending funny clips to selected bloggers. This got the clips into such wide circulation that Fox regularly sends exclusive clips to bloggers when it releases a new season of the series.[24] Walt Disney posts a weekly *podcast* (downloadable audio or video file) with behind-the-scenes views and news of Walt Disney resorts and parks. Disney fans are the target audience, says the company's head of global PR.[25]

Direct Marketing

In direct marketing, the organization reaches out to customers and prospects through mail, broadcast and print media, the Internet, and other media. This IMC tool is

Planning Tip
Research the audience's needs and receptivity as you plan content, media, message, and timing.

cost-effective for precise targeting and the use of customized messages, offers, and timing—even one recipient at a time if enough information is available about each individual's needs and characteristics. Because the audience responds directly to the organization, marketers can easily measure results and see whether objectives have been met—and change the message or medium fairly quickly if necessary. The marketing plan should summarize the objectives, the expected response, how results will be measured, any use of research, relevant issues, and the connection with other IMC objectives.

Many direct marketing programs aim for an immediate sale; other objectives may be building awareness, influencing perceptions and attitudes, continuing customer relationships, obtaining leads for sales staff, and encouraging prospects to take the next step toward buying. Not-for-profit organizations typically set objectives such as generating contributions, signing up volunteers, and selling products to benefit the cause. Heifer International has done this.

Heifer International. This not-for-profit organization uses its Web site, fund-raising letters, and printed catalogs to bring in donations. The objective for its Hope for the Future campaign is to obtain $800 million in contributions by 2010. With the money, Heifer is buying livestock and bees for families in poor areas so they can make a living in an environmentally sustainable way. Because the organization's Web site is easy to navigate and clearly communicates the benefits of giving as well as where the money goes, Heifer raises about $8 million yearly through its online marketing. It also benefits from cause-related marketing activities by large and small companies. Organic Bouquet, an online organic florist, donates 10 percent of the price of selected bouquets to Heifer.[26]

To be effective, the direct marketing message must be relevant to the target audience and not be perceived as junk mail or spam. The Cosmetique Beauty Club handled this challenge by inviting prospects to opt in for e-mail offers. It clearly marked e-mails as containing cosmetics offers from Cosmetique and allowed recipients to opt out at any time. By sending e-mails only to people who elected to receive them, the company was able to attract more than 100,000 new members in just nine months.[27]

Personal Selling

Personal selling is appropriate if the target audience requires customized goods or services, needs assistance assessing needs, makes large purchases, or requires individual attention for other reasons. This is an important IMC tool for pharmaceutical firms, equipment manufacturers, and many other B2B marketers, as well as for some marketers that target consumers. The one-to-one nature of personal selling (in person or by phone) supports strong customer relationships; therefore, the emphasis may not be on making an instant sale but on building connections for the future. "Focus on developing a win-win relationship for both the company and the customer," advises Larry Panattoni, a sales representative for Servatron in Spokane, Washington, and "orders will follow."[28]

Planning Tip
Support personal selling with communications to build awareness, interest, and demand.

Decisions that marketers face in planning for personal selling are whether to hire salespeople or work with an outside sales agency; how to recruit, train, manage, motivate, and compensate sales staff; how many salespeople are needed; and how they will be organized (e.g., by product, by market, or by type of customer). A growing number of Web-based businesses are planning for personal selling activities at different points in the buying process.

> **Bluefly.** When a visitor searches this designer clothing discount retailer's site and lingers on three or more items within a five-minute period, Bluefly launches a pop-up window to suggest an online chat with a sales representative. Another situation that triggers a friendly offer of chat help occurs when a customer begins but does not complete the checkout process. Offering chat help adds a personal touch to Bluefly's positioning as a must-see site for price-sensitive customers seeking fashion finds. "This lets us give customers a three-dimensional experience, in the sense that you're adding the voice of someone you can communicate with in real time," explains Bluefly's CEO.[29]

A number of decisions about structuring the sales process itself draw input directly from the marketing plan:

- *Identifying and qualifying prospects.* Based on earlier segmentation and targeting decisions, management identifies the audience for personal selling activities and determines how prospects will be qualified for sales contact.
- *Planning the presales approach.* Data from earlier market and customer analyses informs the approach that a salesperson plans in contacting prospects.
- *Making sales contact.* Based on the prospect's needs and the firm's positioning, the salesperson opens a dialogue with a prospect, determines specific needs, and explains how the offering will provide value.
- *Addressing objections.* Using knowledge of the product, the prospect's needs, and the competition, the salesperson responds to specific concerns and questions raised by the prospect.
- *Closing the sale.* The salesperson completes the sale, arranges payment, and schedules delivery with an understanding of pricing and logistics strategies.
- *Following up after the sale.* To continue building the relationship, the salesperson must understand the customer service strategy, the customer's needs, and applicable IMC support, such as frequent-buyer programs.

SUMMARY

Integrated marketing communication is an approach that coordinates the content and delivery of all marketing communications for a brand, product, or organization to ensure consistency and support the chosen positioning and direction. IMC strategy covers advertising, sales promotion, public relations, direct marketing, and personal selling. Some IMC strategies push products by addressing the channel as the target audience; others pull products through the channel by addressing customers as the target audience; and some combine push and pull, targeting both customers and the channel.

Depending on the plan's overall objectives, IMC may be used to move the target audience through responses corresponding to beliefs, behavior, and feelings about the product or brand. In planning IMC strategy, marketers should look at legal, regulatory, ethical, technological, social, cultural, and competitive issues before selecting appropriate IMC tools. The marketing plan should allow for pretesting and postimplementation research to evaluate and fine-tune the IMC strategy and specific activities. Planning for each IMC tool entails decisions that link back to the overall objectives and strategies set during the marketing planning process.

10

Planning Performance Measurement and Implementation Control

In this chapter:

PREVIEW

The final step in formulating a marketing plan is preparing to check the organization's progress toward performance targets after implementation. Because macroenvironmental or microenvironmental changes are inevitable, marketers will be better able to cope if they define procedures and standards for tracking results and are prepared to address significant problems.

This chapter discusses four tools for checking marketing performance during the period covered by the marketing plan: forecasts of future sales and costs, budgets allocating financial resources, schedules identifying the timing of marketing tasks, and metrics to gauge movement toward achieving objectives. The second part of the chapter looks at how marketing control is used to identify, analyze, and correct variations from expected results.

After reading this chapter and planning your forecasts, budgets, schedules, and metrics, record them with *Marketing Plan Pro* software or in a written plan. Also document any contingency plans you have developed. Think about the questions in the checklist below when planning a marketing audit.

CHAPTER 10 CHECKLIST   Planning a Marketing Audit

Marketing Strategy

✔ Does the mission focus on market and customer needs?

✔ Are marketing-mix strategies appropriate in light of the situation analysis?

✔ Do all marketing objectives support the strategies, goals, and mission?

✔ Do employees understand the marketing plan and have the skills, resources, and time to implement it?

Marketing Operations and Results

✔ Is the organization effectively tracking and reporting results and trends for marketing decision makers?

✔ Does the organization have suitable systems for managing marketing-mix activities?

✔ Does the organization have good relationships with channel members, salespeople, suppliers, and partners?

✔ Can the organization benchmark against industry or world-class standards?

✔ How are performance problems analyzed?

✔ How are corrective action and contingency plans undertaken?

✔ Is the organization achieving its desired financial, marketing, and societal objectives?

Stakeholder Relations

✔ How are stakeholders' comments, feedback, and priorities obtained, analyzed, and incorporated into marketing decisions?

✔ How do customers and other stakeholders perceive the brand/product/company and how have their perceptions and attitudes changed over time?

MEASURING MARKETING PERFORMANCE

Planning Tip

You can't manage what you don't measure, so plan to track the progress of your marketing plan.

Before implementing the marketing plan, marketers need to be able to predict the probable outcomes of their programs; after implementation, they must periodically measure progress toward achieving objectives. The time to establish checkpoints and rules for measuring performance is during the planning process, so the organization is ready to check interim results regularly. Once implementation is underway, marketers can monitor these measures and analyze progress over time to diagnose any variations and make any changes needed to get back on track.

Marketing plans typically include four main tools for measuring performance progress: (1) forecasts, (2) budgets, (3) schedules, and (4) metrics (see Exhibit 10.1).

Forecasting Sales and Costs

Forecasts are future projections of what sales and costs are likely to be in the months and years covered by the plan. To do a good job of forecasting, companies must weigh external factors such as demand, threats, and opportunities as well as internal factors such as goals, capabilities, and constraints. Many companies prepare forecasts for the best-case, the worst-case, and the most likely scenario. Not-for-profit organizations may prepare forecasts of future contributions, overall need for services, and projected service use, along with future estimates of associated costs. Forecasts can never be more than good estimates, and in fact marketers must allow for some forecast error because

EXHIBIT 10.1   Tools for Measuring Marketing Progress

Tool	Application
Forecasts	Used to predict future sales and costs as checkpoints for measuring progress
Budgets	Used to allocate funding across programs in specified periods and then track expenditures during implementation
Schedules	Used to plan and coordinate the timing of tasks and programs
Metrics	Used to establish measures for specific performance-related outcomes and activities and then track results against measures

these are only projections. Still, forecasts should be as accurate as possible, because the organization relies on them when developing strategies and planning the resources needed to implement the marketing plan.

Here's how United Technologies uses forecasting.

United Technologies. With a product mix as diverse as air conditioners, elevators, aircraft engines, and maintenance services, United Technologies Corp. (UTC) prepares its B2B global forecasts based on geography, politics, economic trends, and many other factors. However, no one could have predicted the precipitous drop in demand for air travel after the 2001 terrorist attacks, which prompted airlines to postpone or reduce aircraft purchases and hurt UTC's engine sales for several years. Yet demand for elevators and air-conditioning equipment soared so high due to Asia's construction boom that UTC recently raised its annual sales forecast by $1 billion. Now that the aircraft engine business has improved, UTC managers worry that soaring industrywide demand could overburden suppliers. Therefore, they have stockpiled parts to avoid shortages; this pushed inventory costs above budgeted levels, but the division has still achieved higher sales and profits.[1]

Clearly, marketers need to review forecasts often, especially in light of internal or external shifts that can influence sales, costs, and marketing performance. To illustrate, Ford's marketers constantly scan the environment for signs that their sales forecasts need to be updated. Having felt the effects of sudden and dramatic economic downturns, they not only look at daily vehicle sales but also check informal sources such as Internet chat rooms to get a sense of consumer confidence. "When you have this month-to-month volatility, it creates a certain level of anxiety," says Ford's director of sales analysis. "You've got to really pay attention."[2]

Forecasting must account for the effect that marketing activities will have on the direction and velocity of sales. For example, the company will probably forecast higher sales for a new product if it plans to use penetration pricing to encourage rapid adoption. On the other hand, if it uses skimming pricing to skim profits from the market, the forecast for introductory sales volume will probably be lower than with penetration pricing. Why does this matter? Relying on a forecast that underestimates sales could leave a company with insufficient inventory or staffing to satisfy demand; on the other hand, relying on an overestimate could lead to overproduction and other costly problems.

McDonald's prepares numerous forecasts in the course of marketing planning.

> **McDonald's.** Like other fast-food chains, McDonald's forecasts sales for each location at different times of the day and days of the week so it can project costs, plan staffing levels, and order food and other supplies. Its forecasts also allow for the effect of holidays, seasonality, economic conditions, competitive actions, and other elements that influence demand. The McDonald's on Broadway near busy Times Square in New York City checks the dates of movie premieres because the restaurant is within walking distance of 35 cinemas, and dinner sales can spike by as much as 25 percent when a blockbuster opens. By forecasting outlet by outlet, country by country, and region by region, McDonald's marketers can more closely estimate overall revenues and costs for each planning period.[3]

Types of Forecasts

Planning Tip
The specific forecasts you prepare depend on your organization and its priorities.

United Technologies and McDonald's, like other companies, use sales and cost forecasts as they develop their marketing plans. The most commonly used types of forecasts are:

- *Forecasts of market and segment sales.* The company starts by projecting a market's overall industrywide sales for up to 5 years, using the definition created during the market analysis. This helps size the entire market so managers can set specific share objectives (as discussed in Chapter 5) and estimate the share competitors will have in future years. If possible, the company also should forecast year-by-year sales in each targeted segment.
- *Forecasts of company product sales.* Based on market and segment forecasts, market and customer analysis, direction decisions, and marketing strategies, the company now projects the number and dollar amount of product (or product line) sales for each market or segment. These are usually presented month by month for a year or for the period covered by the marketing plan and sometimes longer. Toyota, for example, projects sales model by model; one forecast calls for selling 1 million Prius hybrid cars by 2010. Some companies, including, Toyota, also create separate forecasts for each new product so these can be tracked more closely.[4]
- *Forecasts of cost of sales.* Here, management forecasts the costs associated with company product sales forecasts, based on data gathered for the analysis of the current situation and on data about cost trends. These forecasts may be adjusted after marketing budgets have been prepared.
- *Forecasts of sales and costs by channel.* When companies sell through more than one channel level or intermediary, they may want to project monthly unit and dollar sales by product by channel and, if feasible, costs per channel. These forecasts focus attention on channel cost-efficiency and provide a yardstick for measuring and analyzing actual channel results and expenses. Toyota's plan for the China market, for example, forecasts overall vehicle demand of 10 million in 2010. Because the company wants a 10 percent share of the market, its channel forecast includes 1,000 car dealerships, with each selling 1,000 cars yearly.[5]

Creating this series of forecasts is only part of the task. Next, the marketer calculates the month-to-month and year-to-year change for the figures in each forecast to examine trends (such as how much growth in sales is being projected for the coming 12 months) and rate of change (such as how quickly costs are rising). Forecast projections and trend calculations can be used to check on target markets, review objectives, reallocate resources, and measure actual against expected results. Given the rapid rate of change in many markets, many companies update forecasts monthly or more often to reflect current conditions; many also collaborate with key suppliers and channel members for more precise forecasting. Wal-Mart, for instance, provides sales data for forecasting to more than 3,500 suppliers on a weekly basis.[6]

Sources and Tools for Forecasting Data

Just as Wal-Mart shares sales data with its suppliers, many companies obtain data for forecasting purposes from their value-chain partners. Marketers can also tap primary research sources such as studies of buying patterns and buying intentions that suggest demand levels by market, segment, category, or product. However, marketers must use judgment, remembering that customers may not buy in the future as they have in the past, nor will they necessarily make future purchases even though they told researchers they would do so.[7] Trade associations, government statistics, and industry analysts' reports can be valuable secondary sources of data.

Some marketers predict future sales by applying causal analysis methods such as regression analysis, econometric models, and neural networks or using time series methods such as smoothing and decomposition. They may also apply judgmental forecasting tools such as sales force estimates, executive opinion, and the Delphi method, as shown in Exhibit 10.2. Because these tools may be subject to human error or bias, marketers generally use a combination of judgment and statistical analysis updated with estimates from knowledgeable sources for increased accuracy.

As difficult as forecasting can be for existing products, planners face even more challenges in forecasting for new products. Some companies use the Bass model for forecasting initial purchases of new products; this is appropriate when (1) the company has been able to collect sales data for even a brief period, or (2) the product is similar to an existing product or technology with a known sales history.[8] When a product is so innovative that it establishes a new product category—such as digital music players—marketers have no historical or industry data to factor into their forecasts. Instead, some predict sales using the results of simulated test marketing research, while others look at sales patterns of products with similar market behavior for clues to the new product's future sales. Once forecasts are in place, marketers create budgets to allocate resources and prepare to track expenses.

Budgeting to Plan and Track Expenses

Budgets are time-defined allocations of financial outlays for specific functions, programs, customer segments, or geographic regions. Budgeting enables marketing managers to allocate expenses by program or activity over specific periods and compare these with actual expenditures. Some organizations insist that budget preparation

EXHIBIT 10.2   Judgmental Tools for Forecasting

Forecasting Tool	*Use*
Sales force estimates	Composite projection based on estimates made by sales personnel; convenient but accuracy depends on instincts, experience, and objectivity of salespeople.
Executive opinion	Composite projection based on estimates made by managers; convenient but accuracy depends on instincts, experience, and objectivity of managers.
Delphi method	Composite projection based on successive rounds of input from outside experts, who ultimately come to consensus on estimates; time consuming but sometimes helpful when forecasting sales of new products or new markets.

Planning Tip
Combine bottom-up and top-down budget input when allocating marketing funds.

follow internal financial calendars; some specify profit hurdles or particular assumptions about expenses and allocation; some mandate particular formats or supporting documentation; and some require budgets based on best-case, worst-case, and most likely scenarios. A growing number of businesses are no longer fixing budgets annually but instead are adjusting budgets monthly based on market realities or tying budgets to longer-term performance.[9]

Budgeting Methods for Marketing Spending

How much money should be budgeted for marketing programs? Smaller companies often deal with this question using **affordability budgeting,** simply budgeting what they believe they can afford, given other urgent expenses. Affordability budgeting may work for start-ups in the early days, when many entrepreneurs have little to spend. However, this is generally not a good way to set budgets, because it doesn't allow for the kind of significant, ongoing investments often needed to launch major new products or enter intensely competitive markets. In effect, budgeting based on affordability ignores the profit payback that comes from spending on marketing to build sales.

Ideally, the size of the marketing budget should be based on careful analysis of the link between spending and sales (or, for not-for-profit organizations, donations). By building a sophisticated model of how sales actually react to different spending levels, the company can determine exactly how big the marketing budget must be to achieve its sales targets. Companies without such models tend to rely on rule-of-thumb budgeting methods that do not directly correlate spending with sales, such as the percentage-of-sales method, the competitive-parity method, and the objective-and-task method.

With **percentage-of-sales budgeting,** management sets aside a certain percentage of dollar sales to fund marketing programs, based on internal budgeting guidelines or previous marketing experience. Although this is simple to implement, one disadvantage is that sales are seen as the source of marketing funding, rather than as the result of budget investments. Another is that the company may have no justification (other than tradition) for choosing the percentage devoted to marketing. Finally, if the budget is continually adjusted based on month-by-month sales, lower sales may lead to a lower marketing budget—just when the company needs to maintain or even increase the budget to stimulate higher sales.

Planning Tip
Don't match what competitors spend, but do be aware of their budget priorities.

When companies use **competitive-parity budgeting,** they fund marketing by matching what competitors spend (as a percentage of sales or specific dollar amount). Again, this is a simple method, but it ignores differences between companies and doesn't allow for adjustments to find the best spending level for achieving marketing plan objectives. Imagine if competitors of the Web-based software firm Salesforce.com matched its $50 million marketing and sales budget as a percentage of revenues. Salesforce.com currently spends 50 percent of its revenues on marketing and sales, whereas the marketing budgets of rivals Oracle and Microsoft represent a much smaller percentage of sales.[10]

With the widely used **objective-and-task budgeting method,** marketers add up the cost of completing all the marketing tasks needed to achieve their marketing plan objectives. In the absence of a proven model showing how sales levels respond to marketing spending, the objective-and-task method provides a reasonable way to build a budget by examining the cost of the individual programs that contribute to marketing performance—as long as the appropriate objectives have been set.

Budgets within the Marketing Budget

Once the overall budget has been established, marketers start to allocate marketing funding across the various activities in the time period covered by the marketing plan.

Then, when they implement the marketing plan, they can input actual expenditures for comparison with planned expenditures. The marketing plan usually includes:

- *Budgets for each marketing-mix program.*   These budgets list costs for each program's tasks or expense items, presented month by month and with year-end totals. Depending on the company's preferred format, marketing-mix budgets also may show expected sales, gross or net margins, and other objectives and profitability measures. Tracking expenses by program reinforces accountability and helps management weigh expected costs against actual costs—and results.
- *Budgets for each brand, segment, or market.*   Creating these types of budgets forces companies to understand their costs and returns relative to individual brands, segments, and markets.
- *Budgets for each region or geographic division.*   Budgeting by region or geography focuses attention on the cost of marketing by location and allows easy comparisons between outlays and returns.
- *Budgets for each division or product manager.*   These budgets help divisional and product managers track costs for which they are responsible, compare spending with results achieved, and pinpoint problems or opportunities for further investigation.
- *Budget summarizing overall marketing expenses.*   This summary budget may be arranged by marketing program or tool, by segment or region, or by using another appropriate organizing pattern. Typically, this budget shows month-by-month spending and full-year totals; in some cases, companies may project spending for multiple years in one summary budget. And this budget may include expected gross or net margins and other calculations based on sales and expenditures.

All these budgets serve as checkpoints against which actual spending can be measured. In this way, marketers can quickly spot overspending and calculate margins and other profitability measures to check on progress toward financial objectives. Wyndham Worldwide sets overall goals, budgets for marketing to support its growth initiatives, and systematically evaluates its marketing expenditures using specific measures of performance.

Wyndham Worldwide. Wyndham Hotels & Resorts, Ramada, Days Inn, and Super 8 are among the 10 hotel brands marketed by Wyndham Worldwide. To drive sustainable revenue and profit growth, the company plans to expand from its current 530,000 hotel rooms to 700,000 rooms by 2010. Most of this expansion will be in international markets. Although Wyndham invests in print and broadcast advertising to reach consumers and members of the travel industry, 15 percent of its marketing budget (which represents most of its online advertising budget) is devoted to search-engine advertising. Why spend so much on the Web? Wyndham's analysis shows that every $1 spent on search-engine ads yields $14 in sales revenue.[11]

Scheduling Marketing Plan Programs

The next step is to coordinate the timing of each activity through scheduling. **Schedules** are time-defined plans for completing a series of tasks or activities (milestones) related to a specific program or objective. Scheduling helps the company define the timing of these tasks and coordinate implementation to avoid conflicts and measure progress

Planning Tip
Include the timing and
progress of ongoing
activities in your situation
analysis.

toward completion. To create a detailed program-by-program schedule, marketing managers list the main tasks and activities for one program at a time and, through research or experience, assign each a projected start and end date. Some companies create a series of schedules, based on best-case, worst-case, and most likely scenarios for timing. Schedules also identify who is responsible for supervising or completing each task in each program.

Marketing plans typically include a summary schedule showing the timing and responsibility for each planned program; the appendix or separate documents may show detailed schedules for each program along with Gantt charts, critical path schedules, or other project-management tools. The point is to make the timing as concrete as possible so managers can quickly determine whether they are on schedule. Then they use metrics to monitor key performance-related activities and outcomes.

Measuring What Matters: Metrics

Metrics are numerical measures of specific performance-related activities and outcomes used to see whether the organization is moving closer to its objectives and goals. Metrics focus employees on activities that make a difference, set up performance expectations that can be objectively measured, and lay a foundation for internal accountability and pride in accomplishments. Thus, metrics must cover activities that are relevant to the mission.

Exhibit 10.3 shows the main categories of metrics often used to assess marketing performance. Note that the marketing plan need not include all metrics for all

EXHIBIT 10.3   Main Categories of Marketing Metrics

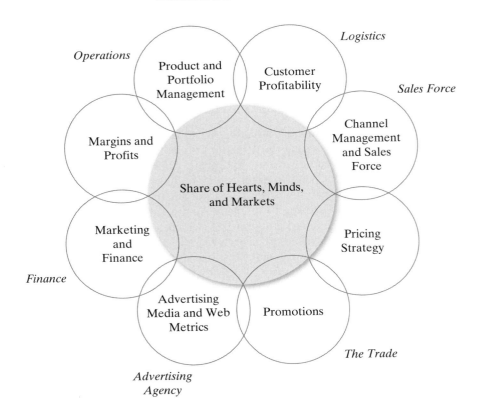

activities. Most important to explain are metrics specifically related to overall achievement of objectives. For example, Nationwide Financial monitors customer retention and 11 other metrics to measure progress toward objectives; to reinforce the importance of this system, the firm links management compensation to achieving preset metrics levels.[12]

All kinds of organizations use metrics to track progress toward meeting objectives and satisfying external and internal customers. The U.S. Navy uses metrics to determine whether personnel are installing new shipboard computer and communication systems on time, within budget, and in fully functioning condition. Simply tracking the accuracy of system installation drawings has reduced error rates by up to 50 percent. Today's metrics may not be appropriate for tomorrow, however. "Good metrics also evolve, and by continually measuring the same things, you may be missing new opportunities to improve," says Rear Admiral David Antanitus.[13] This illustrates another key point: results should be evaluated using suitable metrics, even if these are not the same metrics chosen during the planning process.[14]

A growing number of firms monitor results using a **marketing dashboard,** a computerized, graphical presentation that helps management track important metrics over time and spot patterns that signal deviations from the marketing plan.[15] Like a car dashboard, the marketing dashboard helps marketers see the situation at a glance, based on a limited number of data inputs. In addition to a corporate-level marketing dashboard, management may create dashboards for individual divisions or functions. Cisco Systems, which makes networking equipment, uses marketing dashboards to align marketing and sales activities and to ensure that marketing is accountable for achieving the expected results.[16] The process of creating a marketing dashboard is a useful experience, as Endeca Technologies found out.

Planning Tip

Review recent and previous year's metrics measurements when analyzing the current situation.

> **Endeca Technologies.** Endeca makes software to help companies search, organize, analyze, and interpret data. When its managers decided they wanted a marketing dashboard, they first had to determine exactly what should be included. "It was a catalyst to sit down and really discuss what our key metrics were," says an Endeca executive. Ultimately Endeca adopted 20 metrics, including sales leads and forecasts, that help management monitor marketing and sales effectiveness and gauge the company's overall health.[17]

Identifying Metrics

How can a company like Endeca identify suitable metrics? One approach is to work backward from the mission, goals, and objectives to find specific outcomes and activities that signal progress. For example, companies pursuing growth need metrics to measure changes in customer relationships and sales. Such metrics might include measurements of customer acquisition, customer retention, customer defection, customer satisfaction, customer lifetime value, and sales trends by customer or segment.[18] Exhibit 10.4 shows some sample metrics for a number of marketing plan objectives.

Consider McDonald's, which knows that 60 percent of its U.S. restaurant sales come from drive-through orders. Cutting even six seconds from drivers' waiting time can boost sales by a full percentage point. The company's goal is to cut the wait to no longer than 90 seconds. By one outside survey, however, McDonald's drive-through waiting time hovers above 150 seconds, while the average waiting time at rival Wendy's is much shorter. McDonald's wants more than faster drive-through service; it also wants more accurate order fulfillment. Yet because the menu has expanded, improving both speed and accuracy is a challenge.[19]

EXHIBIT 10.4 Sample Metrics for Marketing Plan Objectives

Type of Objective	Sample Metrics
Marketing	• To acquire new customers: Measure number or percentage of new customers acquired by month, quarter, and year.
	• To retain current customers: Measure number or percentage of customers who continue purchasing during a set period.
	• To increase market share: Measure dollar or unit sales divided by total industry sales during a set period.
	• To accelerate product development: Measure the time needed to bring a new product to market.
Financial	• To increase sales revenue by product: Measure product sales in dollars per week, month, quarter, or year.
	• To improve profitability: Measure gross or net margin for a set period by product, line, channel, marketing program, or customer.
	• To reach break-even: Measure the number of weeks or months until a product's revenue equals and begins to exceed costs.
Societal	• To make products more environmentally friendly: Measure the proportion of each product's parts that are recyclable or have been recycled during a set period.
	• To build awareness of a social issue: Research awareness among the target audience after the program or a set period.
	• To conserve electricity or fuel: Measure amount used by month, quarter, and year.

Planning Tip

Remember to include metrics for any programs that span marketing plan periods.

Metrics that reveal increases in the customer base and customer satisfaction serve as early indicators of future sales performance. Conversely, lower scores on these metrics are warning signs of problems that must be addressed, as Toyota found out.

> **Toyota.** Japan-based Toyota sold 10 percent more Scion cars in the United States than it forecast for the model's first year. However, according to satisfaction surveys conducted by J.D. Power & Associates, Scion customers lodged 158 complaints per 100 cars—far higher than the industry average of 119 complaints per 100 cars. Although the complaints were minor, Toyota needed to bring the score down as it drove toward its second-year objective of selling 8,000 Scions monthly. This is important because Toyota sees Scion as an entry-level vehicle for hip young drivers who could trade up to more expensive Toyota models in the future. Quality is just one of the many metrics Toyota is monitoring as it drives toward its 2010 goal of capturing 15 percent of the global car market.[20]

Good performance as measured by customer satisfaction, market share, social responsibility targets, and other nonfinancial metrics sometimes means accepting the trade-off of lower short-term financial performance.[21] In terms of financial outcomes, common metrics are return on investment (ROI) and gross or net profit margins for each product and line, channel, promotion, and price adjustment, among other measures. Note, however, that while marketers believe such measures are vital, the way certain outcomes are measured can vary from company to company; moreover, finance executives may be accustomed to using different metrics than marketing executives use.[22]

Not-for-profit organizations frequently work backward from their objectives to create metrics that quantify periodic results and trends for donations received (metrics such as donations by source and productivity of fund-raising by program or source), number of people being helped (metrics such as use of service by segment or location), and public image (metrics such as awareness and attitude by stakeholder segment).

A second way to identify metrics is by looking for key components or activities related to customer buying behavior, using research gathered during the analysis of markets and customers. This means finding measurements that signal customer movement toward a purchase. Although many companies measure brand preference as an indicator of future buying behavior, this metric is not right for all organizations.

To illustrate, the chief marketing officer of Morrison Foerster, a multinational law firm, recognizes that corporate decisions about hiring legal counsel are rarely made primarily on the basis of brand preference. "A firm's brand says something about its teamwork, its global resources, and other key attributes," explains the chief marketing officer. "For instance, it helps that the firm may have a brand reputation for intellectual property law. But in the final analysis, what companies buy when they buy legal services is the provider of legal services—and that is not the firm but the individual attorneys."[23]

Once customers start buying, the company can use metrics to measure sales by transaction or by segment, customer or segment purchase frequency, sales by channel or intermediary, and so forth. Exhibit 10.5 presents sample metrics keyed to some basic stages in the buying process (compare with the audience response models in Exhibit 9.2).

Businesses that rely on personal selling usually set up metrics to measure the sales pipeline, such as number of prospect inquiries, number of qualified leads generated, number of meetings with qualified leads, number of bids accepted, percentage of prospects converted to customers, and number of orders received. Channel productivity may be judged using metrics such as number or percentage of customers or sales generated per channel or intermediary, cost and profits per sale by channel or intermediary, speed of order fulfillment, and percentage of stock-outs. Of course, the exact metrics depend on each organization's situation and priorities.

EXHIBIT 10.5 Metrics Based on Customer Behavior

Behavior	Sample Metrics
Customer becomes aware of a product.	Measure customer awareness of product and competing products, by segment.
Customer learns more about the product.	Measure number of information packets or catalogs requested; number of hits on Web site; number of people who visit store; number who subscribe to e-mail newsletter.
Customer has a positive attitude toward the product.	Measure customer attitudes toward the product and competing products, by segment; feedback from hotlines, letters and e-mail, channel and sales sources, etc.
Customer tries the product.	Measure number of people who receive free samples; number who redeem coupons for trial sizes.
Customer buys the product.	Measure sales by transaction, segment, product, channel, payment method; conversion from trials and information requests.
Customer is satisfied.	Measure customer satisfaction by product and by segment; satisfaction feedback from hotlines, letters and e-mails, channel sources, etc.
Customer becomes loyal.	Measure customer retention; size and frequency of repeat purchases; utilization of frequent buyer program.

Using Metrics

Planning Tip
Plan for metrics needed by top-level managers and those needed by marketing managers.

Marketers must find practical ways to measure meaningful outcomes and activities. Not every outcome or activity can be measured, nor is every possible metric actually meaningful. For example, if a company lacks the budget to conduct valid attitudinal research, it cannot use customer attitudes as a metric. Another potential problem is that marketers will simply aim to meet each metrics target without watching the overall effect on strategic outcomes.[24]

Although metrics start with periodic measurements of marketing plan activities and outcomes, they are most valuable to marketers when viewed in the context of:

- *Expected outcomes.* How do the outcomes measured by metrics compare with the expected outcomes in the marketing plan? If the metric is dollar sales by segment, the marketer will compare actual segment sales over a given period with expected segment sales for that period to evaluate progress.
- *Historical results.* How do the outcomes measured by metrics compare with the actual outcomes in previous periods? Because marketers review previous results as part of their internal environmental analysis, they have the data to weigh current outcomes against previous outcomes, which can reveal unusual trends and suggest possible problems that could affect performance.
- *Competitive or industry outcomes.* How do the outcomes measured by metrics compare with competitors' outcomes or average outcomes for the industry? When comparable competitive or industry information is available, marketers can check these against their own organization's outcomes to gauge relative performance and reveal strengths and weaknesses. However, marketers must remember that competitors operate under different circumstances and have very different goals, costs, and outcomes, so competitive comparisons are useful only in relative terms.
- *Environmental influences.* How do the outcomes measured by metrics appear in relation to environmental trends, such as an economic boom or a parts shortage? Marketers need to interpret metrics in the context of everything else affecting the organization. If metrics indicate that sales objectives are barely being achieved when an economic boom has dramatically boosted

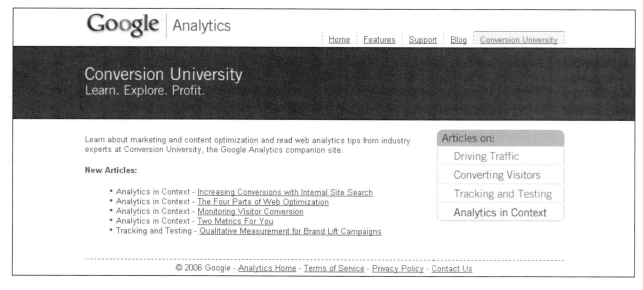

Google helps companies understand the metrics of Web page traffic.

demand, the organization should reevaluate its metrics or create new ones to find out why sales aren't higher still.

Here's how Wal-Mart used metrics to make decisions about its disappointing performance in Germany.

Wal-Mart. Wal-Mart entered the German market in 1998 by buying stores from two local chains. Despite the company's highly efficient buying power and merchandising expertise, metrics showed that the German stores never gained sales and profit momentum. Why? Local deep-discount retailers with extensive store networks and well-established supply chains dominated the market, posing a competitive challenge that Wal-Mart could not overcome. After carefully analyzing years of performance metrics, Wal-Mart decided to sell its 85 stores to a German retail chain in 2006. A spokesperson explained: "As we looked at our competitive environment here, we realized it was going to be hard to achieve the results we expect." Analysts estimate that Wal-Mart lost hundreds of millions of dollars in Germany.[25]

Many companies check performance metrics on a monthly basis, although some check weekly and some daily—or more often, when they have access to fresh data and know they can gain or lose a sale at the click of a mouse. Americanas.com, a Brazilian dot-com retailer of electronics and appliances, checks sales data every 20 minutes. If sales are lower than the day's objectives, managers find out which products are selling the slowest, then change some aspect of their marketing—such as posting a new photo of the product or e-mailing customers with a special offer—to boost sales.[26] Remember that metrics are merely tools to track the progress of programs after implementation, nothing more. Management must make decisions and take action when metrics show that the expected results are not being achieved.

CONTROLLING MARKETING PLAN IMPLEMENTATION

Planning Tip
You may want to control performance on other financial measures, including costs.

To implement a marketing plan most effectively, the organization must "own" the plan, support it, and adapt it as needed (see Exhibit 10.6). During the planning process, a manager (or, ideally, a team) inside the company must be responsible for laying out both strategies and details, championing the plan internally, seeing that rewards are based on marketing performance, and involving senior management. The plan needs support

EXHIBIT 10.6   Successful Marketing Plan Implementation

EXHIBIT 10.7 Types of Marketing Plan Control	
Control	*Use*
Annual plan control	Gauge the organization's progress toward achieving overall marketing plan objectives and individual program objectives.
Profitability control	Gauge the organization's performance in achieving profit-related objectives through measures such as return on investment, return on equity, return on assets, contribution margin, gross/net profit margin.
Productivity control	Gauge the organization's efficiency in managing the sales force, channels, marketing communications, and products.
Strategic control	Gauge the organization's effectiveness in managing marketing, customer relationships, and social responsibility and ethics.

during development and during implementation—support in the form of sufficient time, funding, and staffing as well as internal marketing. Finally, marketers must be persistent and ready to adapt the plan if metrics indicate that there is room for improvement.

Four types of marketing control help marketers gauge the effectiveness of plan implementation: annual plan, profitability, productivity, and strategic control (see Exhibit 10.7). Because marketers generally formulate new marketing plans every year, they need **annual plan control** to assess the progress of the current year's marketing plan. This type of control covers broad performance measures, performance toward meeting marketing plan objectives, and performance toward meeting marketing strategy and program objectives.

Profitability control assesses the organization's progress and performance based on key profitability measures. The exact measures differ from organization to organization, but often include return on investment (or other return measures), contribution margin, and gross or net profit margin. Many companies measure the monthly and yearly profit-and-loss results of each product, line, and category, as well as each market or segment and each channel. By comparing profitability results over time, marketers can spot significant strengths, weaknesses, threats, and opportunities early enough to make appropriate changes.

Productivity control assesses the organization's performance and progress in managing the efficiency of key marketing areas. Closely related to profitability control, productivity control usually covers the efficiency of the sales force, promotions, channels and logistics, and product management. Productivity is so important to the bottom line that some companies appoint marketing controllers to establish standards, measure performance, and boost marketing efficiency without compromising customer satisfaction or other objectives. Moreover, some companies measure the productivity of their product development and manufacturing activities as well as order fulfillment and other tasks, knowing that behind-the-scenes inefficiencies can damage customer relationships. GlaxoSmithKline applies this type of control to its product-development process, bringing new drugs into the pipeline more quickly and screening out low-potential drugs much earlier than in the past.[27]

Strategic control assesses the organization's effectiveness in managing the marketing function, customer relationships, and social responsibility and ethics issues— three areas of strategic importance. Whereas other types of control are applied monthly or more often, strategic control may be applied once or twice a year, or as needed to clarify the organization's performance in these strategic areas. To assess the effectiveness of the marketing function, companies should conduct a yearly **marketing audit,** a detailed, systematic analysis of marketing capabilities and performance (see this chapter's checklist). After an audit is conducted, a summary of the findings should be included in the internal environmental analysis section of the marketing plan.

Auditing the marketing function helps management gauge its strengths, pinpoint areas for improvement, and hold marketing personnel accountable for performance. To illustrate, consider the marketing audit conducted by Onslow Memorial Hospital in Jacksonville, North Carolina.

Onslow Memorial Hospital. After Onslow Memorial emerged from a period of financial difficulty, it completed a marketing audit to see how well the hospital's marketing activities had been working. A survey of the local community revealed that people who had used the hospital were satisfied with its care but were not recommending it to others. Benchmarking against the national average of medical facilities of similar size, the executives found that Onslow Memorial's marketing budget was slightly lower. Despite the disparity, the hospital did not increase its expenditures; instead, it fine-tuned its messages and media to maximize the marketing impact in advance of plans to expand the facility.[28]

Applying Control

The control process, introduced in Chapter 1, is essential for guiding the implementation of any marketing plan to determine whether programs are working out as planned and to give marketers information to make decisions about changing, continuing, or abandoning marketing programs. This assumes that the organization is willing to make changes; despite today's volatile business environment, fewer than 25 percent of companies responding to a recent survey said they always develop plans for corrective action.[29]

After setting the marketing plan's objectives, marketers set standards and measurement intervals (drawn from marketing plan budgets, forecasts, metrics, and schedules) to measure interim progress. For example, assume that the forecast calls for selling 1,000 units of Product A and the budget assumes an average price of $40. The next step is to periodically measure actual results and then compare these actual results with preset standards to diagnose any variances. In this example, the company might compare actual monthly sales and price results with the forecast and budget standards. It can be helpful to diagnose results in the context of historic, competitive, or industrywide results and research the macroenvironmental and microenvironmental issues affecting performance.

The final step is to take corrective action, if necessary, by making adjustments or implementing a contingency plan formulated in advance. One approach is to change the program, the strategy, or the implementation in a bid to achieve the planned results. A second approach is to change the standards or objectives by which performance is measured, appropriate when the variance is not a one-time occurrence and the company understands the underlying influence(s) on performance. Although corrective action is the last step in marketing control, its outcome becomes input for setting or reevaluating objectives at the start of the next control or marketing planning cycle.

Preparing Contingency Plans

Contingency plans are plans that organizations have ready to implement if one (or more) of their original strategies or programs is disrupted by significant, unexpected changes. Hospitals, banks, telecommunications firms, and other organizations that must operate without interruption are especially meticulous about contingency planning, Consider Ent Federal Credit Union's approach to contingency plans.

Ent Federal Credit Union. Based in Colorado, Ent has a series of contingency plans to keep the financial institution operating even if computer connections with the head office are unexpectedly cut off. One of the plans calls for providing service support from a different location; another details how backup data and systems will be brought online when needed. Ent also rehearses its contingency plans to check that the proper procedures are in place and that personnel know what to do. "In addition to a crisis plan, we believe in continuously testing systems and employees to ensure our members and the community will have access to financial services, even in a time of crisis," says Ent's CEO.[30]

Marketers usually prepare contingency plans showing how their organization will respond in the case of emergencies such as: computer systems outages; prolonged power or telecommunications interruptions; natural disasters; sudden bankruptcy of a major customer or supplier; contamination or other environmental disasters; sudden technological breakthrough by a competitor; major failure of a program or strategy; price war or other extreme competitive development; and significant criminal, sabotage, or terrorist activities.

Contingency plans should be outlined as marketing plans are being developed, then periodically reviewed and updated as the situation changes. When preparing a contingency plan, think creatively about the organization's options, priorities, and resources to come up with alternatives that minimize the impact of the disruption and allow the organization to recover as quickly as possible. Like Ent, try to test the plans to be sure they work and are as complete as possible. And use the lessons learned from dealing with the emergency as input for analyzing the current situation when preparing the next marketing plan.

SUMMARY

As preparation for implementation, marketing plans typically specify four main tools for measuring performance progress: forecasts, budgets, schedules, and metrics. A forecast is a future projection of what sales and costs are likely to be in the months and years covered by the plan. Most companies forecast by market, segment, product, and channel. Budgets are time-defined allocations of financial outlays for specific functions, programs, customer segments, or geographic region; four budgeting methods are affordability, percentage-of-sales, competitive-parity, and objective-and-task. Schedules are time-defined plans for completing a series of tasks or activities (milestones) related to a program or objective, used to manage marketing plan implementation.

Metrics are numerical measures of performance-related activities and outcomes that marketers apply to determine whether they are moving closer to their objectives. Metrics focus employees on activities that make a difference, set up performance expectations that can be objectively measured, and lay a foundation for internal accountability and pride in accomplishments. Metrics should be examined in the context of expected outcomes, previous results, competitive/industry outcomes, and environmental influences. Organizations use four types of marketing control: annual plan, profitability, productivity, and strategic control (including the marketing audit). If results are disrupted by significant, unexpected changes, the organization should have contingency plans ready for implementation.

Sample Marketing Plan: SonicSuperphone

Sonic, a hypothetical start-up company, is about to introduce a new multimedia, multifunction "smartphone," a cell (mobile) phone handset with unique features and functions. This product is entering a U.S. market crowded with offerings from Nokia, BlackBerry, Motorola, and numerous other rivals. Yet significant profit potential exists for cutting-edge products that can deliver the specific benefits most valued by targeted segments. The following sample marketing plan shows how Sonic is preparing to launch its first product.

Executive Summary

Early next year, Sonic will introduce a new product in the fast-maturing U.S. market for smartphones. Competing against well-established multinational rivals, we plan to launch a high-quality, slim handset combining a number of useful, innovative features that eliminate the need for users to carry multiple devices. We are targeting specific segments in the consumer and business markets, matching our features to the benefits sought by these customers. After our initial product is established in the U.S. market, we plan to market it in Canada and in Europe.

We will differentiate this first product, the SonicSuperphone, on the basis of innovation and versatile communication, convenience, and entertainment capabilities, supported by skimming pricing to emphasize high quality. Our marketing priorities include building brand awareness among affluent consumers and targeted business customers, reaching specific sales levels, breaking even early in the second year, and operating in an environmentally friendly manner. Sonic's core competencies of technical expertise and efficient assembly procedures will minimize variable costs and enable us to react quickly to market trends and technological advances. For the product's introduction, we will use a push strategy aimed at channel members combined with a pull strategy aimed at customer segments.

Situation Analysis

Sonic was founded 18 months ago by two entrepreneurs with extensive high-tech experience and a creative design for a new smartphone, to be called the SonicSuperphone. The cofounders hold an industry-exclusive license for Wireless Communication Commander software, which makes the handset compatible with Wi-Fi, Wi-Max, and all other wireless communication standards. They also have licensed voice recognition software to manage all of the handset's functions, including entering contacts and other data; accessing the Web, text messages, or e-mail; working with video, audio, and Webcam files; and handling business files and data. Included is a special biometric security system to prevent unauthorized access and protect data.

The SonicSuperphone is designed to be light, slender, and user-friendly, with a touch-screen handset and virtual keyboard that can be projected onto a flat surface as needed. The handset will work with any cell-phone carrier or plan, including free plans such as Skype. In addition to the business functions and global positioning system (GPS) capabilities, the SonicSuperphone can record, store, play, upload, and download photos, videos, and MP3 music files (with 100 GB of storage capacity). As a result, our product's features and functions deliver significantly more benefits than Web-enabled cell phones or phone-equipped personal digital assistants (PDAs) (see Figure A.1).

We will face strong competition: Five manufacturers account for more than 70 percent of the units sold in the global handset market. Nonetheless, our exclusive software license and our core competencies in technology and production should provide an important edge (see the SWOT analysis). Moreover, as the following sections explain, the product's launch will be based on favorable market trends; advanced technology; skimming pricing; selective distribution; extensive knowledge of our markets, customers, and competitors; and tight marketing control.

Market Needs and Trends

The SonicSuperphone can meet a wide variety of customer needs, replacing multiple gadgets and enabling consumers and businesspeople to carry only one

FIGURE A.1   SonicSuperphone Features, Functions, and Benefits

Feature or Function	Benefit
Voice-activated control of all functions	Built-in, hands-free operation for on-the-go users
Compatibility with all wireless communication and peripheral connection standards	Phone, e-mail, text messaging, and Web access possible from any location; Bluetooth or other technologies can be used for headsets or other peripherals
Exclusive Wireless Communication Commander software	Automatically chooses among wireless options for best quality, least expensive Internet or phone connection in each location
Touch-screen technology plus "virtual" keyboard for data entry	Simplifies operation by eliminating need for separate pen or input device; no external keyboard needed, because software projects the image of a keyboard onto a flat surface and follows user's keystrokes
Live Webcam video capture and display	Record and monitor home, children, pets, business areas in real time
Global positioning system (GPS) navigation	Instantly obtain point-to-point directions, traffic and transit updates
Video/photo/audio recording, downloading, uploading, storage, playback	Convenient for entertainment purposes and fully compatible with Windows and Apple operating systems; large 100 GB storage capacity accommodates numerous multimedia files
Biometric security device	Fast and convenient identity recognition to prevent unauthorized access
Expansion slots for removable storage and third-party devices	Users can add peripherals, video game accessories, storage capacity, and more

device. These needs include:

1. *Communication.* Stay in touch on the go by voice, e-mail, text and multimedia messaging, photo and video images, Webcam, file exchange.

2. *Convenience.* Easy-to-use voice-recognition system, touch-screen handset, and virtual keyboard simplify operation; exclusive Wireless Communication Commander software automatically selects the highest-quality and lowest-price wireless method, guided by preset user preferences.

3. *Store and manage information.* Receive and access documents and files; make changes or record data; store files; and transmit to home or office systems through voice commands, touch screen, or virtual keyboard. In particular, adequate storage for large audio and video files is a growing need that our model will fill.

4. *Navigation.* Obtain driving directions, traffic and transit information; GPS navigation uses both voice commands and on-screen maps.

5. *Monitor from a remote location.* With Webcam, watch and listen to what happens in a child's room, anywhere in a home, in a pet's enclosure, or within a business building.

6. *Entertainment.* Record, download or upload, store, play, organize video, photo, music, ringtones; share files on choice of Windows or Apple operating systems.

Targeted Segments

Within the consumer market, our primary target segment is middle- to upper-income professionals who want one portable device to communicate with family and colleagues while on the go. This segment wants to access wireless connections from different locations, obtain navigation assistance, and monitor home or family security. Consumers in this segment are well educated (attended or completed college or graduate school), and have annual household incomes above $75,000. A secondary target segment is young adults, aged 18 to 30, who are early adopters of (and can afford to buy) new electronics; this segment will be particularly interested in the SonicSuperphone's entertainment and imaging features and the ability to add video game units or other peripheral devices.

Within the business market, our primary target segment consists of executives, entrepreneurs, and small business owners who travel; want to access company files and use basic software via a hands-off operation; need to stay in touch with customers and coworkers; and value software that will automatically choose the best-quality, lowest-cost phone and Internet services in any particular location. An additional business segment being considered for second-year entry: medical users, doctors and nurses

FIGURE A.2	Worldwide Mobile Handset Sales	
2005 (actual)	*2007 (actual)*	*2009 (projected)*
610 million units	800 million units	1 billion units

who want to access and update patients' medical records; photograph, video, or remotely monitor patients; and consult reference materials stored in expanded memory.

Market Growth

Global sales trends for cell phones show steady growth over the long term (see Figure A.2). Actual mobile handset sales increased 31 percent from 2005 to 2007. Projections suggest that growth will slow to 25 percent between 2007 and 2009—still a healthy increase but evidence of the maturing world market. By the end of this year, an estimated 2.6 billion consumers and business customers worldwide will be cell-phone subscribers; this represents a 13 percent increase over the previous year, another indication of continued growth.

Other market trends point to positive acceptance of our SonicSuperphone. Widespread media attention to developments in the smartphone industry has increased awareness and interest among targeted segments. Also, reviewers have focused on the specific advantages and disadvantages of new smartphone models, providing us with clues to competitive weaknesses that we can exploit through marketing. Although we are targeting only the U.S. market at this time, we are preparing for expansion into other markets.

SWOT Analysis

In taking advantage of growth opportunities in the U.S. market, Sonic can build on several powerful strengths, including our license for Wireless Communication Commander software (a feature unmatched by competitors at this time); our advantageous contracts for raw materials, parts, components, and packaging; and our efficient, high-quality production expertise. We expect that some competitors will have voice-recognition systems for all handset functions within 6 to 12 months and will be able to match the Commander software within 18 months; still, our head start should provoke positive brand associations and contribute to strong sales.

Our major weakness is the lack of brand awareness and image; we also lack the financial resources and global sourcing contacts of the largest handset manufacturers. Moreover, the SonicSuperphone will have a virtual keyboard only (to keep the device small and reinforce the voice-activation feature), a possible competitive weakness. We see opportunities in higher demand for multimedia, multifunction phones; wider availability of chips for multifunction devices; wider availability of high-capacity storage for smartphones; and frequent media coverage of technologies for personal and business use. We see potential threats from intense competition; pressure to keep prices low; and the future obsolescence of existing wireless standards. Figure A.3 summarizes these strengths, weaknesses, opportunities, and threats.

Competition

On the broadest level, our SonicSuperphone will compete with all smartphone products in the global

FIGURE A.3	SWOT Analysis for SonicSuperphone
***Strengths** (internal capabilities that support achievement of objectives)*	***Weaknesses** (internal factors that might prevent achievement of objectives)*
1. Exclusive license for software to manage wireless connections and compatibility 2. Advantageous supply and packaging partnerships 3. Production quality, efficiency	1. Lack of brand awareness and image 2. Virtual keyboard instead of built-in keyboard may become a competitive issue 3. More limited resources than competitors
***Opportunities** (external circumstances that may be exploited to achieve objectives)*	***Threats** (external circumstances that might interfere with achievement of objectives)*
1. Higher demand for multimedia, multifunction phones 2. Availability of smaller, faster chips to power multifunction devices and higher-capacity storage for multimedia files 3. Media interest in technologies for everyday use	1. Intense domestic and international competition 2. Downward pricing pressure due to maturing market and competitive forces 3. Existing wireless connection standards may become obsolete

FIGURE A.4 Top Competitors in the Global Smartphone Market

Competitor	Current Estimated Share
Nokia	43.0 percent
Panasonic	10.0 percent
NEC	9.5 percent
Research in Motion (BlackBerry)	7.7 percent
Sharp	5.7 percent
Other companies	24.1 percent

market. These competitors have formidable resources, high brand recognition, and extensive experience in product development and management.

As shown in Figure A.4, Finland's Nokia dominates in smartphones, with a 43 percent share of the worldwide market. Panasonic and NEC, both based in Japan, are second and third in terms of global market share. Canada's Research in Motion, which makes the popular BlackBerry wireless PDAs, has the fourth-largest share; and Sharp, a Japanese manufacturer, has the fifth-largest share. Other key competitors active in the U.S. market include: Motorola, which markets the slick Q smartphone; T-Mobile, which markets the stylish Sidekick; Apple's iPhone; and Palm, which markets the Treo PDA/phone combination favored by many businesspeople.

Some competing handsets allow voice-recognition dialing but none of them offers voice activation of every function, including data input, file access, storage, and exchange. This feature has special appeal for our targeted segment of business customers. No other handset is equipped with Wireless Communication Commander software, which facilitates connection through any wireless technology and automatically chooses the best-quality, least-expensive method in a given location. According to our research, both consumers and business customers place a high value on the benefits of this feature. Most important, no competing product has the exact mix of features and benefits offered by the SonicSuperphone.

Critical Issues and Environmental Factors

One issue critical to our success is proper promotion of the Wireless Communication Commander software that Sonic has licensed. Potential buyers may be skeptical that the software is actually compatible with all wireless communication standards and can select the best-quality, least-expensive connection available at any location. Therefore, we will join with the software firm to demonstrate the benefits through a public relations campaign. Also, we will launch a product-specific radio advertising campaign featuring celebrities voicing a variety of commands as the SonicSuperphone responds.

One of our print campaigns will show how quickly SonicSuperphone users can accomplish tasks and access functions using voice recognition. Another will focus on Wireless Communication Commander. Both campaigns will be posted on our Web site. Finally, we will give SonicSuperphones to certain opinion leaders as a way of stimulating buzz and positive word-of-mouth communication.

Macroenvironmental factors likely to affect Sonic include demographics (such as trends in household income); economic issues (such as the purchasing power of targeted segments); technology (such as changes in wireless communication standards); laws and regulations (such as state and federal rules governing telecommunications); ecological concerns (such as being able to recycle product parts); and cultural trends (including the popularity of multifunction, multimedia devices such as smartphones).

Microenvironmental factors likely to affect Sonic include suppliers (especially our industry-exclusive Wireless Communication Commander license); marketing intermediaries (such as relations with retailers and with phone service providers); competitors; and customers (including their perceptions of the SonicSuperphone and the value of its benefits).

Marketing Strategy

SonicSuperphone's positioning will be based on superior innovation, high quality, and status. We will segment our consumer and business markets using demographic factors such as income, behavior, and benefits sought. Through differentiated marketing, we will target selected segments for initial entry and add secondary segments (such as medical users) later.

Using all elements of the marketing mix, supported by service and internal marketing, we will educate the market about our product's features and benefits to motivate purchases by first-time users as well as by consumers and businesspeople who switch from competing handsets. Although television advertising is not affordable in our start-up situation, we will use creative radio, magazine, online, and other media to reach targeted segments. Skimming pricing will reflect our positioning consistent with the high-end brand image we seek to create.

Mission, Direction, and Objectives

Sonic's mission is to make innovative electronics that help consumers and businesspeople become more productive, connected, informed, and entertained in their daily lives. We will pursue rapid growth through the achievement of the following objectives:

- *Marketing objectives.* Achieve first-year unit sales volume of 240,000; gain 40 percent brand awareness among targeted consumer segments and 50 percent among targeted business segments by the end of next year; establish strong channel relationships with upscale retailers and major phone service carriers within 90 days.
- *Financial objectives.* Restrict first-year losses on the SonicSuperphone to less than $10 million; reach the break-even point within 18 months of introduction; earn an annual ROI of 15 percent within the first 4 years.
- *Societal objectives.* Earn the U.S. government's Energy Star designation for power efficiency by the time of introduction; recycle 25 percent of the product's parts after its useful life is over; build community relations by offering deeply discounted SonicSuperphones to not-for-profit organizations and charitable groups.

Product Strategy

As shown in Figure A.1, our product will have features and functions that deliver a number of benefits highly valued by the targeted segments. Some of these features are exclusive to our initial model, although competitors may be able to match one or two key features in a matter of months. We are partnering with a major accessories manufacturer to provide a full line of SonicSuperphone branded accessories. All products carrying our brand must meet rigorous quality and technical standards, as verified by an independent testing laboratory. Moreover, power-supply components will have to be more efficient than competing models, offering the dual benefits of longer use when charged and minimal environmental impact.

Depending on market needs, competitive pressure, and demand, we will lengthen the product line by introducing a language-translation–enabled model within 18 months of launching our first model. This new product will reinforce our innovation positioning, encourage business customers who travel internationally to trade up to the new model with more features, and support longer-term market-share objectives. It also will solidify channel relationships and satisfy additional needs of certain targeted segments. We are currently interviewing designers as we decide whether to create limited-edition fashion handsets soon after our first model is introduced.

The SonicSuperphone brand name will be presented in lettering suggesting speed, linked with a stylized, iridescent lightning bolt logo on the product and all accessories, store displays, Web pages, and other communications. We will cobrand models sold through our phone service providers to show channel support and reinforce customer recognition. All brand elements will be carefully coordinated to contribute to salience, distinctiveness, and image.

(In an actual marketing plan, the product strategy section would include more information about branding, product design and features, packaging and labeling, product compatibility, and other details. Such information is not included in this sample plan.)

Pricing Strategy

Our financial pricing objectives are to achieve profitability within 18 months of introducing the new product and achieve a second-year ROI of 12 percent. We aim to hold first-year losses at $10 million or less, including product-development and production expenses as well as IMC and channel costs related to the introduction. We will use a skimming pricing strategy to support an image of innovation and high quality: the first SonicSuperphone model will carry an average wholesale price of $375 and an average retail price of $500. Thus, first-year revenues are projected to be $90 million based on sales of 240,000 units.

Typically, multifunction phones are priced above $300; the iPhone's initial price was much higher.

Customers perceive high value in the additional benefits of these full-featured products, and our targeted segments are less price-sensitive with regard to leading-edge technology. Often carriers bundle handsets with phone-service contracts, resulting in lower handset prices. Product prices and features vary widely, as this brief competitive sample of smartphones indicates:

- Nokia 7370 ($399 retail) is stylish and equipped with a keyboard that swivels out plus voice-command capability, video ringtones, camera and video recording, and multimedia messaging.

- Blackberry 8700 ($299 when purchased from a phone carrier) is configured for access to 10 e-mail accounts; it features Web browsing, an ergonomic keyboard, 64 MB storage, and multimedia messaging.
- Motorola Q ($349 with one-year phone service subscription) is fashionable and features a keyboard for input, has a high-resolution screen for Web browsing and an expansion slot for storage and other devices.
- Palm Treo 700p ($399 when purchased from a phone carrier) features a camera, plays music and video, has full PDA/phone functionality, and includes a relatively large screen.

Our research shows that business customers who pay for a smartphone with a data-service bundle are more likely to remain loyal. Therefore, we are researching optimal price points for bundling the SonicSuperphone with subscriptions to various data storage and transmission services.

(In an actual marketing plan, the pricing strategy section would include more information about the expected break-even volume, fixed and variable costs, pricing by channel, promotional pricing, segment price sensitivity, competitive pricing, and other details. Such information is not shown in this sample plan.)

Promotion Strategy

Two marketing objectives for our promotion strategy are to generate 40 percent brand awareness within the consumer target market and to generate 50 percent brand awareness within the business target market by the end of next year. To achieve these objectives, we will create a multimedia brand-building campaign that differentiates the product from competing handsets. We also will use trade sales promotion to support our distribution strategy and hold high-profile launch events to stimulate publicity and media coverage in consumer media. Through our catalog partners, we will deliver customized direct marketing packages to prospects with a specific demographic and behavioral profile. Highlights of our initial 6-month promotion activities are shown in Figure A.5.

FIGURE A.5	Highlights of IMC Activities
Month	*Activity*
January	• Start trade campaign to educate channel partners for push strategy supporting product launch. • Give SonicSuperphones to selected product reviewers, bloggers, opinion leaders, media representatives, and celebrities as part of public relations strategy. • Train sales personnel to explain Sonic's features, benefits, and competitive advantages. • Post product preview information on company and retailer Web sites. • With phone service providers, plan sales activities targeting businesspeople. • With Wireless Communication Commander software firm, plan sales activities targeting consumers.
February	• Begin integrated print/radio/Internet pull campaign targeting professionals, businesspeople, affluent consumers. • Distribute point-of-sale materials and schedule in-store demonstrations. • Through catalog retailers, send direct-mail packages to high-potential prospects. • Hold a launch party to spark media coverage and buzz.
March	• Rotate messages as consumer advertising campaign continues. • Add sales promotions such as discounting accessories to encourage switching from competing handsets. • Distribute new in-store displays. • Arrange targeted e-mail promotions through retail partners.
April	• Announce trade sales contest for May–June. • Launch a trade campaign focusing on May–June sales opportunities. • Temporarily reduce frequency of consumer ad messages.
May	• Roll out new radio commercials and print ads featuring celebrities and well-known businesspeople using the SonicSuperphone. • Send retailers display blow-ups of new print ads.
June	• Exhibit at semiannual electronics industry show. • Provide channel partners with new feature/benefit sales aids. • With retailers, plan year-end holiday promotions and sales contests.

We will soon begin pretesting message and creative elements for specific target audiences. During the launch period, we will advertise in magazines such as *Forbes FYI* to reach high-income consumers and business segments. Also, we will use cooperative advertising to have the SonicSuperphone featured in upscale catalogs and on retailers' Web sites. We are fine-tuning our media plan to deal with clutter, competitive advertising, and audience fragmentation. In addition, we are working with channel partners to develop policies for communicating pricing by market.

(In an actual marketing plan, the promotion strategy section would include more information about integrating messages and media, specific tools to be used, and communication programs. Such information is not shown in this sample plan.)

Channel Strategy

Consistent with skimming pricing and our high-quality image, we are using selective distribution to market the SonicSuperphone through two main channels. The first consists of upscale catalog/online/store retailers such as Hammacher Schlemmer, Neiman Marcus, Brookstone, and Skymall. These retailers have extensive customer databases that we can leverage for customized, product-specific direct-marketing promotions; they also are known for good customer service and speedy order fulfillment.

The second channel consists of cell-phone service providers. We have reached agreement to offer the initial model through Verizon, which gives us access to their stores in major markets and opportunities for co-branded promotions. Soon we expect to have agreements with two other phone-service providers and will negotiate with non-U.S. carriers when we expand to global markets.

Although channel costs are a factor, we have decided to emphasize customer service and logistical efficiency. Channel partners will access a secure extranet to place orders, track shipments, and handle other functions. Our suppliers will have sufficient parts and components ready for peak production periods, and our flow of goods will ensure proper inventory levels during the introduction. On the other hand, we do not want to have excess inventory, because of the threat of technological obsolescence.

(An actual marketing plan would include more information about channel functions, criteria for selection and evaluation, customer requirements, competitors' channel strategies, and other details. Such information is not shown in this sample plan.)

Service and Internal Marketing

As part of our customer service strategy, the SonicSuperphone will carry a one-year warranty on parts and labor. In the United States, repairs will be handled by a nationwide firm whose technicians have been trained by our engineers. We will receive weekly reports so we can pinpoint any problems to be addressed through manufacturing or design adjustments. To ensure that customers receive the expected level of warranty service, we will conduct quarterly customer satisfaction surveys.

Sonic will provide comprehensive training and point-of-sale service for channel partners. Customers and retailers will be able to obtain service support 24 hours a day, 7 days a week, on the Web, on a toll-free hotline, or by pressing the "Service" button on the SonicSuperphone. Because we are establishing a new brand, we have high service standards and will measure results to ensure that we consistently meet those standards. We will survey a sample of customers monthly and annually to track satisfaction and plan improvements.

To build internal support and improve product and customer knowledge, our internal marketing activities will include monthly staff meetings; weekly e-mail bulletins; beta-testing by staff and channel members; coordination of marketing and production schedules; and recognition rewards for meeting sales and customer-satisfaction objectives.

Marketing Research

Sonic's use of marketing research includes:

- *Product development.*   Through concept testing, surveys, focus groups, and market tests, we have identified the features and benefits that targeted segments most value in enhanced phones and related electronics. We are collecting additional data on usability, quality and value perceptions, and new features of interest to medical users.

- *Integrated marketing communication.*   We plan to measure brand awareness before, during, and after our campaigns to determine the effectiveness of each medium in reaching the targeted audience and stimulating the desired response. We also want to analyze customers' attitudes toward competitors' campaigns and learn how customers receive and interpret our messages so we can refine promotions for more impact.

- *Customer satisfaction.*   We are planning comprehensive studies to gauge customer satisfaction and identify product defects or other issues that require immediate attention. We will also solicit feedback from retail partners and phone-service providers.

FIGURE A.6	First Year Sales Forecasts
By Market	**Unit Sales**
Consumer	88,000
Business	152,000
Total	240,000
By Channel	**Unit Sales**
Catalog/online/store retailers	180,000
Phone service carrier(s)	60,000
Total	240,000

Financials and Forecasts

Total first-year revenue for the SonicSuperphone is projected at $90 million, based on sales of 240,000 units at an average wholesale price of $375. We anticipate first-quarter sales of $18 million, second-quarter sales of $22 million, third-quarter sales of $21 million, and fourth-quarter sales of $29 million. These projections assume cumulatively higher business sales and a spike in year-end consumer sales. Figure A.6 shows unit forecasts by market and channel.

Heavy investments in product development, promotion, and channel support will mean a first-year loss of up to $10 million. However, we should reach the break-even point of 267,500 units early in the second year, a realistic objective given the narrow margins in this market. Once we introduce a second model, we plan to lower the wholesale price of the first model—in line with standard industry practice—to lower the retail price and increase sales volume. Our first-year marketing budgets cover advertising, sales materials, point-of-purchase displays, consumer and trade sales promotions, public relations, online marketing, channel costs, travel, marketing research, sales training and support, shipping, and customer-service support.

(In an actual marketing plan, each action program would carry its own financial assumptions, management assignments, and schedules. The full marketing plan also would include a detailed profit-and-loss analysis, month-by-month forecasts by product and channel, and summary and detailed budgets by program and activity, market/segment, region, and manager. None of these is shown in this sample plan.)

Performance and Control

We plan stringent control activities to monitor quality and customer service satisfaction so we can respond immediately to any problems. We also are monitoring customer-service communications to detect any early signs of customer concern or confusion. Other metrics to be monitored include weekly and monthly sales (to gauge progress toward revenue and unit sales objectives), weekly and monthly costs (to gauge progress toward the break-even point), quarterly awareness levels (to gauge progress toward brand awareness targets), weekly and monthly sales by channel (to gauge progress in channel relationships), and the number of not-for-profit organizations making special purchases (to gauge progress toward community-relations objectives). In addition, we are tightly controlling schedules to ensure timely implementation.

A contingency plan has been developed to deal with severe downward pricing pressure on enhanced handsets. This may occur if a major competitor initiates a price war or develops a lower-cost technology. Our contingency plan calls for introducing a significant but short-term price promotion such as a rebate to remain competitive while gauging the price sensitivity of different segments. Based on the outcome of this short-term promotion, we would revise the marketing plan as necessary to defend market share while retaining a minimally acceptable level of profitability.

(An actual marketing plan would include detailed schedules and management assignments by program and activity. For control purposes, the plan also would allow for month-by-month comparison of actual versus projected sales and expenses; and it would summarize any contingency plans. None of these is shown in this sample plan.)

Sources for Appendix

Some background information for the fictional sample plan was adapted from: Chris Noon, "Nokia's Kallasvuo Puts Brave Face On iPhone," Forbes, February 12, 2007, www.forbes.com; Walter S. Mossberg, "The Q Review," *SmartMoney*, October 2006, p. 129; Brad Stone, "It's Sweet Home Chicago for a Silicon Valley Vet," *Newsweek*, September 11, 2006, p. 33; "Nokia Tops Converged Mobile Devices Market," *First Glimpse*, September 2006, p. 22; Matt Richtel, "The Wi-Fi in Your Handset," *New York Times*, July 29, 2006, pp. C1, C6; Jay Greene, "One Slick Sidekick," *BusinessWeek*, August 7, 2006, p. 20; Peter Lewis, "License to Thrill?" *Fortune*, July 10, 2006, p. 142; Roger O. Crockett, "Putting It All

Together," *BusinessWeek,* July 3, 2006, pp. 70+; "Go Figure," *Wireless Week,* June 1, 2006, p. 24; Arik Hesseldahl, "Unmaking Motorola's Q," *BusinessWeek Online,* July 20, 2006, www. businessweek. com; Rob Pegoraro, "New Cellphones from BlackBerry, T-Mobile Play Against Type," *Washington Post,* July 2, 2006, p. F5; Shihoko Goto, "Emerging Markets Pushing Cell-Phone Growth," *UPI Hi-Tech,* July 20, 2005; Brad Stone, "Your Next Computer," *Newsweek,* June 7, 2004, pp. 51+; Andy Reinhardt, "Can Nokia Get the Wow Back?" *BusinessWeek,* Mary 31, 2004, pp. 48–50; "A Few Who Got Us Here," *Newsweek,* June 7, 2004, pp. 74+.

Glossary

affordability budgeting   Method of budgeting for marketing in which the company plans to spend what it believes it can afford. (Chapter 10)

annual plan control   Type of marketing control used to assess the progress and performance of the current year's marketing plan. (Chapter 10)

attitudes   An individual's lasting evaluations of and feelings toward something. (Chapter 3)

B2B marketing   Business-to-business marketing. (Chapter 1)

benefits   Need–satisfaction outcomes that customers desire from a product offering. (Chapter 6)

brand equity   Extra value perceived in a brand that enhances long-term loyalty among customers. (Chapter 6)

brand extension   Putting an established brand on a new product in a different category, aimed at a new customer segment; also known as *category extension*. (Chapter 6)

branding   Using words, designs, or symbols to give a product a distinct identity and differentiate it from competing products. (Chapter 6)

break-even point   Point at which revenues cover costs and beyond which a product becomes profitable. (Chapter 7)

budget   Time-defined allocation of financial outlays for a specific function or program. (Chapter 10)

business market   Companies, not-for-profit organizations, and institutions that buy products for operations or as supplies for production; also known as the *organizational market*. (Chapter 3)

buzz marketing   More intense, company-stimulated word-of-mouth communication about a product or brand that may both spread and fade quickly; sometimes involves rewarding communicators with coupons or samples. (Chapter 9)

cannibalization   Allowing a new product to cut into sales of one or more existing products. (Chapter 6)

cause-related marketing   Marketing a product or brand through a link to benefiting a charitable cause. (Chapter 5)

channel   The set of functions and the structure of organizations performing them outbound on the value chain to make a particular offering available to customers; also known as the *distribution channel*. (Chapter 8)

competitive-parity budgeting   Method in which the company creates a budget by matching what competitors spend, as a percentage of sales or a specific dollar amount. (Chapter 10)

concentrated marketing   Focusing one marketing strategy on one attractive market segment. (Chapter 4)

consumer market   Individuals and families that buy products for themselves. (Chapter 3)

contingency plan   Plan that is ready to implement if significant, unexpected changes in the situation disrupt the organization's strategy or programs. (Chapter 10)

core competencies   The set of skills, technologies, and processes that allow a company to effectively and efficiently provide value and satisfy its customers in a competitively superior way. (Chapter 1)

cost leadership strategy   Generic competitive strategy in which the company seeks to become the lowest-cost producer in its industry. (Chapter 2)

customer churn   Turnover in customers during a specific period; often expressed as a percentage of the organization's total customer base. (Chapter 6)

customer lifetime value   Total amount a customer spends with a company over the course of a long-term relationship. (Chapter 6)

derived demand   In B2B marketing, the principle that demand for a business product is based on demand for a related consumer product. (Chapter 3)

differentiated marketing   Creating a separate marketing strategy for each targeted segment. (Chapter 4)

differentiation strategy   Generic competitive strategy in which the company creates a unique differentiation for itself or its product based on some factor valued by the target market. (Chapter 2)

diversification   Growth strategy of offering new products to new markets through internal product-development capabilities or by starting (or buying) a business for diversification purposes. (Chapter 5)

dynamic pricing   Approach to pricing in which prices vary from customer to customer or situation to situation. (Chapter 7)

emotional appeal   Message strategy that relies on feelings rather than facts to motivate audience response. (Chapter 9)

ethnographic research   Type of marketing research in which customers are observed in actual product purchase or usage situations. (Chapter 3)

features   Specific attributes that enable a product to perform its function. (Chapter 6)

financial objectives   Targets for performance in managing specific financial results. (Chapter 5)

fixed pricing   Approach to pricing in which prices do not vary; the customer pays the price set by the marketer. (Chapter 7)

focus strategy   Generic competitive strategy in which the company narrows its competitive scope to achieve a competitive advantage in its chosen segments. (Chapter 2)

focus group   Marketing research in which a small group of customers or prospects is brought together for a guided discussion of their needs and behavior relative to a product or product category. (Chapter 3)

forecast   Future projection of what sales and costs are likely to be in the period covered by the plan. (Chapter 10)

frequency   How many times, on average, the target audience is exposed to the message during a given period. (Chapter 9)

goals   Longer-term performance targets for the organization or a particular unit. (Chapter 1)

integrated marketing communication   Coordinating content and delivery so all marketing messages are consistent and support the positioning and direction in the marketing plan. (Chapter 9)

internal marketing   Marketing that targets managers and employees inside the organization to support the marketing mix in the marketing plan. (Chapter 5)

lifestyle   The pattern of living that an individual exhibits through activities and interests. (Chapter 3)

line extension   Putting an established brand on a new product added to the existing product line. (Chapter 6)

logistics   Managing the movement of goods, services, and related information from the point of origin to the point of sale or consumption and balancing the level of service with the cost. (Chapter 8)

macroenvironment   Largely uncontrollable external elements that can potentially influence the ability to reach goals; these include demographic, economic,

ecological, technological, political–legal, and social–cultural forces. (Chapter 2)

market   All the potential buyers for a particular product. (Chapter 3)

market development   Growth strategy in which the company identifies and taps new segments or markets for existing products. (Chapter 5)

market penetration   Growth strategy in which the company sells more of its existing products to customers in existing markets or segments. (Chapter 5)

market segmentation   Grouping customers within a market according to similar needs, habits, or attitudes that can be addressed through marketing. (Chapter 4)

market share   The percentage of sales in a given market held by a particular company, brand, or product; can be calculated in dollars or units. (Chapter 3)

marketing   An organizational function and a set of processes for creating, communicating, and delivering value to customers and for managing customer relationships in ways that benefit the organization and its stakeholders. (Chapter 1)

marketing audit   A detailed, systematic analysis of an organization's marketing capabilities and performance. (Chapter 10)

marketing control   The process of setting goals and standards, measuring and diagnosing results, and taking corrective action when needed to keep a marketing plan's performance on track. (Chapter 1)

marketing dashboard   A computerized, graphical presentation enabling management to monitor marketing results by tracking important metrics over time and spotting patterns that signal deviations from the plan. (Chapter 10)

marketing objectives   Targets for performance in managing specific marketing relationships and activities. (Chapter 5)

marketing plan   A document that summarizes marketplace knowledge and the strategies and steps to be taken in achieving the objectives set by marketing managers for a particular period. (Chapter 1)

marketing planning   The process of determining how to provide value to customers and the organization by researching and analyzing the market and situation; developing and documenting marketing objectives, goals, strategies, and programs; and implementing, evaluating, and controlling marketing activities to achieve the objectives. (Chapter 1)

mass customization   Creating products, on a large scale, with features tailored to individual customers. (Chapter 6)

metrics   Numerical measures of specific performance-related activities and outcomes. (Chapter 10)

microenvironment   Groups that have a more direct effect on the organization's ability to reach its goals: customers, competitors, channel members, partners, suppliers, and employees. (Chapter 2)

mission Statement of the organization's fundamental purpose, its focus, and how it will add value for customers and other stakeholders. (Chapter 2)

motivation What drives the consumer to satisfy needs and wants. (Chapter 3)

North American Industry Classification System (NAICS) Method of classifying businesses according to industry designation; used in the United States, Canada, and Mexico. (Chapter 3)

niche Smaller segment within a market that exhibits distinct needs or benefit requirements. (Chapter 4)

objective-and-task budgeting Method in which the budget is determined by totaling the cost of all marketing tasks needed to achieve the marketing plan objectives. (Chapter 10)

objectives Shorter-term performance targets that support the achievement of an organization's or unit's goals. (Chapter 1)

penetration pricing Pricing a product relatively low to gain market share rapidly. (Chapter 7)

percentage-of-sales budgeting Method of budgeting in which the company allocates a certain percentage of sales revenues to fund marketing programs. (Chapter 10)

perception How the individual organizes environmental inputs such as ads and derives meaning from the data. (Chapter 3)

personas Detailed but fictitious profiles representing how individual customers in a targeted segment behave, live, and buy. (Chapter 4)

positioning Using marketing to create a distinctive place or image for a brand or product in the mind of customers. (Chapter 1)

price elasticity of demand Percentage change in unit sales of demand divided by the percentage change in price; where customers are price-sensitive and demand changes considerably due to small price changes, the demand is elastic. (Chapter 7)

primary research Research conducted specifically to address a certain situation or answer a particular question. (Chapter 3)

product development Growth strategy in which the company sells new products to customers in existing markets or segments. (Chapter 5)

product life cycle The stages of introduction, growth, maturity, and decline through which a product moves in the marketplace. (Chapter 6)

product line Group of products made by one company that are related in some way. (Chapter 6)

product mix Assortment of all product lines marketed by one company. (Chapter 6)

productivity control Type of marketing control used to assess the organization's performance and progress in managing the efficiency of key marketing areas. (Chapter 10)

profitability control Type of marketing control used to assess the organization's progress and performance based on profitability measures. (Chapter 10)

psychographic characteristics Variables used to analyze consumer lifestyle patterns. (Chapter 3)

pull strategy Using marketing to encourage customers to ask intermediaries for a product, thereby pulling it through the channel. (Chapter 9)

push strategy Using marketing to encourage channel members to stock a product, thereby pushing it through the channel to customers. (Chapter 9)

quality How well a product satisfies customer needs. (Chapter 6)

rational appeal Message strategy that relies on facts or logic to motivate audience response. (Chapter 9)

reach How many people in the target audience are exposed to the message during a particular period. (Chapter 9)

schedule Time-defined plan for completing work that relates to a specific purpose or program. (Chapter 10)

secondary research Research data already gathered for another purpose. (Chapter 3)

segments Groups within a market having distinct needs or characteristics that can be effectively addressed by specific marketing offers and programs. (Chapter 1)

service recovery How an organization plans to recover from a service lapse and satisfy its customers. (Chapter 5)

skimming pricing Pricing a new product high to establish an image and more quickly recover development costs in line with profitability objectives. (Chapter 7)

societal objectives Targets for achieving specific results in social responsibility. (Chapter 5)

stakeholders People and organizations that are influenced by or that can influence an organization's performance. (Chapter 1)

strategic control Type of marketing control used to assess the organization's performance and progress in the strategic areas of marketing effectiveness, customer relationship management, and social responsibility and ethics. (Chapter 10)

subcultures Distinct groups within a larger culture that exhibit and preserve distinct cultural identities through a common religion, nationality, ethnic background, or lifestyle. (Chapter 3)

sustainable marketing Forming, maintaining, and enhancing customer relationships to meet all parties' objectives without compromising the achievement of future generations' objectives. (Chapter 1)

SWOT analysis Summary of an organization's strengths, weaknesses, opportunities, and threats in preparation for marketing planning. (Chapter 2)

target costing Using research to determine what customers want in a product and the price they will pay, then finding ways of producing the product at a cost that will accommodate that price and return a profit. (Chapter 7)

target market   Segment of the overall market that a company chooses to pursue. (Chapter 4)

targeting   Decisions about which market segments to enter and in what order, and how to use marketing in each. (Chapter 1)

undifferentiated marketing   Targeting all market segments with the same marketing strategy. (Chapter 4)

value   The difference between total benefits and total costs, as perceived by customers. (Chapter 1)

value-based pricing   Approach to setting prices that starts with customers' perspective of a product's value and the price they are willing to pay; marketers then work backward to make the product at a cost that also meets the company's objectives. (Chapter 7)

value chain   The series of interrelated, value-added functions and the structure of organizations that perform these functions to get the right product to the right markets and customers at the right time, place, and price; also known as *supply chain*. (Chapter 8)

word-of-mouth communication   People telling other people about an organization, a brand, a product, or a marketing message. (Chapter 9)

Endnotes

CHAPTER 1

1. Diana T. Kurylko, "CEO: Plan for MG's Launch, Growth Is Solid," *Automotive News*, October 30, 2006, p. 50; Nick Bunkley, "A Revival in Oklahoma," *New York Times*, July 12, 2006, pp. C1, C2; Kelvin Chan, "Nanjing Auto Starts European Drive," *South China Morning Post*, March 10, 2006.

2. "Oasis Claims PR Boon Over Delay," *Travel Trade Gazette UK & Ireland*, November 3, 2006, p. 24; Jeffrey Ng, "Hong Kong Airline Plans Launch," *Wall Street Journal*, June 30, 2006, http://online.wsj.com.

3. Carol Matlack, "Nestlé: Fattening Up on Skinnier Foods," *BusinessWeek*, July 3, 2006, pp. 48–50; "Nestlé's Marketing Crisis," *Marketing*, February 19, 2004, pp. 24+; "Selling to the Developing World," *The Economist*, December 13, 2003, p. 8; Amie Smith Hughes, "Home Improvement," *Promo*, September 1, 2003; "Nestlé: A Dedicated Enemy of Fashion," *The Economist*, August 31, 2002, pp. 47–48.

4. Sir George Bull, "What Does the Term Marketing Really Stand for?" *Marketing*, November 30, 2000, p. 30.

5. David Pringle, "Nokia Takes Leap into Wi-Fi Arena with New Phone," *Wall Street Journal*, February 23, 2004, p. B4; Justin Fox, "Nokia's Secret Code," *Fortune*, May 1, 2000, pp. 160+.

6. Brendan I. Koerner, "Fried Chicken Dinner, on the Fly," *New York Times*, August 6, 2006, Sec. 3, p. 2; Kenneth Hein, "Yum! Develops Taste for Multibranding," *Brandweek*, May 15, 2006, p. 13; "As Yum! Brands Plots a 1,100-Unit International Expansion, Its KFC Brand Is Poised to Extend Its Dominance in Much of Asia," *Nation's Restaurant News Daily NewsFax*, May 26, 2006; "Yum! Brands Inc. Subsidiary KFC Has Launched KFC Famous Bowls," *Nation's Restaurant News Daily NewsFax*, May 18, 2006; Julia Boorstin, "Yum Isn't Chicken of China—Or Atkins," *Fortune*, March 8, 2004, p. 50.

7. William Spain, "Noncarbonated Drinks, Snacks Lift PepsiCo Profit by 14%," *Wall Street Journal*, July 13, 2006, http://online.wsj.com; Chad Terhune, "Pepsi Marketer's Quest: Find Fizz Amid Flatness," *Wall Street Journal*, June 14, 2006, p. B3C.

8. "Sony: Playing a Long Game," *The Economist*, November 18, 2006, pp. 63–64; Marc Gunther, "The Welshman, the Walkman, and the Salarymen," *Fortune*, June 12, 2006, pp. 70+; Martin Fackler, "Cutting Sony, a Corporate Octopus, Back to a Rational Size," *New York Times*, May 29, 2006, pp. C1, C4; "Sony Corp.," *Wall Street Journal*, May 20, 2004, p. 1; Ken Belson, "As Newcomers Swarm, Sony Girds for a Fight," *New York Times*, February 8, 2004, Sec. 3, p. 4; Bolaji Ojo, "Sony, Matsushita Slash Supply Base to Cut Costs," *EBN*, August 23, 2003, p. 1; Jonathan Silverstein, "PlayStation 3: A Bust or a Boon for Sony?" *ABC News*, January 4, 2007, http://abcnews.go.com.

9. Stephanie Balzer, "Suns Search for Fan Rebound," *Phoenix Business Journal*, May 4, 2001, p. 3; http://www.nba.com/suns/community.

10. Ken Belson, "As DVD Sales Slow, the Hunt Is On for a New Cash Cow," *New York Times*, June 13, 2006, p. C1+; Paul Sweeting, "Netflix Out to Conquer New Worlds," *Video*

Business, January 26, 2004, pp. 1+; Christopher Null, "How Netflix Is Fixing Hollywood," *Business 2.0,* July 2003, pp. 41–43.

11. "Poor Sales Doom McDonald's Spicy Sandwich," *Wall Street Journal,* July 13, 2006, http://online.wsj.com; Martin Fackler, "Will Ratatouille Bring Japanese to McDonald's?" *Wall Street Journal,* August 14, 2003, pp. B1, B5.

12. Maureen Tkacik, "Markdown-onomics," *New York,* January 23, 2006, pp. 38+; Jeanette Borzo, "Get the Picture," *Wall Street Journal Europe,* January 16, 2004, pp. R2+; George Anders, "Why Real-Time Business Takes Real Time," *Fast Company,* July 2001, pp. 158–161.

13. Kevin J. Clancy and Peter C. Krieg, *Counterintuitive Marketing* (New York: Free Press, 2000), pp. 199–201.

14. Garance Burke, "Banks Tailor Products for Latino Immigrants," *Marketing News,* April 1, 2006, p. 37; www.bankofthewest.com.

15. Christopher Hosford, "Selling Strategies for Small Businesses," *Sales and Marketing Management,* April, 2006, pp. 30+.

16. Susan Chandler, "Designers Find Their Target," *News-Times* (Danbury, CT), September 4, 2001, p. C8; www.target.com.

17. See Philip Kotler and Kevin Lane Keller, *Marketing Management,* 12th ed. (Upper Saddle River, N.J.: Prentice Hall, 2006), Chapter 2; and Alan R. Andreasen and Philip Kotler, *Strategic Marketing for Non-Profit Organizations,* 6th ed. (Upper Saddle River, N.J.: Prentice Hall, 2003), pp. 80–82.

18. Joe Nocera, "A Good Chief Just Stays Out of the Way," *New York Times,* June 17, 2006, pp. C1, C4.

19. George S. Day, "Feeding the Growth Strategy," *Marketing Management,* November–December 2003, pp. 15+.

20. Frances Brassington and Stephen Pettitt, *Principles of Marketing,* 3rd ed. (Harlow, Essex, UK: Financial Times Prentice Hall, 2003), p. 19.

21. "FedEx Kinko's Expands 'Green Power' Buys," *Traffic World,* January 16, 2006, p. 31; "FedEx Delivers Cleaner Air," *Hartford Courant,* April 6, 2004, p. A8; Charles Haddad, "FedEx and Brown Are Going Green," *BusinessWeek,* August 11, 2003, pp. 60–62.

22. Patricia Cobe, "How to Plan a Grand Opening," *Restaurant Business,* June 2006, p. 12; Gregg Cebrzynski, "Local Marketing Keeps Rock Bottom's Fire Chief Promo Ablaze," *Nation's Restaurant News,* March 20, 2006, p. 14.

23. See Paul W. Farris, Neil T. Bendle, Phillip E. Pfeifer, and David J. Reibstein, *Marketing Metrics: 50+ Metrics Every Executive Should Master* (Upper Saddle River, N.J.: Wharton School Publishing, 2006), Chapter 10.

24. Holly Vanscoy, "Life After Living.com," *Smart Business,* February 2001, pp. 68–70.

25. U.S. Census Bureau, "State and County QuickFacts," www.quickfacts.census.gov/cgi-bin/usa.

26. Ralph A. Oliva, "Seeds of Growth," *Marketing Management,* November-December 2003, pp. 39–41.

27. See "Model of Exchange Shifts Towards Services," *Marketing News,* January 15, 2004, p. 25.

28. Mark Rechtin, "Lexus Checks into the Four Seasons for Ideas," *Marketing News,* June 6, 2005, p. 6.

29. Bret Begun, "The Italian Stallion," *Newsweek,* December 1, 2003, p. 12.

30. Michael Fielding, "Brand Marketing: No Longer Plain, Simple," *Marketing News,* May 15, 2006, pp. 11–15; Matthew Boyle, "Brand Killers," *Fortune,* August 11, 2003, pp. 88+.

31. Julie Schlosser, "Markdown Lowdown," *Fortune,* January 12, 2004, p. 40; "Zilliant," *Fortune,* November 24, 2003, p. 210.

32. Yukari Iwatani Kane, "Nintendo Shares Hit Record High, Thanks to the DS," *Wall Street Journal,* July 7, 2006, p. C14; Seth Schiesel, "The Video Game Goes Minimalist," *New York Times,* June 4, 2006, Sec. 2, p. 1; Phred Dvorak, "Nintendo Steers Away from the Pack," *Wall Street Journal,* May 11, 2004, p. B10; Phred Dvorak, "Nintendo's GameCube Sales Surge after Price Cut," *Wall Street Journal,* November 4, 2003, p. B4.

33. "Manufacturing Complexity," *The Economist,* June 17, 2006, pp. 6–9.

34. Chris Gaither, "Small Business Innovation: Looking Online for Local Customers," *Los Angeles Times,* May 16, 2006, p. S5.

35. Jane Spencer, "Cases of 'Customer Rage' Mount as Bad Service Prompts Venting," *Wall Street Journal,* September 17, 2003, pp. D4+.

36. "Federal Government Makes Improvements to Customer Service," *Wall Street Journal,* July 31, 2003, p. D2.

37. Michael Garry, "Tech Award Winners Take Advantage of IT's Rapid Growth," *Supermarket News,* January 30, 2006, p. 8; Susan Greco, "The Best Little Grocery Store in America," *Inc.,* June 2001, pp. 54–61.

38. Jean Patteson, "Escada Designer Bucking to Lasso a Youthful Look," *Orlando Sentinel,* April 7, 2006, www.orlandosentinel.com; Cecilie Rohwedder, "Style & Substance: Making Fashion Faster," *Wall Street Journal,* February 24, 2004, p. B1.

39. "Analysis: eBay's Growth to Come from Community, Not Acquisitions," *InformationWeek,* June 19, 2006; Matthew Creamer, "A Million Marketers," *Advertising Age,* June 26, 2006, p. 1; Patrick Dillon, "Peerless Leader," *Christian Science Monitor,* March 10, 2004, p. 11.

40. Irene M. Kunii, "Websmart 50: Shiseido," *BusinessWeek,* November 24, 2003, p. 100.

41. See Kotler and Keller, *Marketing Management* 12th ed., Chapter 1.

42. Day, "Feeding the Growth Strategy."

43. John S. McClenahan, "New World Leader," *Industry Week,* January 2004, pp. 36+; Bob Donath, "Irritations Lead Users to Innovations," *Marketing News,* October 9, 2000, p. 16; Michael Arndt, "3M: A Lab for Growth?" *BusinessWeek,* January 21, 2002, pp. 50–51.

44. Brian Grow, "The Debate Over Doing Good," *BusinessWeek,* August 15, 2006, pp. 76+.

45. R. S. Flinn, "Big Bank Mergers Create Space for the Little Guy," *New York Times,* December 21, 2003, Sec. 14, p. 17.

46. Carol Hymowitz, "For Now, the Focus Is More on Innovation Than on Budget Cuts," *Wall Street Journal,* July 17, 2006, p. B1.

47. Glen A. Beres, "Blue Nile Looks Past Grooms-to-Be, Toward Other Jewelry Categories," *National Jeweler,* May 16, 2006, p. S34; Timothy J. Mullaney, "Jewelry Heist," *BusinessWeek,* May 10, 2004, pp. 82+; "Niche Internet Retailers Hit Their Stride," *News-Times* (Danbury, CT), February 5, 2004, p. B8.

48. Ross Sneyd, "Cohen, Greenfield Re-emerge for Ben & Jerry's New Campaign," *Associated Press,* July 11, 2006, www.boston.com; "Ben & Jerry's Coffee for a Change," *Specialty Coffee Retailer,* January 2004, p. 6; Andy Serwer, "Economic Crunch," *Fortune,* December 8, 2003, pp. 64+.

CHAPTER 2

1. Don E. Schultz, "Others' Benchmarks Overlook *Your* Brand," *Marketing News,* March 15, 2004, p. 7.

2. Geoff Colvin, "Lafley and Immelt," *Fortune,* December 11, 2006, pp. 70+; George S. Day and Paul J. H. Schoemaker, "Scanning for Threats and Opportunities," *Harvard Business School Working Knowledge,* May 15, 2006, http://hbswk.hbs.edu.

3. "General Electric Co.: Unit to Spend $1.4 Billion on Senior-Housing Portfolios," *Wall Street Journal,* June 27, 2006, p. B14; Richard Thompson, "Developing Markets: A Boom in Infrastructure Investments in the Middle East Is Central to GE's Growth Strategy," *MEED Middle East Economic Digest,* February 3, 2006, p. 8; "General Electric Gets $38M Navy Pact," *Associated Press,* January 3, 2007, www.businessweek.com.

4. James C. Collins and Jerry I. Porras, *Built to Last* (New York: HarperBusiness, 1994), pp. 220–221.

5. Quoted in Maureen Jenkins, "What's Our Business? Why Every Employee Needs to Know the Company's Mission Statement," *Black Enterprise,* October 2005, p. 71; Jeffrey Abrahams, *The Mission Statement Book* (Berkeley, CA: Ten Speed Press, 1999).

6. Ben Elgin, "So Much Fanfare, So Few Hits," *BusinessWeek,* July 10, 2006, p. 26; Google Web site (www.google.com).

7. Médecins Sans Frontières Web site, www.msf.org.

8. Simon Romero, "Big Tires in Short Supply," *New York Times,* April 20, 2006, pp. C1, C4.

9. Yuval Rosenberg, "What's Next for Netflix?" *Fortune,* December 11, 2006, p. 172; Paul Sweeting, "Netflix Out to Conquer New Worlds," *Video Business,* January 26, 2004, pp. 1+; Calmetta Coleman, "Pruning Costs," *Wall Street Journal,* February 12, 2001, p. R30.

10. "P&G Back to Basics with Crest," *Advertising Age,* July 3, 2006, p. 12; Sarah Ellison, "Crest Spices Up Toothpaste War with New Tastes," *Wall Street Journal,* September 15, 2003, pp. B1, B10; www.pg.com.

11. Jeffrey E. Garten, "Wal-Mart Gives Globalism a Bad Name," *BusinessWeek,* March 8, 2004, p. 24.

12. Lisa Sanders, "How to Target Blacks? First, You Gotta Spend," *Advertising Age,* July 3, 2006, p. 19; Lisa M. Keefe, "P&G's Multiculti Marketing DNA," *Marketing News,* March 1, 2004, pp. 13+.

13. "Caterpillar to Power Coal Methane Gas Project in China," *Xinhua News Agency,* May 19, 2006; Mark Tatge, "Cat's in the Bag," *Forbes,* March 15, 2004, p. 178; James B. Arndorfer, "Cat Looking to Make Inroads in Asia," *Crain's Chicago Business,* November 10, 2003, p. 24.

14. Robert Johnson, "Incognito, Polyester Boogies Onto the Playing Field," *New York Times,* March 21, 2004, Sec. 4, p. 5.

15. John Carey, "Business on a Warmer Planet," *BusinessWeek,* July 17, 2006, pp. 26+.

16. Thea Singer, "Can Business Still Save the World?" *Inc.,* April 2001, pp. 58–72.

17. Daniel Wolfe, "Search for E-Pay Edge Leads Citi to Google," *American Banker,* June 30, 2006, p. 1; Michelle Conlin, "Champions of Innovation," *BusinessWeek IN,* June 2006, p. 26.

18. Bruce Einhorn, "Trophy TVs: Thin, but Not Quite So Rich," *BusinessWeek,* June 26, 2006, p. 10.

19. Eric J. Savitz, "Bull Market for Red Tape," *Smart Money,* May 2004, pp. 56+.

20. David Jonas, "Low-Cost Carriers Launching Slew of New Services," *Business Travel News,* October 31, 2005, p. 8.

21. Steven Lee Myers, "Russia Returns $15 Million in Phones to Motorola," *New York Times,* August 25, 2006, p. A7; Steven Lee Myers, "Phone Seizure Seen as Example of Russian Corruption," *New York Times,* June 14, 2006, p. A3; "4 Million Handsets Sold in Russia in 2005," *Europe Intelligence Wire,* June 21, 2006; Guy Chazan, "Russia Puts Motorola on Hold," *Wall Street Journal,* June 8, 2006, p. B1.

22. Krissana Parnsoonthorn, "Thai-Owned Producer of Food Business Set for Rapid Expansion in Scandinavia," *Bangkok Post,* February 20, 2003, www.bangkokpost.com; Sofia Javed, "Ethnic E-Tailer Builds Expertise in Untapped Market," *Marketing News,* October 9, 2000, p. 24.

23. Cooperative Insurance Web site, www.cis.co.uk; "U.K. Insurance Firm Asks Customers to Help Prioritize Its Socially Responsible Investments," *Financial Times,* March 1, 2004, www.ft.com.

24. Jen Haberkorn, "Competition Gnaws at Giant Food Lead; Chain to Respond with New Stores," *Washington Times,* June 17, 2006, p. C10; "Grocery Scene Sees New Players," *MMR,* June 13, 2005, p. 200.

25. Discussion is based on Michael Porter, *Competitive Advantage* (New York: Free Press, 1985), pp. 11–26.

26. "Coach's Net Income Jumps 37%, Driven by Strong Japanese Sales," *Wall Street Journal,* January 25, 2006, p. B11; Robert Berner, "Coach's Driver Picks Up the Pace," *BusinessWeek,* March 29, 2004, pp. 98–100.

CHAPTER 3

1. "McDonald's Reports Sales Were Up 7.7% in September," *New York Times,* October 13, 2006, p. C2; Gordon Fairclough and Geoffrey A. Fowler, "Drive-Through Tips for China," *Wall Street Journal,* June 20, 2006, p. B1; John Tagliabue, "A McDonald's Ally in Paris," *New York Times,* June 20, 2006, pop. C1, C5; Janet Adamy, "How Jim Skinner Flipped McDonald's," *Wall Street Journal,* January 5, 2007, pp. B1+.

2. Based on Gary L. Lilien and Arvind Rangaswamy, *Marketing Engineering,* 2nd ed. (Upper Saddle River, N.J.: Prentice Hall, 2003), p. 159.

3. For more on market potential, see Roger J. Best, *Market-Based Management,* 4th ed. (Upper Saddle River, N.J.: Pearson Prentice Hall, 2005), Chapter 3.

4. "RV Retail Market: Monaco Rises to Fifth Place in Trailers," *RV Business,* May 2006, p. 7; Jonathan Fahey, "Lord of the Rigs," *Forbes,* March 29, 2004, pp. 67–72.

5. Don Clark, "Net at Texas Instruments Rises 11%," *Wall Street Journal,* October 24, 2006, p. B3; Damon Darlin, "Cashing In Its Chips," *New York Times,* July 9, 2006, Sec. 3, pp. 1, 7.

6. Fahey, "Lord of the Rigs."

7. "Kirin Tops Asahi in Beer Shipments in Jan.–June, 1st Time in 5 Yrs.," *Kyodo News International,* July 12, 2006; "Kirin Brewery Co.," *Wall Street Journal,* February 21, 2006, p. C9.

8. "More than 50% of Consumers Buy Fairtrade Goods," *Marketing,* March 4, 2003, p. 3.

9. John Adams, "Payments: Looking Forward, with a Nod to the Old," *Bank Technology News,* November 2005, p. 32; Mara Der Hovanesian, "Websmart 50: Wells Fargo," *BusinessWeek,* November 24, 2003, p. 96.

10. Philip Kotler and Kevin L. Keller, *Marketing Management,* 12th ed. (Upper Saddle River, NJ: Prentice Hall, 2006), p. 24.

11. "Hering's World-Class Harmonicas," *Music Trades,* February 2004, pp. 222+; Tony Smith, "Resurrected Harp-Maker Plays to Win," *Marketing News,* February 26, 2001, p. 47; www.heringusa.com.

12. Elliot Zweibach and Jon Springer, "Kroger, United Debut Hispanic Formats," *Supermarket News,* July 3, 2006, p. 8; Brian Grow, "Hispanic Nation," *BusinessWeek,* March 15, 2004, pp. 58+.

13. Kathryn Martin, "Unique Flip-Top Closure for 'Silly Squirts' Ketchup," *Food Engineering,* March 2006, p. 19; Keven T. Higgins, "Competition Can't Ketchup to Heinz," *Marketing Management,* January/February 2004, pp. 22+; "The Latest Crazy Color from Heinz in Its Kid-Targeted EZ Squirt Condiment Line Is Stellar Blue," *DSN Retailing Today,* May 5, 2003, p. S12.

14. Eric Wilson, "Don't I Know You from the Party Pages?" *New York Times,* June 25, 2006, Sec. 9, pp. 1, 11.

15. Lawrence Kudlow and Jim Kramer, "Carnival Cruise Lines: VC and COO Interview," *America's Intelligence Wire,* March 2, 2004; Rebecca Tobin, "In the Hot Seat: Bob Dickinson," *Travel Weekly,* December 29, 2003, p. 9.

16. Rob Bates, "New DTC Director: 'We're Still Transforming Ourselves,'" *Jewelers Circular Keystone,* June 2006, pp. 168+; Rob Bates, "DTC Introduces 'Journey' Concept," *Jewelers Circular Keystone,* March 2006, p. 46; Rob Walker, "The Right-Hand Diamond Ring," *New York Times Magazine,* January 4, 2004, p. 16; Blythe Yee, "Ads Remind Women They Have Two Hands," *Wall Street Journal,* August 14, 2003, pp. B1, B5.

17. Tobias Mayer, "The Breaker and the Box," *New York Times,* March 14, 2004, Sec. 3, p. 8.

18. Peter Kafka, "Apple Seed," *Forbes,* February 16, 2004, p. 50.

19. Jerry Useem, "Another Boss, Another Revolution," *Fortune,* April 5, 2004, pp. 112+.

20. Clay Boswell, "Beauty and Brains," *Chemical Market Reporter,* May 15, 2006, pp. 18+.

21. Leslie Wayne and Mark Landler, "Duo Atop EADS Promise Needed Repairs," *New York Times,* July 19, 2006, p. C4.

22. Richard Durante and Michael Feehan, "Watch and Learn," *Marketing News,* February 1, 2006, pp. 59–60.

23. Spencer E. Ante, "The Science of Desire," *BusinessWeek,* May 29, 2006, pp. 98+.

24. Peter Burrows, "Stopping the Sprawl at HP," *BusinessWeek,* May 29, 2006, pp. 54+.

25. David H. Freedman, "Why Privacy Won't Matter," *Newsweek International,* April 3, 2006.

CHAPTER 4

1. "Breaking: Royal Mail Develops Personalized Stamps," *New Media Age,* March 16, 2006, p. 3; Alicia Henry, "You Oughta Be In . . . Stamps?" *BusinessWeek,* August 25, 2003, p. 14; "Customized Postage Goes Commercial," U.S.P.S. news release, May 16, 2006, www.usps.com.

2. Molly Prior, "Avon Profits Plunge 47% in 3rd Quarter," *WWD,* October 30, 2006, p. 2; Elisabeth Butler, "For Avon, Rocky Start to Critical Makeover," *Crain's New York Business,* August 14, 2006, p. 1; "Avon Calls, China Opens the Door," *BusinessWeek,* February 28, 2006; Molly Prior, "Andrea Jung's Call to Break the Mold," *WWD,* May 26, 2006, p. 12; Monica Roman, "Avon Looks Fabulous," *BusinessWeek,* February 16, 2004, p. 44; Jill Jusko, "Avon Calling—On Russia," *Industry Week,* December 2003, p. 48.

3. Joseph Weber, "Harley Just Keeps On Cruisin'," *BusinessWeek,* November 6, 2006, p. 71; Russell Pearlman, "Getting New Riders High on the Hog," *SmartMoney,* August 2006, pp. 28–29.

4. "Dollar General Corp.," *BusinessWeek,* April 5, 2004, p. 116; Nichole Monroe Bell, "Family Dollar December Sales Rise," *Charlotte Observer,* January 4, 2007, www.charlotte.com.

5. Hassan Fattah, "The Rising Tide," *American Demographics,* April 2001, www.americandemographics.com.

6. Louise Lee, "Courting the 'Mass Affluent,'" *BusinessWeek,* March 8, 2004, pp. 68–69.

7. Matt Richtel and Ken Belson, "Cell Carriers Seek Growth by Catering to Hispanics," *New York Times,* May 30, 2006, pp. C1, C4.

8. "Tesco Merges Its C-Store Ops," *Grocer,* March 13, 2004, p. 5; "Taste the Differences," *Grocer,* January 20, 2001, pp. S10+.

9. "Taste the Differences."

10. Richard H. Levey, "Home Depot Embraces Mail Order," *Direct,* January 1, 2006; Fara Warner, "Yes, Women Spend (and Saw and Sand)," *New York Times,* February 29, 2004, Sec. 3, p. 3; Peg Tyre, "Trading Spaces, and Jabs," *Newsweek,* April 5, 2004, p. 46.

11. Michael Arndt, "3M's Rising Star," *BusinessWeek,* April 12, 2004, pp. 62+.

12. Scott Van Camp, "Esselte in Supplies Strategy," *Brandweek,* February 9, 2004, p. 18.

13. "U.S.: AOL, WebEx Start Beta Tests on New AIM Pro Service," *The America's Intelligence Wire,* June 20, 2006; Marcus Lillkvist, "Macromedia Plans to Branch into Web-Based Conferencing," *Wall Street Journal,* February 9, 2004, p. B8.

14. Lynn Crandall, "The Nose Knows," *Inform,* March 2006, pp. 140–141; John Tagliabue, "Sniffing and Tasting with Metal and Wire," *New York Times,* February 17, 2002, Sec. 3, p. 6.

15. "Harrah's Entertainment at Goldman Sachs Lodging, Gaming, Restaurant, and Leisure Conference," *The America's Intelligence Wire,* June 5, 2006; Julie Schlosser, "Teacher's Bet," *Fortune,* March 8, 2004, pp. 158+.

16. Mara Der Hovanesian, "Coffee, Tea, or Mortgage?" *BusinessWeek,* April 3, 2006, pp. 48–49.

17. Dale Buss, "Marketing Personas: Reflections of Reality," *Advertising Age Point,* June 2006, pp. 10–11.

18. *Ibid.*

19. Bruce Mohl, "JetBlue, Southwest to Raise Air Fares," *Boston Globe,* February 23, 2006; Michael Arndt, "Flying Budget, But in Style," *BusinessWeek,* March 15, 2004, pp. 114–115; Micheline Maynard, "Are Peanuts No Longer Enough?" *New York Times,* March 7, 2003, Sec. 3, pp. 1, 9.

20. Dana James, "Play It Straight," *Marketing News,* May 21, 2001, p. 15; "Agfa's Second Crack at Cracking Digital," *Print Week,* January 15, 2004, p. 17; http://www.agfa.com/en/gs/solutions/index.jsp.

21. Jim Farrell, "Marketing Their Way to a Better Image," *Hartford Courant,* November 14, 2003, p. B3.

CHAPTER 5

1. RadioShack Layoff Notices Are Sent by E-Mail," *New York Times,* August 31, 2006, p. C2; Denise Trowbridge, "Retailer Closing 9 Area Locations: Moves Part of Radio Shack Recovery Plan," *Columbus (OH) Dispatch,* March 28, 2006.

2. H. Igor Ansoff, "Strategies for Diversification," *Harvard Business Review,* September–October 1957, pp. 113–124; Philip Kotler, *Kotler on Marketing* (New York: The Free Press, 1999), pp. 46–48.

3. Brian Bremner, "Slow Growth, Bad Loans Weigh on HSBC," *BusinessWeek Online,* December 7, 2006, www.businessweek.com; Ben Marlow, "HSBC to Go Global with Its Giant Branches," *Sunday Business (London),* July 9, 2006, www.thebusinessonline.com; Sherman So, "HSBC Gears Up for Seven-Day Services," *The Standard (Hong Kong),* July 7, 2006; Raymond Wang, "BOCHK Loses to HSBC in Loan War," *The Standard,* January 4, 2007, n.p.

4. Tommy Fernandez, "Small Business: Union Square Businesses Cell Themselves," *Crain's New York Business,* December 15, 2003, p. 17.

5. Abigail Goldman, "Mattel Tries to Get Back into Game with Preteen Console," *Los Angeles Times,* July 20, 2006, p. C1.

6. "HP Passes Dell to Become the World's Largest PC Seller," *InformationWeek*, December 1, 2006, www.informationweek.com; Ellen Florian Kratz, "Picture This," *Fortune*, September 4, 2006, p. 34; Damon Darlin, "Dell Is Trying to Bounce Back from a Bad Year," *New York Times*, June 15, 2006, p. C1; Lee Gomes, "Can Dell Ever Transfer Its PC-Making Talent to Other Ventures?" *Wall Street Journal*, May 17, 2006, p. B1; Mike Musgrove, "Dell's New Approach to Retail," *Washington Post*, May 30, 2006, p. D1.

7. "Turnaround Candidates: Rallis India," *Asia Africa Intelligence Wire*, March 7, 2004.

8. Teri Agins, "King of Midprice Basics Regroups," *Wall Street Journal*, June 16, 2006, p. B1.

9. Scott Hornstein, "Use Care with That Database," *Sales and Marketing Management*, May 2006, p. 22; "New Metrics for Tracking a CRM Program's Success," *Report on Customer Relationship Management*, February 2002, p. 1.

10. "Flight of the Bumblebee," *The Economist*, July 1, 2006, p. 61.

11. Mary Boltz Chapman, "A Little More Friday's," *Chain Leader*, June 2006, p. 2.

12. Jeremy Mullman, "Travelers: We Didn't Spend Enough," *Advertising Age*, June 12, 2006, pp. 4, 37.

13. Diane Toops, "Rising Stars," *Food Processing*, March 2006, pp. 26+; Jon Gertner, "Newman's Own," *New York Times*, November 16, 2003, Sec. 3, p. 4.

14. Personal communication with Judy Strauss.

15. Ross Goodwin and Brad Ball, "What Marketing Wants the CEO to Know," *Marketing Management*, September–October 2003, pp. 18+.

16. Guido Reinking, "Bentley Achieves VW Profit Goal," *Automotive News*, January 30, 2006, p. 28; Joann Muller, "Playing Hard to Get," *Forbes*, April 19, 2004, p. 65.

17. "Deccan to Break Even by 2008," *India Business Insight*, May 15, 2006; "Air Deccan IPO Falls Flat," *Airline Business*, June 27, 2006; "Air Deccan Records 90–100% Load Factors in May 2006," *India Business Insight*, June 18, 2006.

18. "It's Not Easy Being Green—But Big Business Is Trying," *Fortune*, August 7, 2006, p. 54.

19. Jack Hayes, "Industry, Communities Profit with Cause-Related Marketing," *Nation's Restaurant News*, March 3, 2003, p. 98.

20. "Resurgent PdV Champions State Interests," *Weekly Petroleum Argus*, June 26, 2006, p. 7; Brian Ellsworth, "The Oil Company as Social Worker," *New York Times*, March 11, 2004, pp. W1, W7.

21. Charles Keenan, "Translating Customer Service to the Front Lines," *American Banker*, May 7, 2001, pp. 18A+.

22. David Rynecki, "Putting the Muscle Back in the Bull," *Fortune*, April 5, 2004, pp. 162–170.

23. Rod Stiefbold, "Dissatisfied Customers Require Recovery Plans," *Marketing News*, October 27, 2003, pp. 44–46.

24. "Awards for Excellence: Internal Marketing," *Marketing*, June 21, 2006, p. 17.

25. Bruce Orwall and Emily Nelson, "Small World: Hidden Wall Shields Disney's Kingdom," *Wall Street Journal*, February 13, 2004, p. A1; "Working Their Magic: Disney Culture Molds Happy Employees," *Employee Benefit News*, September 1, 2003, www.benefitnews.com.

CHAPTER 6

1. Vivian Marino, "From Cereal to Juice, a Year of Innovation," *New York Times*, January 4, 2004, Sec. 3, p. 7.

2. Jena McGregor, "How Failure Breeds Success," *BusinessWeek*, July 10, 2006, pp. 41+.

3. Steve Hamm, "More to Life Than the Office," *BusinessWeek*, July 3, 2006, pp. 68+; Scott Gilbertson, "MS Winning Office Doc Battle," *Wired News*, January 5, 2007, www.wired.com.

4. Roland T. Rust, Debora Viana Thompson, and Rebecca W. Hamilton, "Defeating Feature Bloat," *Harvard Business Review*, February 2006, pp. 98–107.

5. Faith Keenan, "A Mass Market of One," *BusinessWeek*, December 2, 2002, pp. 68+.

6. Melissa Allison, "An Annual Meeting Minus the Fizz," *Seattle Times*, May 19, 2006, www.seattletimes.com.

7. David Kirkpatrick, "Why 'Bottom Up' Is on Its Way Up," *Fortune*, January 26, 2004, p. 54.

8. Charles Forelle, "IBM's Net Rises 11%, but Contract Signings Slip," *Wall Street Journal*, July 19, 2006, p. A3; Steve Lohr, "Big Blue's Big Bet: Less Tech, More Touch," *New York Times*, January 25, 2004, Sec. 3, p. 1.

9. Scott Leith, "Cingular Gains Users," *Atlanta Journal-Constitution,* July 21, 2006, www.ajc.com; "Wireless Carriers Cutting Churn Rates," *InformationWeek,* November 30, 2005; Janet Guyon, "Will Godzilla Defeat King Kong?" *Fortune,* March 8, 2004, p. 46.

10. Peter Landers, "Hospital Chic: The ER Gets a Makeover," *Wall Street Journal,* July 8, 2003, pp. D1, D3.

11. Gail Edmondson, "Designer Cars," *BusinessWeek,* February 16, 2004, pp. 56+.

12. David Kiley, "Blurred Focus," *BusinessWeek,* June 19, 2006, p. 69; "Ford Design Chief Seeking to Turn Optimism into Auto Sales," *Pittsburgh Post-Gazette,* July 6, 2006, www.post-gazette.com; Keith Naughton, "Detroit's Hot Buttons," *Newsweek,* January 12, 2004, pp. 38–39.

13. "Making Milk More Vending Friendly," *Dairy Foods,* November 2006, p. F1; Deborah Ball, "The Perils of Packaging: Nestlé Aims for Easier Openings," *Wall Street Journal,* November 16, 2005, pp. B1, B5; Deborah L. Vence, "The Lowdown on Trans Fats," *Marketing News,* March 15, 2004, pp. 13–14.

14. Kate Murphy, "Thinking Outside the Can," *New York Times,* March 14, 2004, Sec. 3, p. 3.

15. Catherine Arnold, "Way Outside the Box," *Marketing News,* June 23, 2003, pp. 13+.

16. "Japan's Konica Minolta Back in Profit in H1 on Weak Yen, Restructuring," *Europe Intelligence Wire,* November 3, 2006, n.p.; "Down with the Shutters: Photography," *The Economist,* March 25, 2006, p. 69; "Konica Minolta, a Photo Giant, Quitting Cameras and Color Film," *New York Times,* January 20, 2006, p. C6.

17. Steve Hamm, "Speed Demons," *BusinessWeek,* March 27, 2006, pp. 68+.

18. "Kraft Looks Outside the Box for Inspiration," *Wall Street Journal,* June 2, 2006, p. A15.

19. Ann Harrington, "Who's Afraid of a New Product," *Fortune,* November 10, 2003, pp. 189+.

20. Bob Tedeschi, "After Delving into 32 Other Lines, Amazon Finally Gets Around to Food," *New York Times,* July 24, 2006, p. C4.

21. Hamm, "Speed Demons;" "Intel Unveils Next-Generation Pentium 4," *Information Week,* February 2, 2004, www.informationweek.com.

22. "Intel Further Slashes Prices as New PC Chips Are Rolled Out, *America's Intelligence Wire,* July 27, 2006, n.p.; "Intel Unveils Next-Generation Pentium 4," *Information Week,* February 2, 2004, www.informationweek.com.

23. Stephanie Thompson, "'Small-Ball' Marketing Comes Up Big for Kellogg," *Advertising Age,* April 24, 2006, p. 6; "Special K Snack Bites," *Stagnito's New Products Magazine,* May 2006, p. 12.

24. Kevin Lane Keller, *Strategic Brand Management* (Upper Saddle River, N.J.: Prentice Hall, 2003), p. 175.

25. Marc Gobé, *Emotional Branding* (New York: Allworth Press, 2001), p. 99.

26. James Gleick, "Get Out of My Namespace," *New York Times Magazine,* March 21, 2004, pp. 44+.

27. Pete Engardio, "Taking a Brand Name Higher," *BusinessWeek,* July 31, 2006, p. 48; Rob Walker, "Haier Goals," *New York Times Magazine,* November 20, 2005, p. 38; Claudia H. Deutsch, "G.E.'s Bland Appliances Grow Sexier and Pricier," *New York Times,* June 17, 2006, pp. C1, C5.

28. "The Luxury Sector's Rich Times," *BusinessWeek Online,* March 6, 2006, www.businessweek.com/globalbiz/content/marc2006/gb20060306_296309.htm; Carol Matlack, "The Vuitton Machine," *BusinessWeek,* March 22, 2004, pp. 98+.

29. Don E. Schultz, "Understanding Total Brand Value," *Marketing Management,* March/April 2004, pp. 10–11.

30. Johny K. Johansson and Ilkka A. Ronkainen, "The Brand Challenge," *Marketing Management,* March/April 2004, pp. 54+.

31. "In Brief: Loving Shanghai . . . Denim Appointment," *WWD,* April 7, 2006, p. 2; "Brand Extension, with Jacuzzi," *The Economist,* February 28, 2004, pp. 61–62.

CHAPTER 7

1. See John Hogan, "Is Your Pricing Strategy a Tactical Anchor or a Strategic Lever for Growth?", speech delivered at the American Marketing Association Strategic Marketing Conference in Chicago, May 11, 2006.

2. "Mylan to Acquire Matrix for $736 Million," *Chain Drug Review,* September 25, 2006, pp. 57+; Eric Bowen, "Mylan Pharmaceuticals: Mylan Aims for New Products, Direction for Coming Year," *Dominion Post (Morgantown, WV),* April 16, 2006; "Knockoff Pill Pushers," *Fortune,* May 3, 2004, pp. 168–170; "Mylan Gets Go-ahead for Generic Levothroid," *Pittsburgh Business Times,* January 3, 2007, http://phoenix.bizjournals.com.

3. Jack Neff, "Maurice Coffey," *Advertising Age,* August 7, 2006, p. S-2; "P&G Introduces Swiffer Wetjet PowerMop," *MMR,* February 9, 2004, p. 19; Nancy Einhart, "Clean Sweep of the Market," *Business 2.0,* March 2003, p. 56.

4. Thomas T. Nagle and John E. Hogan, *The Strategy and Tactics of Pricing,* 4th ed. (Upper Saddle River, N.J.: Prentice Hall, 2006), p. 130.

5. Jeremy Kahn, "Beg, Borrow, and Steel," *Fortune,* March 8, 2004, p. 44.

6. Charles Oliver, "When the Olympics Come to London in 2012," *Reason,* March 2006, p. 12; Brendan Sainsbury, "Charge Ahead," *Alternatives Journal,* January–February 2006, pp. 34+; Robert W. Poole, Jr., "What the Traffic Will Bear," *Forbes,* May 10, 2004, p. 44; "London Traffic Starts to See Benefits of Toll Levied on Motorists," *Wall Street Journal,* May 6, 2003, p. 1; "Ken Livingstone's Gamble," *The Economist,* February 15, 2003, pp. 51–53.

7. Nagle and Hogan, *The Strategy and Tactics of Pricing,* chapter 1.

8. "Dollar General: New President, Strategic Changes," *Home Textiles Today,* December 4, 2006, p. 6; "Dollar General Corporation 2006 Analyst Day," *The America's Intelligence Wire,* June 7, 2006; "Dollar General Adds 2 Brands," *DSN Retail Fax,* October 24, 2005, p. 2; Robert Berner and Brian Grow, "Out-Discounting the Discounter," *BusinessWeek,* May 10, 2004, pp. 78–79; www.dollargeneral.com.

9. Nagle and Hogan, *Strategy and Tactics of Pricing,* pp. 8–9.

10. Evan Perez and Melanie Trottman, "Major Airlines Fuel a Recovery by Grounding Unprofitable Flights," *Wall Street Journal,* June 5, 2006, p. A1.

11. "Verizon Wireless Offers Additional 'Worry-Free' Guarantees," *The America's Intelligence Wire,* November 20, 2006, n.p.; Kevin Fitchard, "Untethering the Bundle," *Telephony,* August 14, 2006; Yuki Noguchi, "Verizon Wireless to Lower Exit Fee," *Washington Post,* June 29, 2006, p. D1.

12. Wayne D. Hoyer and Deborah J. MacInnis, *Consumer Behavior,* 3rd ed. (Boston: Houghton Mifflin, 2004), p. 262.

13. "Q4 2006 Monro Muffler Brake Earnings Conference Call," *The America's Intelligence Wire,* May 23, 2006; James Covert, "Monro Muffler Puts Focus on Trust," *Wall Street Journal,* June 11, 2003, p. B5G.

14. Philip Siekman, "The Struggle to Get Lean," *Fortune,* January 12, 2004, pp. 128(B)–128(H).

15. Steven Levingston, "Newspapers Weigh Cutting Stock Pages; Print-Web Relationship Is Evolving," *Washington Post,* March 2, 2006, p. D3; Ian Mount, "If They Have to Pay, Will They Come?" *Business 2.0,* February 2003, p. 45; "WSJ.com launches Personal Journal," *Information Today,* January 2004, p. 40.

16. Matt Nannery, "Digital Depot," *Chain Store Age,* January 2004, pp. 18A+.

17. Christopher Lawton, "H-P Net Jumps Amid a Shift in Strategic Focus," *Wall Street Journal,* May 17, 2006, p. A3.

18. Teril Yue Jones, "Speedier Intel Chips Take Aim at AMD," *Los Angeles Times,* July 28, 2006, p. C1; "Chip Price War Helps Customers, Hurts Intel and AMD," *InformationWeek,* July 25, 2006; Don Clark, "Intel Profit Sinks 57%, Pinched by a Price War," *Wall Street Journal,* July 20, 2006, p. A3.

19. Geoffrey Colvin, "Pricing Power Ain't What It Used to Be," *Fortune,* September 15, 2003, p. 52.

20. Berner and Grow, "Out-Discounting the Discounter."

21. Timothy J. Mullaney, "Jewelry Heist," *BusinessWeek,* May 10, 2004, pp. 82–83.

22. See Nagle and Hogan, *The Strategy and Tactics of Pricing,* Chapter 14.

23. Tim Matanovich, "Fees! Fees! Fees!" *Marketing Management,* January–February 2004, pp. 14–15.

24. "Southwest Raises Fares Amid Higher Fuel Costs," *Los Angeles Times,* July 7, 2006, p. C4; Adam Edström, "By the Numbers: Fueling Speculation," *Fortune,* May 17, 2004, p. 32.

25. See Chapter 9 and Appendix 9A in Nagle and Hogan, *Strategy and Tactics of Pricing,* for more detail on break-even formulas and calculations.

26. Steve Bills, "Deluxe Profit Slips as Checks Slide," *American Banker,* April 29, 2005, p. 9; Sheryl Jean, "As Check Sales Slow, Deluxe Corp. Begins Selling Personal Accessories," *Saint Paul Pioneer Press,* January 15, 2004, www.twincities.com/mld/pioneerpress; Sheryl Jean, "Shoreview, Minn.-Based Check Printer Reports Third-Quarter Profit," *Saint Paul Pioneer Press,* October 17, 2003, www.twincities.com/mld/pioneerpress; Deluxe Chairman's Letter and Form 10-K for 2003.

27. Carol Matlack, "The Vuitton Machine," *BusinessWeek,* March 22, 2004, pp. 98+.

28. "Chip Price War Helps Customers."

29. "The Asian Invasion Picks Up Speed," *BusinessWeek,* October 6, 2003, pp. 62–64.

30. Melanie Warner, "Salads or No, Cheap Burgers Revive McDonald's," *New York Times,* April 19, 2006, p. A1, C4.

31. "P&G Tries to Absorb More Low-End Sales," *Brandweek,* September 26, 2005, p. 4.

32. Robert H. Frank, "How Much Is That Laptop? It Depends on the Color of the Case. And That's Fair," *New York Times,* July 6, 2006, p. C3.

33. "Gillette Hits Mach 4," *BusinessWeek,* November 17, 2003, p. 52; Charles Forelle, "Schick Puts a Nick in Gillette's Razor Cycle," *Wall Street Journal,* October 3, 2003, p. B7; Claudia H. Deutsch, "For Mighty Gillette, There Are the Faces of War," *New York Times,* October 12, 2003, Sec. 3, pp. 1, 11.

34. "The Price Is Wrong," *The Economist,* May 25, 2002, pp. 59–60.

35. Victoria Murphy Barret, "What the Traffic Will Bear," *Forbes Global,* July 3, 2006.

36. "Shop Affronts," *The Economist,* July 1, 2006, p. 59.

37. "The Commoditization of Brands and Its Implications for Businesses," *Copernicus* and *Market Facts,* December 2000, pp. 1–6.

CHAPTER 8

1. "P&G's End-to-End RFID Plan," *Baseline,* June 28, 2006; "Manufacturing Complexity," *The Economist,* June 17, 2006, pp. 6–9.

2. Jeff O'Neill, "CVS Rolls Out the Fusion," *Modern Materials Handling,* February 2006, p. 9.

3. "LG's enV Joins Crowded U.S. Smart Phone Market," *eWeek,* November 27, 2006, n.p.; "LG VX8300," *PC Magazine Online,* June 29, 2006; Roger O. Crockett, "Cell Phones," *BusinessWeek,* April 26, 2004, pp. 48–49.

4. "A MinuteClinic Milestone," *Chain Drug* Review, November 20, 2006, p. 2; Daniel Yi, "Latest Retail Niche: Clinics," *Los Angeles Times,* July 18, 2006, p. C1.

5. Olga Kharif, "Travelocity's Helpful Human Touch," *BusinessWeek Online,* April 27, 2006, www.businessweek.com; Jim Fuquay, "Travelocity to Unveil New Website Design, Logo," *Fort Worth Star-Telegram,* March 25, 2004, www.dfw.com.

6. Grainger David, "The Passion of the *Da Vinci* Reader," *Fortune,* March 8, 2004, p. 48; Jenna Schnue, "Adrienne Sparks and Suzanne Herz," *Advertising Age,* March 1, 2004, p. S4.

7. Donna Fuscaldo and Don Clark, "Dell Plans to Open Pilot Stores, but Orders Stay on Phone, Web," *Wall Street Journal,* May 24, 2006, p. B2; Vauhini Vara, "'That Looks Great on You': Online Salespeople Get Pushy," *Wall Street Journal,* January 3, 2007, p. D1.

8. "Distributing Fun," *Confectioner,* June 2006, p. 44.

9. http://www.staplesrecyclefored.com.

10. Anjali Fluker, "Shifting Technology Helps ReCellular Grow from Humble Roots," *Crain's Detroit Business,* November 20, 2006, p. 12; James S. Granelli, "Laws to Give New Life to Used Cellphones," *Los Angeles Times,* July 1, 2006, p. C1.

11. Alina Tugend, "Getting Movies from a Store or a Mailbox (or Just a Box)," *New York Times,* August 5, 2006, p. C5; "McDonald's Pushes Redbox to Boost Traffic," *DSN Retailing Today,* May 22, 2006, p. 12; "Redbox Expands in Northeast," *Cardline,* February 3, 2006, p. 1; William Conroy, "Redbox Lets Consumers Rent Movies for $1 a Night from Vending Machine," *Asbury Park (NJ) Press,* May 6, 2006.

12. David Strom, "Wired for Power," *VARbusiness,* March 15, 2004, pp. 54+.

13. Kerry A. Dolan, "Outmuscling Wal-Mart," *Forbes,* May 10, 2004, pp. 80–81.

14. Lisa Napoli, "QVC, a Talent Show for Those Who Dream of Dollars," *New York Times,* May 1, 2006, p. F-11; Martin Forstenzer, "In Search of Fine Art Amid the Paper Towels," *New York Times,* February 22, 2004, Sec. 3, p. 4.

15. Timothy Aeppel, "Too Good for Lowe's and Home Depot?" *Wall Street Journal,* July 24, 2006, p. B1.

16. "Arctic Cat Forms Distribution Ties with Italian Motorcycle, Motor Scooter Manufacturer," *Grand Forks (N.D.) Herald,* March 6, 2006.

17. Yi, "Latest Retail Niche: Clinics."

18. "Royal Philips Electronics and Home Depot," *Private Label Buyer,* June 2002, p. 11.

19. Sunil Chopra and Peter Meindl, *Supply Chain Management,* 2nd ed. (Upper Saddle River, N.J.: Prentice Hall, 2004), p. 73.

20. "Wal-Mart to Customize Stores to Boost Neighborhood Appeal," *Los Angeles Times,* September 8, 2006, p. C3; Mark Landler and Michael Barbaro, "No, Not Always," *New York Times,* August 2, 2006, pp. C1, C4; William Hoffman, "Mixing It Up," *The Journal of Commerce,* May 29, 2006, pp. 64A+; Wendy Zellner, "Wal-Mart Eases Its Grip," *BusinessWeek,* February 16, 2004, p. 40; Mike Troy, "Logistics Still Cornerstone of Competitive Advantage," *DSN Retailing Today,* June 9, 2003, pp. 209+; Michael Garry and Sarah Mulholland, "Master of Its Supply Chain," *Supermarket News,* December 2, 2002, pp. 55+.

21. Jim Carlton, "Weyerhaeuser's Supply-Side Strategy," *Wall Street Journal,* June 27, 2006, p. B4.

22. Roy Furchgott, "Wi-Fi Technology Moves from Storeroom to Store," *New York Times,* August 25, 2003, p. C1.

23. Claudia H. Deutsch, "Planes, Trucks, and 7.5 Million Packages," *New York Times,* December 21, 2003, Sec. 3, pp. 1, 9.

24. Amanda Bower, "True Green," *Time Inside Business,* August 2006, p. A20.

25. Katie Hafner, "Postal Service Finds a Friend in the Internet," *New York Times,* August 2, 2006, pp. A1, C6.

26. Chuck Moozakis, "No-Slack Supply Chain: General Mills Maximizes Truck Loads to Cut Logistics Spending," *InternetWeek,* January 29, 2001, pp. 1+.

CHAPTER 9

1. Stephanie Kang, "Nike Taps Outsider for Post to Guide Global Online Sales," *Wall Street Journal,* October 24, 2006, p. B9; Stanley Holmes, "Nike: It's Not a Shoe, It's a Community," *BusinessWeek,* July 24, 2006, p. 50; Brian Steinberg, "Look—Up in the Sky! Product Placement!" *New York Times,* April 18, 2006, p. B1; Mark Landler, "The Hard Sell at the Cup," *New York Times,* June 7, 2006, p. C1; Stephanie Kang, "Nike Targets Women with New Hip-Hop Line," *Wall Street Journal,* February 15, 2006, p. B4; Matt Vella, "Nike + iPod Equals Smooth Runnings," *Business Week Online,* January 3, 2007, www.businessweek.com.

2. See Kenneth E. Clow and Donald Baack, *Integrated Advertising, Promotion, and Marketing Communications,* 3rd ed. (Upper Saddle River, N.J.: Pearson Prentice Hall, 2007), p. 15.

3. Roger J. Best, *Market-Based Management,* 4th ed. (Upper Saddle River, N.J.: Pearson Prentice Hall, 2005), p. 312.

4. Chekitan S. Dev, "Carnival Cruise Lines: Charting a New Brand Course," *Cornell Hotel & Restaurant Administration Quarterly,* August 2006, pp. 301+; Ann Carrns, "Carnival Lowers Profit Targets as Hurricane Fears Hurt Bookings," *Wall Street Journal,* May 17, 2006, p. B3.

5. Rick Kranz, "Volvo Plans Offbeat Mini-Style Marketing for C30," *Automotive News,* October 2, 2006, p. 24; Burt Helm, "For Your Eyes Only," *BusinessWeek,* July 31, 2006, p. 66.

6. "Media Multi-Taskers," *Marketing Management,* May–June 2004, p. 6; Don E. Schultz, "Include SIMM in Modern Media Ad Plans," *Marketing News,* May 15, 2004, p. 6.

7. David Page, "Oklahoma Beef Council Beefs Up Advertising Budget," *Journal Record (Oklahoma City),* June 27, 2006.

8. Lexie Williamson, "Healthcare: Consumer Health," *PR Week (UK),* September 19, 2003, p. 14.

9. Stuart Elliott, "A Survey of Consumer Attitudes Reveals the Depth of the Challenge That the Agencies Face," *New York Times,* April 14, 2004, p. C8.

10. Miriam Jordan, "Cerveza, Si or No? The Beer Industry's Embrace of Hispanic Market Prompts a Backlash from Activists," *Wall Street Journal,* March 29, 2006, p. B1.

11. Margaret Webb Pressler, "Turning the Job into a Party," *Washington Post,* July 6, 2003, p. F6.

12. Larry Yu, "How Companies Turn Buzz into Sales: The Good Word from Devoted Customers May Not Always Be the Most Effective Promotional Tool," *MIT Sloan Management Review*, Winter 2005, pp. 5+

13. "Diary: The Cream of It," *Marketing Event*, June 14, 2006, p. 58; "Nivea Hires Consumers for Sunkissed Marketing Plan," *Marketing Week*, April 27, 2006, p. 4.

14. Todd Davenport, "ING Direct Recasts the Internet Model," *American Banker*, December 1, 2006, p. 17A; Jane J. Kim, "ING Direct Plans Checking Account with High Yield," *Wall Street Journal*, April 11, 2006, p. D2; Matthew Swibel, "Where Money Doesn't Talk," *Forbes*, May 24, 2004, p. 176.

15. Arundhati Parmar, "Attitude Adjustment," *Marketing News*, May 1, 2004, pp. 10–12.

16. Coeli Carr, "Fortified with Vitamins, Minerals, and Tragedy," *New York Times*, May 7, 2006, sec. 2, p. 20; www.smartstart.com.

17. Mya Frazier, "Rush Is on to Rule In-Store TV Ads," *Advertising Age*, June 26, 2006, p. S-13.

18. Alice Z. Cuneo, "P&G Tries Out Mobile-Marketing," *Advertising Age*, June 19, 2006, p. 2.

19. "Field Marketing: Right People, Place, Time," *Marketing*, January 8, 2004, p. 23.

20. Belinda Gannaway, "Hidden Danger of Sales Promotions," *Marketing*, February 20, 2003, pp. 31+; Philip Kotler, *A Framework for Marketing Management*, 2nd ed. (Upper Saddle River, N.J.: Prentice Hall, 2003), pp. 318–319.

21. "Back to Basics: Devising a Media Plan," *PR Week (US)*, January 12, 2004, p. 22.

22. Scott Malone, "Gap Report Cites Action against Violating Factories," *WWD*, May 12, 2004, p. 23.

23. Claudia H. Deutsch, "Shunning the Traditional Route for Trade Shows, Siemens Is Showcasing Its Technology by Railway," *New York Times*, March 26, 2004, p. C6.

24. "Podcast Marketing: The Next Big Thing?" *Hotels*, March 2006, p. 22; Kim Hart, "Barging into the Bloggers' Circle," *Washington Post*, August 5, 2006, p. D1.

25. "Podcast Marketing: The Next Big Thing?"

26. "Heifer International Partners with Organic Bouquet," *Europe Intelligence Wire*, October 10, 2005; "Heifer International Has Been Named the Winner of the 2004 Award," *Arkansas Business*, March 22, 2004, p. 10.

27. Paul Soltoff, "Taking the Spam Out of Your E-mail Marketing," *DSN Retailing Today*, November 10, 2003, pp. 10+.

28. Chris Penttila, "The Art of the Sale," *Entrepreneur*, August 2003, pp. 58+.

29. Bob Tedeschi, "Salesmanship Comes to the Online Stores, but Please Call It a Chat," *New York Times*, August 7, 2006, p. C9; "Campaign: Widespread Press Push Helps Bluefly Tout Its New Focus," *PR Week*, November 7, 2005, p. 31.

CHAPTER 10

1. Rob Varnon, "UTC 2nd-Quarter Profit Rises 14 Percent," *Connecticut Post*, July 19, 2006; Michael Remez, "UTC Raises Revenue Forecast 3%," *Hartford Courant*, May 5, 2004, p. E2.

2. "Downturn in Fast-Forward," *BusinessWeek*, February 19, 2001, pp. 32+.

3. Amy Garber, "John McDonnell: It's Showtime," *Nation's Restaurant News*, January 26, 2004, pp. 120+.

4. "Toyota Sets Lofty Prius Sales Goals," *Ward's Dealer Business*, November 1, 2006, n.p.; Martin Fackler, "With $12 Billion in Profit, Toyota Has G.M. in Sight," *New York Times*, May 11, 2006, p. C4; Norihiko Shirouzu, "Toyota Revs Up Its Push in U.S.," *Wall Street Journal*, January 4, 2007, p. A3.

5. "Toyota Motor Corp.: Sales Push in China Includes Plan to Open 1,000 Dealers," *Wall Street Journal*, June 9, 2006.

6. Philip Bligh, Darius Vaskelis, and John Kelleher, "Taking the Frenzy Out of Forecasting," *Optimize*, March 2003, www.optimizemag.com.

7. See David B. Whitlark, Michael D. Geurts, and Michael J. Swenson, "New Product Forecasting with a Purchase Intention Survey," *Journal of Business Forecasting* 12, Fall 1993, pp. 18–21

8. Gary L. Lilien and Arvind Rangaswamy, *Marketing Engineering*, 2nd ed. (Upper Saddle River, N.J.: Prentice Hall, 2003), p. 253.

9. Loren Gary, "Why Budgeting Kills Your Company," *HBS Working Knowledge,* August 11, 2003, www.hbsworkingknowledge.hbs.edu.

10. "Salesforce.com Announces Record Fiscal First Quarter 2007 Results," Salesforce.com, May 2006, www.salesforce.com; Adam Lashinsky, "By the Numbers: Sales Data," *Fortune,* January 12, 2004, p. 34.

11. David Eisen, "Cendant Reveals Hotel Strategy," *Business Travel News,* April 3, 2006, p. 4; Kevin J. Delaney, "Wisdom for the Web: Search-Engine Advertising Is Crucial These Days," *Wall Street Journal,* July 10, 2006, p. R4.

12. Russ Banham, "The Revolution in Planning," *CFO,* August 1999, pp. 47+.

13. Dave Antanitus, "The Business of Metrics," *Program Manager,* March–April 2003, pp. 10+.

14. Tim Ambler, "Why Is Marketing Not Measuring Up?" *Marketing,* September 24, 1998, pp. 24+.

15. Paul W. Farris, Neil T. Bendle, Phillip E. Pfeifer, and David J. Reibstein, *Marketing Metrics: 50+ Metrics Every Executive Should Master* (Upper Saddle River, N.J.: Wharton School Publishing, 2006), p. 331.

16. Richard Karpinski, "Making the Most of a Marketing Dashboard," *B to B,* March 13, 2006, p. 18.

17. Karpinski, "Making the Most of a Marketing Dashboard."

18. Christopher Ittner and David Larcker, "Non-Financial Performance Measures: What Works and What Doesn't," *Wharton Knowledge,* October 16, 2000, www.knowledge.wharton.upenn,edu/articles.cfm?catid=1&articleid=279.

19. "Fast-Food Orders Go Long Distance," *New York Times Upfront,* September 4, 2006, p. 7; Julie Jargon, "McD's Service Stalls at Drive-Thru," *Crain's Chicago Business,* January 2, 2006, p. 1; Daniel Kruger, "You Want Data with That?" *Forbes,* March 29, 2004, pp. 58+.

20. Jean Halliday, "Marketer of the Year: Toyota," *Advertising Age,* November 13, 2006, pp. M-1+; Mark Rechtin, "Scion's Dilemma: Be Hip but Avoid the Mainstream," *Automotive News,* May 22, 2006, p. 42; Christopher Palmeri, "Toyota's Youth Models Are Having Growing Pains," *BusinessWeek,* May 31, 2004, p. 32; Yuzo Yamaguchi, "Upbeat Toyota Revises Forecast for Global Sales," *Automotive News,* July 28, 2003, p. 18.

21. Ittner and Larcker, "Non-Financial Performance Measures."

22. Ed See, "Bridging the Finance-Marketing Divide," *Financial Executive,* July–August 2006, pp. 50+; Kate Maddox, "ANA Explores Marketing Accountability," *B to B,* August 8, 2005, p. 3.

23. Lynda Radosevich, "Brand Preference Monitoring Debated," *B to B,* July 10, 2006, p. 17.

24. Gordon A. Wyner, "The Right Side of Metrics," *Marketing Management,* January–February 2004, pp. 8–9.

25. Kyle Wingfield, "Aldi Right Moves," *Wall Street Journal,* August 16, 2006, www.wsj.com; Mark Landler, "Wal-Mart to Abandon Germany," *New York Times,* July 29, 2006, pp. C1, C6.

26. Jonathan Karp, "From Bricks to Clicks," *Wall Street Journal,* September 22, 2003, p. R7.

27. Reed Abelson, "For Glaxo, the Answers Are in the Pipeline," *New York Times,* May 4, 2003, Sec. 3, p. 4.

28. Roselee Papandrea, "Hospital Maps Out Marketing Strategy," *Daily News* (*Jacksonville, NC*), January 29, 2006.

29. Banham, "The Revolution in Planning."

30. Toni Kistner, "One Smart Contingency Plan," *Network World Fusion,* October 6, 2003, www.nwfusion.com.

Credits

Chapter 1

Exhibit 1.3   Six Approaches to Growth
Adapted from Alan R. Andreasen and Philip Kotler, *Strategic Marketing for Non-Profit Organizations*, 6th ed. (Upper Saddle River, N.J.: Pearson Prentice Hall, 2003), p. 81.

Exhibit 1.5   The Marketing Mix
Adapted from Gary Armstrong and Philip Kotler, *Marketing: An Introduction*, 8th ed. (Upper Saddle River, N.J.: Pearson Prentice Hall, 2007), p. 53.

Need Help Checking Vegetables Off Your Daily "To Do" List?
© CSC Brands, LP, 2006. Used with permission.

Chapter 2

Exhibit 2.1   Environmental Scanning and Marketing Strategy
Marian Burk Wood, *Marketing Planning: Principles into Practice* (Harlow, Essex, England: Pearson Education, 2004), p. 40.

Federal Trade Commission—Facts For Business

Exhibit 2.4   Competitive Forces Affecting Industry Profitability and Attractiveness
Michael E. Porter, *Competitive Advantage*. © 1985 The Free Press, imprint of Simon & Schuster. Reprinted with permission.

Exhibit 2.5   Judging Organizational Strengths and Weaknesses
Mary K. Coulter, *Strategic Management in Action* (Upper Saddle River, N.J.: Pearson Prentice Hall, 1998), p. 141.

Chapter 3

In Opinion polls, 100% of our readers had one.
© The Economist Newspaper Limited, London, 2006.

Chapter 4

Ok, nobody's perfect. Good thing there's a snack that's perfect for you.
Advertisement reprinted with permission of The Quaker Oats Company. All rights reserved. Copyright © 2006.

Exhibit 4.4   Assessing Segment Attractiveness
Adapted from Graham Hooley, John Saunders, and Nigel Piercy, *Marketing Strategy and Competitive Positioning*, 3rd ed. (Harlow, Essex, England: FT Prentice Hall, 2004), p. 354.

Chapter 5

Exhibit 5.1   Options for Marketing Plan Direction
Marian Burk Wood, *Marketing Planning: Principles into Practice* (Harlow, Essex, England: Pearson Education, 2004), p. 124.

The Impact of Public Service Advertising
© 2006 Ad Council. Used with permission.

Exhibit 5.4   Strategy Pyramid
Adapted from Tim Berry and Doug Wilson, *On Target: The Book on Marketing Plans* (Eugene, OR: Palo Alto Software, 2001), p. 107.

Chapter 6

Exhibit 6.2   Designing a Service
Adapted from Christopher Lovelock and Jochen Wirtz, *Services Marketing,* 5th ed. (Upper Saddle River, N.J.: Prentice Hall, 2004), Fig. 1-5, p. 15.

Do You Have It? Total Peace Of Mind.
Reprinted with permission of Underwriters Laboratories, Inc. Copyright © Underwriters Laboratories, Inc.

Exhibit 6.6   Marketing Advantages of Strong Brands
Philip Kotler and Kevin Lane Keller, *Marketing Management,* 12th ed. (Upper Saddle River, N.J.: Pearson Prentice Hall, 2006), p. 277.

Exhibit 6.7   Pyramid of Brand Equity
Adapted from Kevin Lane Keller, *Strategic Brand Management,* 2nd ed. (Upper Saddle River, N.J.: Prentice Hall, 2003), p. 76, Fig. 2.5.

Chapter 7

Exhibit 7.3   Cost-Based versus Value-Based Pricing
Thomas Nagle and John Hogan, *Strategy and Tactics of Pricing,* 4th ed. (Upper Saddle River, N.J.: Pearson Prentice Hall, 2006), p 4.

Rebate Page
© 2007 Staples, Inc.

Exhibit 7.6   Break-Even Analysis
Tim Berry and Doug Wilson, *On Target: The Book on Marketing Plans* (Eugene, OR: Palo Alto Software, 2000), p. 163.

Exhibit 7.7   Skim Pricing and Penetration Pricing Compared
Roger J. Best, *Market-Based Management,* 4th ed. (Upper Saddle River, N.J.: Pearson Prentice Hall, 2005), pp. 242, 248.

Exhibit 7.8   Alternative Reactions to Competitive Price Cuts
Philip Kotler, *Framework for Marketing Management* (Upper Saddle River, N.J.: Prentice Hall, 2001), p. 231.

Chapter 8

Exhibit 8.2   Channel Levels
Philip Kotler and Gary Armstrong, *Principles of Marketing,* 11th ed. (Upper Saddle River, N.J.: Pearson Prentice Hall, 2006), Fig. 12.4, p. 369.

USPS screen capture
© 2007 United States Postal Service.

Chapter 9

Exhibit 9.1   Push and Pull Strategies
Gary Armstrong and Philip Kotler, *Marketing: An Introduction,* 8th ed. (Upper Saddle River, N.J.: Pearson Prentice Hall, 2007), p. 369.

Exhibit 9.2   Models for Audience Response to IMC
Adapted from Michael R. Solomon, *Consumer Behavior,* 5th ed. (Upper Saddle River, N.J.: Pearson Prentice Hall, 2002), pp. 200–202.

Exhibit 9.4   The Media Mix
Kenneth Clow and Donald Baack, *Integrated Advertising, Promotion, Marketing Communication,* 2nd ed. (Upper Saddle River, N.J.: Pearson Prentice Hall, 2002). Reprinted by permission of Pearson Education Inc., Upper Saddle River, NJ.

Watch them say "YES!" to veggies
photo © Marcus Lyon/Photographer's Choice/Getty Images, Inc. Ad used courtesy of Unilever US, Inc. Copyright © 2006.

Chapter 10

Exhibit 10.3   Main Categories of Marketing Metrics
Paul W. Farris, Neil T. Bendle, Phillip E. Pfeifer, and David J. Reibstein, *Marketing Metrics: 50+ Metrics Every Executive Should Master* (Upper Saddle River, N.J.: Wharton School Publishing, 2006), Figure 1.1, p. 5.

Google Analytics screen capture
© Google, Inc. Google Desktop Search, Google Directory, Google Glossary, Google Groups, Google Images, Gmail, Google News, Google Print, Google Scholar, Google Toolbar, Google Zeitgeist, Blogger and Orkut online community are trademarks of Google, Inc. Used with permission.

Exhibit 10.6   Successful Marketing Plan Implementation
Roger J. Best, *Market-Based Management,* 4th ed. (Upper Saddle River, N.J.: Pearson Prentice Hall, 2005), p. 453.

Name/Company/Brand Index

Subject Index